21 Days
To A Healthy Heart

Alan Watson

Diet Heart Publishing
Sebeka, Minnesota

21 Days To A Healthy Heart
By Alan L. Watson

Published by:
Diet Heart Publishing
PO Box 330
Sebeka, MN 56477- 0330
noko@wcta.net

Book design and typography by Bryan Haggerty
Cover Design by Mike Pakonen

ISBN 0-9720481-0-3

First printing April 2002
Printed in the United States of America

Library of Congress Control Number: 2002091726

Table of contents

DEDICATED
TO THE
MEMORY OF
DICK QUINN

Acknowledgments

Truth cannot be suppressed by the majority or decreed by consensus.

Uffe Ravnskov, M.D.

I would like to thank Mike Pakonen, Dr. Coco March, and Bryan Haggerty of Nokomis Nutrition. Without their collaboration and unfailing support, this book would not have been possible.

Special thanks to my brother Jim and sister-in-law Iris Watson who never stopped believing in the good ship "Cayenne."

I am also indebted to the doctors, medical researchers, nutritionists and other health professionals whose published results, clinical data, and dedication to teaching and healing form the scientific basis of this book.

I would also like to thank Karla Caspari, Alan Norton, Jim Robinson, Shirley Sellner, and George Town for their key support and many valuable comments during the preparation of "21-Days."

A particular note of gratitude goes to the thousands of loyal customers who have supported us these many years. Your letters, phone calls, and many pestering questions were the true catalyst behind this effort.

Finally, to my family and friends, I love and thank you all.

Alan L. Watson

21-Day Plan Key Principles

1:    Eat eggs – not cereal - for breakfast.

2:    A change of heart can reduce your risk of a heart attack.

3:    Remove elevated homocysteine with B-complex vitamins.

4:    Use L-Carnitine to prevent heart attacks and promote weight loss.

5:    Supplement with the antioxidants vitamin C and vitamin E.

6:    Avoid pasteurized milk. Attempt to replace low fat and powdered milk or non-dairy products with whole raw milk.

7:    If you supplement with just one mineral, make it magnesium.

8:    Monitor your fasting blood sugar

9:    Select low glycemic index carbohydrates.

10:    Monitor and reduce elevated triglycerides. Promote HDL cholesterol.

11:    Don't be a couch potato and don't over-exercise.

(continued)

12: If you eat grains, eat whole grains that have been properly prepared. Ignore the USDA Food Guide Pyramid recommendation to eat 6-11 servings of grain everyday.

13: Use herbs to stimulate, cleanse, and nutritionally support healthy blood circulation.

14: Do not eat margarine or hydrogenated or partially hydrogenated fats

15: Use butter, olive oil, coconut butter or lard for cooking.

16: Eat two tablespoons of omega-3 rich milled flax-seed everyday.

17: Eat plenty of protein: High quality pasture raised grass-fed beef, lamb and wild game are best.

18: Eat deep-sea cold-water fish as often as possible.

19: Monitor and restore health promoting hormone levels.

20: Replace excess coffee and soft drinks with green tea, herb tea, and plenty of pure water. High quality red wine is beneficial for some people.

21: Ask for a complete lipid evaluation. Understand all of your risk factors.

Author's preface:
breakfast at Jim's Cafe

My grandparents were dairy farmers in a township called Meadow just outside of the small town of Sebeka, Minnesota. My Finnish grandfather worked a small, productive "mixed farm," producing a variety of crops and grazing animals.

In 1910, small mixed farms dotted the countryside. Pasture raised beef and raw, creamy whole milk were daily fare. Outdoor pigs raised under open skies develop optimal amounts of vitamins A and D, providing nutritious lard - the preferred cooking fat.

My grandmother's many chores included baking coarse whole grain bread. My mother helped with meals and looked after the chickens. My mother's older sister was a field hand. They were poor but all remembered, "eating well."

My mother graduated from high school in 1937, and later met my father on a blind date in wartime 1940s Minneapolis. They married, moved north to Sebeka, opened a restaurant, and had five children.

My job was filling the pop cooler. My brother peeled potatoes. My sister charmed the customers. "Jim's Cafe" was once famous for excellent hot roast beef sandwiches, real mashed potatoes, five-cent coffee, homemade ice cream – and thick, tempting cinnamon rolls.

In the late 40s and 1950s, breakfast was a busy place at Jim's Cafe, particularly in the summer when tourists travelling US Highway 71 competed for seats "owned" all winter long by local farmers and town's people.

My father did all the cooking, and he made everything from scratch. But, by the end of the decade, things were changing in

Jim's Café, Summer, 1956. Lil and Jim Watson are on the left. Al Watson and his sister are 3rd and 4th from the right.

places like Sebeka. The creamery closed and the train made it's last trip through town in 1959, For my father, too, time was running out.

Throughout the 1950s, my father, who was a smoker, experienced increasingly frequent chest pains (angina). In 1958, unable to continue working, he sold the restaurant and we moved to Minneapolis where he could be treated at the Veterans Administration Hospital.

He died there one year later during open-heart surgery at age 50. The young English doctor told my grief-stricken mother that he had done everything possible to save her husband's life.

My father died during the heyday of coronary heart disease mortality, which peaked in 1963. His younger brother died suddenly of a heart attack a few years later while square dancing at age 47. Premature coronary heart disease was "running in the family."

By 1974, I had served in the army, graduated from college, got married, and had a decent management job at AT&T. My young wife and I were *margarine*-eating vegetarians. I was afraid to die of heart disease (and she didn't want to kill helpless animals.)

For breakfast, we ate granola or dry cereal, pasteurized skim milk, wheat toast or bagels - washed down with orange juice or coffee. We used *"Promise"* margarine on our pancakes. It didn't taste as good, but this was a heart-healthy breakfast, right?

Or, wrong?

When something as simple as what to eat for breakfast takes on cosmic - if not "comic" proportions – then I knew that one more book about heart disease was needed - especially if written by someone who is challenging outdated prevailing ideas.

You can call me a "patient advocate." My bias is with the patient, friend, or family member whose life is on the line. Heart disease demands a better approach – a much greater emphasis on prevention and clear, easy to follow dietary advice.

Go ahead, order eggs for breakfast - as many as you like. Free range brown eggs are best. Limit bacon, unless it's made the old fashioned way (without nitrates and nitrites). Otherwise, less processed lamb chops may be a better choice.

In the winter months, homemade soups with fish and vegetables or whole oats soaked overnight are good choices. Try not to add sweetener to your cooked oats - instead use milled flaxseed, butter, or, if you can find some, cream or whole raw milk.

Eat fresh fruit instead of juice, which raises blood sugar. If you have blood sugar problems, you may have to limit the fruit too. Green tea is better than black tea which is better than coffee. If you drink coffee (I do), buy certified organic. (Regular coffee is pesticide-laden.)

Like alcohol, a little coffee is beneficial; too much may hurt you. These are ideas – not rules. A construction worker in Minneapolis in the winter may need a heartier breakfast than an office worker in warm, sunny San Diego, California.

There is no one diet for everyone, but all of us should start our day with wholesome nutritious foods. Don't get shoehorned into the official low fat way of eating or pay too much attention to the high carbohydrate USDA Food Guide Pyramid.

We are biochemically unique - everyone a deviant - more different from each other than we are alike. There is no one "desirable" cholesterol number that's best for everyone. "Average person" does not exist. Anti-cholesterol medications can't make it so.

To prevent and reverse heart disease, you must educate yourself by learning about all the risk factors that apply to you. Success, ultimately, depends on whether you are regarded as a unique individual or simply treated as a disease with harsh drugs and failed diets.

In the words of Tristan Jones - Welch author, sailor and adventurer - "*Don't let the bastards grind you down.*"

Introduction:
A brief history of the number one killer

"Today, if a physician challenges – or even simply questions – the importance of cholesterol in heart disease, one faces professional loss of credibility or even banishment, usually by shunning,"

Stephen L DeFelice, M.D.

By everyone's account, heart attacks are the number one killer, the single largest cause of death today in the United States. Heart-related disease will claim nearly one million lives this year - one death every 30 to 40 seconds. Heart disease is a problem of pandemic proportions, and billions are spent managing – not curing-the disease.

Common today, heart attacks were not a major cause of death before 1930 when infectious diseases like tuberculosis killed more people. While turn-of-the century mortality statistics are not always reliable, they consistently indicate that only 3 to 8 percent of all deaths were heart-related.[1]

In 1910, infections threatened the newly born and the mother. Infant mortality was high. Influenza killed millions between 1900 and 1920, including my grandparents' first infant daughter. Even most heart-related deaths were due to infections and congenital conditions. The old died of pneumonia – not heart attacks.

Heart attacks were so rare early in the 20th century that the first case was not described until 1912 – when the words "heart attack" first appeared. In 1930, according to the US Bureau of the Census, heart attacks caused no more than 3,000 deaths.[2]

Dr. Paul Dudley White, Harvard cardiologist, early promoter of the German EKG machine (electrocardiograph), and later President Eisenhower's personal physician, didn't observe a single heart attack at Harvard between 1921 and 1928. The great increase in heart attack mortality occurred between 1930 and 1960.[3]

In 1960, 500,000 people died of heart attacks – a 100-fold increase in just thirty years.[4] Improved emergency response, successful anti-smoking campaigns, and expanded use of nutritional supplements cut the heart attack death rate after the 1960s, but heart-related mortality remains high.

Today, over 50 percent of all deaths are heart-related – and the numbers are still rising.[5] While you're more likely to survive a heart attack today than in the 1950s, your chances of dying within one year are still high – 42 percent for women and 24 percent for men.[6]

Heart attack survivors on drug treatment often die years later from slow, suffocating heart failure. The heart's left ventricle, which pumps blood out to the body, has reduced pumping ability, less "ejection fraction." Often there is edema (water retention) starting around the ankles that spreads to the lungs.

Rare throughout most of the 20th century, the incidence of heart failure doubled between 1989 and 1999. Today, heart failure is the number one Medicare expenditure - responsible for the majority of hospitalizations among people 65 and older.[8]

A family history of heart disease, as in my father's family, is a key risk factor. "A family history of premature coronary artery disease makes it five times more likely that you too will develop coronary heart disease at an early age," writes Thomas Yannios, M.D., in *Heart Disease Breakthrough*.[7]

Coronary heart disease (CHD) is the hardening or narrowing

of the arteries that carry blood to the heart. The heart, itself, can be pumping fine, but its blood supply is reduced or interrupted by clogged, constricted, or poorly functioning blood vessels.

Injured blood vessels beget sludgy, dangerous clots. A heart attack (myocardial infarction) occurs when a clot obstructs a coronary artery and chokes off blood to a portion of the heart. *Ischemia* is the technical term for a decrease in the heart's blood supply.

CHD is also called coronary artery disease, or simply heart disease. Atherosclerosis refers to the thickening of a coronary artery. Arteriosclerosis is damage to arteries anywhere in the body.

Plaque forms after the smooth, slick surface of the artery wall sustains a cut or injury - say from cigarette smoke. The *lesion* or area of damaged tissue soon attracts blood platelets (the clotting factor), cholesterol, specialized white blood cells, and other "patch" materials.

Chronic injury – say from habitual smoking - increases the number and size of lesions. There are slow growing, hard fibrous lesions capped by calcium plaque; and faster growing, more dangerous soft lesions that easily rupture and, like blood clots, often cause sudden death.[9]

Blood clots cause most heart attacks - not blockage. In fact, the majority of people who develop fatal blood clots have less than 50 percent blockage.[10] Heart attacks can be mild, cause extensive damage, or in one third of cases, cause sudden death.[11]

Although heart attacks can occur suddenly and without warning, damage to the arteries typically begins early in life.[12] A postmortem study conducted in the 1990s in Louisville, Kentucky, showed significant hardening or thickening of the coronary arteries in 80 percent of young adults (average age, 26). One in ten had an almost completely blocked coronary artery.[13]

Exactly what causes this clogging or hardening of the arteries is controversial. Beginning in the 1950s, based on early Russian animal experiments, international diet-heart comparisons, and a

Korean War pathology study, influential people in the medical establishment blamed blocked arteries on cholesterol and saturated fats, foods like eggs, butter, red meat, coconut and palm oil.

According to their *diet-heart hypothesis*, dietary cholesterol and saturated fats increase blood cholesterol levels, which, in turn, clog arteries and promote blood clots. Two long-term, hundred million dollar government studies conducted in the 1970s provided no additional scientific support, but the diet-heart idea nonetheless gained momentum and in 1985, the "War on Cholesterol" was declared.

Since then, "cholesterol reduction" has been the single focus of medical research, education and treatment. "Exercise and eat a low fat diet," they say, and if that doesn't lower your cholesterol enough, "take a drug for the rest of your life." No other explanations or solutions are allowed.

An increasing number of medical doctors are speaking out. "The truth is the cholesterol theory has never been proven. The studies that set out to show a connection between dietary cholesterol and heart disease have failed," writes Kilmer McCully, M.D., in *The Heart Revolution*.[14]

"What you have been told about cholesterol and heart disease may not be true," writes Howard H. Wayne, M.D. "Scientific data that shows only a weak relationship between cholesterol and heart disease has been deliberately manipulated, and statistical relationships twisted, to make our cholesterol level seem more important than it really is."[15]

Although heart disease is diet-related, cholesterol and saturated fat are not to blame. There are multiple dietary causes, including our replacing traditional animal foods with excess carbohydrates, especially refined carbohydrates and highly processed vegetable fats.

Following official government and doctors' advice, Americans are consuming a high percentage of calories in the form of sugar, refined carbohydrates, and partially hydrogenated vegetable fats – foods like margarine that contain dangerous **trans fatty acids**.

In combination, the high carbohydrate diet and these modern fabricated foods wreak havoc on our delicate blood sugar regulating mechanisms, cause injury and inflammation in our arteries, and promote the deadly blood clots and ruptured plaques that kill us.

Between 1930 and 1963, during the steep rise in heart attack mortality, we had a substantial increase in our consumption of highly processed vegetable fats and a decrease in our intake of animal fats.[16] During this same period, we had a large increase in our consumption of sugar and refined carbohydrates.[17]

The official low fat high carbohydrate diet is associated with record levels of obesity and diabetes, and the link to CHD is direct: 80 percent of diabetics die of heart disease.[18] While this strong association may not prove that modern highly processed foods cause heart disease, it more than contradicts the notion that dietary cholesterol and saturated fat are solely to blame.

The War on Cholesterol is a losing battle. Instead of light at the end of the tunnel - we have medical tunnel vision. The drug companies and the medical establishment are the only certain winners and there are many losers – including the 30-year delay in finding better prevention and treatment options.

Doctors are treating everyone for cholesterol reduction, while overlooking other important heart disease risk factors, such as elevated fasting blood sugar, high homocysteine, elevated triglycerides, and high levels of dangerous lipoprotein(a).

21 Days To A Healthy Heart provides the missing risk factor information you need to understand and reverse your risk of heart disease. The 21-Day Plan provides key principles – ideas you can learn and apply to your own situation. Start today, and remember, no one can do this for you.

Caution: Something is wrong if you are gaining weight, growing dependent on alcohol, or experiencing reduced tolerance to exercise or strenuous activity. Sudden death is often the initial and only symptom of heart disease.

Do not delay a visit to the doctor or emergency room if you have been experiencing any left-sided pain, tightness, or numbness. Also, a frequent headache, especially if accompanied by nausea or shortness of breath, may be a warning of cardiovascular disease.

Remember, you can have blood vessel damage without knowing it, and blood clots and stress are a deadly combination. Unhappiness on the job, a non-supportive boss or spouse, and feelings of powerlessness at home or at work all increase the risk of a heart attack.

Frequent anger, anxiety, depression, impatience, and a constant sense of haste or urgency can trigger a heart attack. Take any of these warnings seriously. As necessary, seek professional assistance. A healthy lifestyle and reducing emotional stress are ultimately the cures for many an ailing heart.

Are we really living longer today?

It's a commonly held belief that we have more heart disease today simply because of increased life expectancy. A Mayo Clinic health newsletter blamed the rising incidence of heart failure on the basis "we're living longer." Average life expectancy today in the U.S. is about 75 compared to just 49 in 1910.

To prove this out, I visited the old Zion cemetery near Blue Grass, Minnesota on a cold, gray day in November 1997. I walked throughout the cemetery, writing down the names and dates of all the people buried there.

I counted a total of 130 individuals, including 7 people who already had their names and birth dates inscribed on the stones but were not deceased yet. Adding up the total years of these 130 people, I arrived at an average life expectancy of 54.5.

It didn't take me long to record infant mortality. The third stone was August, who died on the day he was born, December 12, 1911. Twenty-one other children died at birth or within months of birth. Infant mortality was brutally high in 1910.

I counted a total of 40 residents who died between birth and age 39, including the 22 children. As was common early last century, several women may have died giving birth. Among them, I counted Emilie (age 34) and Helene (age 23), who died in 1905 and 1912, respectively.

When the 40 early deaths from the Zion average life expectancy calculations are subtracted from the total, the average life expectancy of the remaining residents (who survived age 39) was 76 years - the same as today!

The big surprise: 58 residents (out of 130) reached age 70, including 32 who lived to age 80 or higher. In this group of longest lived people, 50 were born before 1910 when average life expectancy was only 49.

That explains why there are so many old folks in those 1910-era church picnic and family reunion photos. The *Zion Cemetery Study* shows that people born before 1910 who made it into adulthood were just as likely to reach old age as people today.

So don't let the medical establishment blame heart disease on "we're living longer today," or it's due to increased life expectancy.

When *childhood mortality* is removed from average life expectancy, we come face to face with the troubling fact that older Americans today – in spite of one trillion dollars spent on health care in 2001 - do not live any longer than the hearty Americans who lived in 1910.

PART I

The role of cholesterol

Chapter 1

-------- 🐦 --------

Is cholesterol dangerous?

Analyses of the plaques that line the walls of the coronary arteries have shown that only 5 percent of the plaques is cholesterol. Accordingly, the belief that dietary fat and cholesterol cause coronary disease is just a myth, and its perpetuation is a huge scientific hoax.

Howard H. Wayne, M.D.

Is elevated cholesterol a disease? Or, is it like the sensitive canary brought down into the mine shaft to warn of poison gas? Is cholesterol an enemy to fear – or is it a loyal, reliable antioxidant, patching up blood vessel walls injured by stress and dietary abuse?

Cholesterol is fat soluble (dissolves in fat), but it's not a fat. Cholesterol, technically, is a high molecular weight alcohol (but doesn't act like one). The liver and every cell in the body manufacture cholesterol. In humans and in pigs, cholesterol in skin converts sunlight into active vitamin D, promoting mineral absorption and optimum bone density.[1]

Without cholesterol, we could not stand, think, respond to stress, or reproduce. Cholesterol is an essential element in the body's numerous cell membrane systems, "waterproofing" trillions of cells.[2] The highest concentrations of cholesterol are in the brain and nervous system. Cholesterol is the precursor to all adrenal and sex hormones, including pregnenolone, DHEA, and progesterone.

Cholesterol travels in the blood serum (water portion) in combinations of fat and protein called lipoproteins. LDL (low density lipoprotein) carries cholesterol out to the body and HDL (high density lipoprotein) is reverse transport – carrying cholesterol back to the liver for recycling.

LDL is often referred to as "bad" cholesterol; HDL "good." Indeed, high HDL levels protect us from heart disease. The higher the HDL, the lower the risk of heart disease.[3] At the same time, however, there is no proof that LDL causes heart disease. The majority of people who die of heart disease have low or average levels of both LDL and total cholesterol.[4]

LDL delivers fat-soluble antioxidants (vitamin E) and carotenoids (beta carotene, lutein and lycopene) to every cell in the body. LDL is a beneficial antioxidant, unless it's altered or damaged by other blood factors, such as high blood glucose (sugar), which oxidizes cholesterol (see chapter 11).

Cholesterol has no calories; it's not used for energy. Available in tiny milligram amounts from animal food (a milligram is one-thousandths of a gram) - dietary cholesterol is reserved for critical physiological functions. We have 10,000-14,000 milligrams (10-14 grams) of cholesterol coursing through our bloodstream at any given time.[5]

In contrast, one egg, the highest common food source, contains 270 mg. When we eat one egg, says Mary Enig, Ph.D., lipid biochemist, researcher, and author of *Know Your Fats*, we absorb no more than 50 percent or 135 mg of cholesterol. Two eggs for breakfast would add no more than 270 mg of cholesterol - less than 2 percent of blood levels.[6]

"It is not possible for humans to eat enough cholesterol-containing foods every day to supply the amount the body needs," says Enig. To make up the difference, our livers and other organs have "very active cholesterol-synthesis capability."[7]

Your liver and other tissues produce as much as 2,000 mg of cholesterol daily. If you're not eating a dozen eggs per day, your body will simply put cholesterol-synthesis into overdrive.[8] How many million people, warned not to eat more than two eggs per week, have needlessly omitted nutritious eggs from their diet?

For decades, the American Heart Association (AHA) and federal health authorities have conducted an "egg scare," and per capita consumption has plummeted from a high of 402 in 1945 to 233 in 1991.[9] This is unfortunate because eggs are a relatively inexpensive, high protein food.

Approximately 45 percent of the fat in eggs is oleic acid (omega-9), a fat that raises protective HDL cholesterol and is also found in almonds, avocados and olive oil.[10] A recent study published in the *Journal of the American College of Nutrition* (vol. 16, pp. 551-61, 1997) found that eating eggs raised protective HDL cholesterol by 10 percent or more.

If cholesterol and animal fat in our food cause heart disease, then heart disease patients must logically have eaten more cholesterol and saturated fat than people who have no symptoms of heart disease. The research, below, compiled by a Swedish scientist and medical doctor, tells a different story.

Uffe Ravnskov, M.D., Ph.D., author of *The Cholesterol Myths*, analyzed ten major studies, including Framingham (see next chapter), comparing the consumption of cholesterol by healthy individuals to that of heart disease patients. The mean consumption of cholesterol was a little lower in subjects who developed coronary heart disease than in the participants who didn't.[11] (See Ravnskov Summary, next page.)

Dr. Ravnskov, a family doctor and independent researcher from Lund, Sweden, has published 40 papers and letters in peer-reviewed medical journals challenging the scientific evidence linking dietary and blood cholesterol with cardiovascular disease.

Ravnskov has carefully evaluated all published studies that looked at animal fat consumption and heart disease - a total of 150,000 participants in 34 different studies. In just 3 of 34 studies, patients with heart disease had eaten more animal fat; in 1 of

Ravnskov Summary
Cholesterol Eaten Per Day in Mg

		Patients W/ CHD	Healthy Subjects
Framingham citizens	men	708	716
	women	520	477
Participants, LRC study	age 30-59	427	416
	age 60-79	423	355
Puerto Rican men	urban	449	442
	rural	335	358
Honolulu citizens		558	552
Hawaiian men	Hawaiian	510	680
	Japanese	466	587

Comparison of the amount of cholesterol eaten per day by patients with CHD and age- and sex-matched control individuals.
Source: *The Cholesterol Myths*,

34 they had eaten less; and in the remaining 30 studies, investigators found no difference in animal fat consumption.[12]

The Cholesterol Myths was first published in Sweden in 1991, and in Finland in 1992. In Finland, during a heated television program, diet-heart proponents called Ravnskov a crank and set his book on fire. While book burning makes a strong statement, it also raises serious questions about why diet-heart proponents are ignoring so much contrary scientific data?

According to Jeffrey Bland, Ph.D., in *Genetic Nutritioneering*, "Only about 10 percent of the population is genetically predisposed to have elevated blood cholesterol as a result of elevated dietary cholesterol."[13] If Bland is correct, nine out of ten people could not – under any circumstances – raise their cholesterol levels even eating 12 eggs per day. Burp!

Bland goes on to say, "Advising people to omit cholesterol-containing foods from their diet because cholesterol produces heart disease does not balance with the facts."[14] There are things that elevate blood cholesterol levels, but cholesterol-rich foods do not.

Stress hormones are made from cholesterol, and stress raises LDL cholesterol more than anything else. The more stress you suffer, the more cholesterol your body will produce. Anger, anxiety, depression, fear, and stubbornness all involve sympathetic activation of the nervous system, increased adrenaline, loss of magnesium and elevated cholesterol.[15]

Jeffrey Bland says cholesterol is like the body's smoke detector. "The smoke detector does not cause the fire; it alerts us to the presence of fire and forces us to look for its cause." Bland is suggesting that elevated cholesterol doesn't cause heart disease; it's the alarm bell instead.[16]

How, then, did the medical establishment come to blame the smoke detector for the fire – or cholesterol for heart disease? The cholesterol "as culprit" story begins in 1951 during the Korean War.

To learn more about wound ballistics, the Pentagon dispatched a team of pathologists to perform autopsies on fallen American soldiers. Led by Major William Enos, the pathologists had examined 2,000 male casualties, average age 22, by 1954. The results, says Thomas J. Moore, in his book *Heart Failure,* shocked the medical community.[17]

The pathologists found "stringy, streaky yellow deposits of fat and fiber in 35 percent of the casualties." In another 42 percent, "fatty streaks that had already grown into full-fledge lesions."[18] Although the incidence of heart attack had been climbing steadily since the 1930s, no one expected to find fully developed lesions in 22 year-old men.

Like the young people studied in Louisville, Kentucky, in the 1990s, one out of ten examined soldiers already had lesions reducing or blocking blood flow in at least one coronary artery. A new analogy may illustrate how this happens.

Ambulances are always called to accidents involving injuries. The ambulances don't cause the accidents; they are responding to a call for help. The same is true of cholesterol. It's the body's primary healing substance. Cholesterol is among the first substances to arrive when an injury occurs on the smooth, slick surface of a coronary artery.

An injury to the endothelial layer – say from cigarette smoke – mobilizes the body's ambulance crews: Blood platelets, cholesterol, specialized white blood cells, and other materials arrive to patch the injury – similar to a scab forming over a break in the skin.

The army pathologists consistently saw cholesterol in the lesions of the young American soldiers – one component of the stringy, fibrous patchwork the body lays down to heal injuries. The pathologists did not consider or could not see the hundreds or thousands of microscopic cuts or tears below the plaque.

Identified at the scene of the crime, *cholesterol* had no defenders. Like blaming the smoke detector for the fire or the ambulances for the accident, cholesterol and its companion - saturated fat - became the only suspects. The diet-heart hypothesis - blaming only cholesterol and saturated fat - was about to be cast in the firm grip of medical consensus.

Are Statin Drugs dangerous?

In the late 1980s, the drug companies introduced a new type of cholesterol-lowering drug called the statins: Zocor, Mevacor, Pravachol, Lescol, Lipitor, and Baycol. In August 2001, after 31 deaths from a muscle-destroying side effect were documented, Bayer of Germany withdrew Baycol.

It may be just a matter of time before all statins are withdrawn. While clinical studies have demonstrated a small benefit among people with active, late stage heart disease, the threat of muscle-destroying side effects, liver damage, and cancer are on the rise.

As reported in *the Felix Letter*, in the "supposedly successful" simvastatin (Zocor) trial, where the average life extension in the treatment group after 5.4 years was 24 days, Dr. Louis Krut is quoted as saying, "If we were to set a very modest goal to extend their average life by only 1 year, it would require them to take simvastatin for 83 years."

According to Dr. Uffe Ravnskov, the statins may stimulate cancer. Because the latency period between exposure and incidence is as long as 20 years, we do not know the extent to which the statin drugs will increase the rate of cancer in coming decades.

In the CARE study (Pravachol), 12 women in the treatment group developed breast cancer during the trial compared to just one in the control group. And blood levels that cause cancer in rodents were close to those seen in patients taking statin drugs.

Why take a chance with muscle-destroying side effects, liver failure, and cancer? That's what I asked my now deceased mother-in-law a few years ago when she began taking Zocor.

Doris's cholesterol was 285. One year later, as she lay in ICU with a serious blood infection and elevated liver enzymes, her doctor withdrew Zocor. Once she stabilized, we asked her doctor to recheck her cholesterol. Why not see – since the patient had nearly died, if the treatment had nonetheless succeeded.

Reluctantly, the doctor complied. Doris's cholesterol was a 130 – a drop of 155 mg/dl in less than a year. After a few more agonizing hospitalizations, Doris was dead - ZOCORED!

Women - don't let this happen to you. There are no circumstances – ever - when a woman should take a drug to lower cholesterol. The same is true for men unless they have the rare genetic condition, familial hypercholesterolemia.

Statin drug therapy is a colossal step in the wrong direction – a medical mistake chasing after a medical lie. Elevated cholesterol is not a disease to fight with drugs; instead, it's a wake up call - alerting you that something is wrong or broken. Fix the problem - don't attack the messenger.

21-Day Plan key principle #1:
Eat eggs for breakfast

Is this the most important key principle in the 21-Day plan? It could be if you are eating commercial boxed cereals for breakfast every morning. Eating high quality complete protein is a better way of starting your day than loading up on sugar and heat-damaged, highly processed cereal.

Switching from cereal to eggs is a no-brainer – it's easy to do. Eggs are nutritious – the gold standard of protein. Eggs contain all essential amino acids plus the sulfur-containing amino acids (methionine, cysteine, and cystine) important for detoxification and cell membrane integrity.

Egg yolk lecithin is the best source of choline, a B-vitamin like nutrient. In the bloodstream, choline helps keep cholesterol moving and helps remove elevated homocysteine. Elevated homocysteine is an independent risk factor for both strokes and heart attacks (see chapter 3).

Eggs are the most concentrated source of the antioxidants, lutein and zeaxanthin. Lutein and zeaxanthin form a yellowish deposit in the macula, the sensitive light-gathering area at the back of the eye. Without these antioxidants, blue and ultraviolet light will cause free radical damage to the eye.

The best protection against macular degeneration is eating free range fresh eggs on a daily basis. Macular degeneration is the leading cause of blindness among people over fifty. This year, about 300,000 people will join the 13 million who have age-related macular degeneration and have already lost their sight.

In his newsletter, Robert Atkins, M.D., asks, "Can you just imagine how much macular degeneration could have been prevented if eggs yolks hadn't been seen as the dietary enemy for so long?"

Lutein and zeaxanthin have been shown to lower the risk of macular degeneration by 43 percent (JAMA 1994; 272: 1413-1420). Green leafy vegetables like kale and spinach contain lutein. Sweet corn and orange peppers provide zeaxanthin. Your body also converts some lutein into zeaxanthin.

Cholesterol:

Very low total cholesterol, less than 160 mg/dl, has been shown to increase the risk of mortality from lung cancer by 1.75 times for men and 3.29 times for women.

Preventive Medicine, 1995; 24: 557-62

"Drawing from a study of 360,000 men, researchers found that 24 percent of those who died of heart attacks had total cholesterol below 200."

Joe Kita, *Men's Health*, pp 105-108, June 2001

The notion that everyone's cholesterol ought to be below 200 mg/dl may be dangerous. In fact, just as many heart attacks occur among people with cholesterol below 200 as occur among individuals with total cholesterol greater than 300. Low total cholesterol is associated with high total mortality in patients with CHD.

European Heart Journal, 1997; 18:52-59

Many people now mistakenly believe that, as long as they keep their cholesterol below 200, they won't have to worry about heart disease.

Jeffrey S. Bland, Ph.D., *Genetic Nutritioneering*

"It's the fibrous tissue [not cholesterol] that's most responsible for narrowing the lumen of arteries, which is the critical factor as far as blood flow is concerned."

Louis H. Krut, M.D.

Supplement companies are busy adding lutein and zeaxanthin to multiple vitamin formulas, but eggs are your best source. Eggs also provide vitamin B-6, vitamin B-12, easy to absorb "heme" iron, plus calcium, magnesium, phosphorus, zinc, and trace minerals.[19]

In January 2002, after recommending no more than 2 eggs per week for decades, the American Heart Association (AHA) announced that it's OK - after all - to eat one egg per day, "*so long as you carefully control cholesterol in the rest of the diet.*"

High sugar Pop Tarts have the American Heart Association's (AHA) heart-check seal of approval, but do not contain choline, lutein, or zeaxanthin. Is it wise to replace lutein and zeaxanthin with high sugar? One wonders, does the AHA want us to limit ourselves to one Pop Tart per day – or can we eat more?

Decades ago, the Cereal Institute, a member of the National Cholesterol Education Program, sponsored a trial in which they gave volunteers "dry egg powder." Using dry egg powder in a scientific trial only makes sense if (1), you are out to prove that dry egg powder raises LDL cholesterol (it does); and (2), you are trying to sell cereal by smearing the reputation of your major competition (it did).

Dry egg powder contains oxidized cholesterol, raises LDL cholesterol, and is harmful to your health. No one eats dry egg powder. Can you believe this is the one and only study that condemned eggs decades ago? And, in spite of the threat they pose to health, damaged dry egg powder is still routinely added to a lot of processed, packaged foods.

What do the Cereal Institute's highly processed cereals have to offer? Do they contain any lutein, zeaxanthin, choline, methionine, cysteine, cystine, vitamin B-6 or vitamin B-12? None at all – but most contain a lot of sugar.

Kellogg's *Corn Pops* and *Raisin Bran* are 40 percent sugar; General Mills' *Golden Grahams,* and *Lucky Charms* are 25 percent sugar; Health Valley *Lite Puffed Corn* and *Lite Puffed Rice* are 25 percent sugar.[20] What, we might ask, are they lite in?

When you pour reduced fat or skim milk on high sugar cereals, you are adding milk sugar to refined sugar to grain sugar. You'll get your sugar all right – in the form of high fasting glucose (see chapter 7) – and you'll get none of the premier antioxidants and sulfur-bearing amino acids found in eggs.

Boycott highly processed, hard-to-digest, heat-damaged Puffs, Charms, Circles, Flakes and Pops. Instead, eat fresh brown eggs for breakfast – as many as you like – poached, scrambled, or fried slowly in butter, lard or olive oil.

Small producer eggs (free range), rich in fat-soluble vitamins A and D and the special omega-3 fatty acids, EPA and DHA, are best. Most important, fresh brown eggs from pasture-fed chickens contain a 1:1 ratio of omega-6 to omega-3 essential fatty acids (see chapter 16).

Foraging chickens eat worms, seeds, bugs and grass and lay nutritious salmonella-resistant eggs. Large producer battery chickens are force-fed grains, soybean mash, antibiotics, and bakery waste. Overcrowded production methods jeopardize the safety and nutritional value of large producer eggs.

High quality eggs are health promoting – one of the healthiest foods on the planet. They're especially important for growing children. If you've been afraid of eggs – or if you have any indication that you may be developing macular degeneration – **get cracking!**

Chapter 2

-------- ❦ --------

What we learned from the people of Framingham

"…In Framingham, Massachusetts, the more saturated fat one ate, the more cholesterol one ate, the more calories one ate, the lower peoples' serum cholesterol."

William P. Castelli, M.D., Director
Framingham Study, 1992

In 1948, a team of Boston University Medical School researchers, sponsored by the National Heart, Lung and Blood Institute (Heart Institute), began a long term population or epidemiological study in Framingham, Massachusetts.

(Epidemiology is the science that deals with the incidence, distribution and control of a disease in a population.)

The purpose of Framingham was to stem the rising tide of heart attacks by learning as much as possible about coronary heart disease. Near Boston, Framingham in the 1950s was a blue-collar community of 28,000 people, primarily ethnic Irish and Italians.

Two out of every three healthy men and women, 5,127 adults between the ages of 30 and 62, volunteered for the study. According to Moore's account in *Heart Failure*, every two years, the participants would undergo physical exams, fill out detailed diet and life-style questionnaires, and be tested on exercise treadmills and electrocardiographs.[1]

The weight, blood, and eating habits of the participants were carefully monitored. Starting at the five-year-point, Framingham researchers filed reports and compiled observations. By the early 1970s, out of the 5,127 study participants, 404 had died of coronary heart disease.

Out of Framingham data, the now familiar heart disease "risk factors" emerged, including being male, increasing age, cigarette smoking, high blood pressure, obesity, and a sedentary life-style. Men were much more likely than women to get coronary heart disease, especially before age 55. Only eleven of 1,600 premenopausal women died of heart attacks.[2]

Participants with a combination of risk factors seemed especially prone to CHD. Overweight male smokers who had high blood pressure, for example, were at much greater risk than female nonsmokers with normal blood pressure.

Statistically associated with a disease, risk factors are usually not the cause. In Framingham, for example, coffee drinking was positively associated with increasing risk of CHD. Warnings were sounded. When it was discovered that coffee drinkers were more likely to smoke cigarettes and smoking was the culprit, the warning about coffee was withdrawn.

One early finding drew special attention: Men between the ages of 30 and 47 who had higher than normal blood cholesterol were more likely to die of heart attacks. There was a statistical relationship between young men dying of heart attacks and high blood cholesterol, but like the link between CHD and coffee drinking, this wasn't proof that high cholesterol caused heart disease.[3]

In fact, young and middle age men (under age 48) with high cholesterol who die of heart attacks often have diabetes or familial hypercholesterolemia, a rare genetic condition that inactivates cholesterol receptors, causing extremely high levels of blood cholesterol to build up.[4]

This positive association in young men between high blood cholesterol and risk of CHD weakened and *disappeared entirely* once a man reached age 48. In Framingham, high blood cholesterol was generally not a risk factor for men or women over 48.[5] Because 95 percent of all heart attacks occur in people who are over 48, Framingham taught us that blood cholesterol levels are not a risk factor for the majority of people who die of heart disease.[6]

After 20 years, Framingham data showed extensive heart disease (22 percent) among people with low or borderline cholesterol and extensive heart disease (18 percent) among those with the highest cholesterol levels.

Average Serum Cholesterol Level	Occurrence of CHD
Low/Borderline TC (below 239)	22%
High TC (240 and above)	18%
(Average of 10 measurements over 20 years)	
TC = Total Cholesterol	

According to Framingham data, most people who die of heart disease have low or average LDL and total cholesterol values. "This study proved there is an 80 percent overlap of the total cholesterol levels of those who do and do not get heart disease," wrote Thomas Yannios, M.D., in *Heart Disease Breakthrough*.[7]

Reflecting on Framingham data, Yannios wrote, "In fact, many more people have heart disease and die of heart attacks at the lower levels of cholesterol."[8] Why do people with low or average cholesterol levels get heart disease? Why do people with elevated cholesterol get heart disease? In both cases, the answer can't be high cholesterol.

Framingham data, at the 30-year point, found that participants whose cholesterol levels had *declined* over time ran a greater risk of dying from all causes than those whose cholesterol had *increased* over time.

In fact, in Framingham, a declining cholesterol value was the best predictor of overall mortality. "For each 1 mg/dl drop of cholesterol, there was an 11 percent increase in coronary and total mortality."[9] Never refuted, this finding should give us pause. If declining cholesterol values predict mortality, can deliberate cholesterol reduction be dangerous?

Yes, according to a study published in the *Journal of the American Geriatric Society.* "Declining total cholesterol levels in nursing home residents – losses greater than 45 mg/dl per year – increased the odds of mortality by more than six times," as reported in *Nutrition Science News.*[10]

Conversely, in older adults, high serum cholesterol may be protective. Dr. Bernard Forette and a team of French researchers found that the death rate among women who had very low cholesterol was five times higher than the death rate of women with the highest cholesterol levels.[11]

The body's cholesterol regulation is very complex; its increase in young men or decline over time can tell us something is wrong. Low serum cholesterol is associated with death from accidents, cancer, and suicide. In a study of 7,603 male government employees, French researchers found that "the incidence of cancer began to climb steadily as cholesterol levels fell below 200 mg/dl."[12]

Framingham also provided evidence that dietary cholesterol and saturated fat do not raise blood cholesterol values or predispose a person to heart disease. Issued in 1970, *"Diet and the Regulation of Serum Cholesterol"* was a study of 912 Framingham residents that compared the cholesterol in their diets with the cholesterol in their blood.

The researchers could find no relationship between their dietary cholesterol and blood cholesterol levels; nor was there any relationship between their saturated fat or caloric intake and their blood cholesterol levels:[13]

"There is a considerable range of serum cholesterol levels within the Framingham Study Group. Something explains this inter-individual variation, but it is not diet (as measured here)."

Twenty-two years later, in 1992, the director of the Framingham Study, Dr. William P. Castelli, said, "…In Framingham, Massachusetts, the more saturated fat one ate, the more cholesterol one ate, the more calories one ate, the lower peoples' serum cholesterol."

Castelli continued, "…we found that the people who ate the most cholesterol, ate the most saturated fat, ate the most calories, weighed the least, and were the most physically active."[14]

This should have put an end to the theory that dietary fats and cholesterol increase blood cholesterol levels and cause heart disease. But like all other findings in the Framingham Study that did not support the diet-heart hypothesis – they were simply ignored.

The lessons of Framingham:

- Most people who die of heart disease have low or average levels of blood cholesterol.

- For most people, LDL and total cholesterol have little "predictive significance" for heart disease.

- High intake of dietary cholesterol doesn't increase blood cholesterol levels.

- High intake of dietary cholesterol doesn't increase the risk of CHD.

- Something other than cholesterol and saturated fat are causing coronary heart disease.

21-Day Plan key principle #2:

A change of heart can reduce your risk of a heart attack

"Stress is not all bad. It can motivate and create self-confidence. The body's true enemy is constant haste."

Barnard Christian, M.D.

"Never cry over things that can't cry over you."

Sophia Loren

In medicine today, the healing potential of love, meditation, prayer, and spiritual faith are being explored. Nowhere could this be more important than in the prevention and treatment of heart disease. In matters of the heart, a positive, optimistic attitude and cheerful self-motivation are as important as diet, exercise, and visits to a knowledgeable doctor.

Hogwash? Not necessarily.

We live in the "Age of Rage" - road rage, sporting event rage, and now even computer rage, with screens and mice flying through the air. People are killing each other - in more ways than one. Too many of us process negative thoughts and feelings for hours, weeks, months, or years. This is hard on the heart.

Scientists at the *Institute of HeartMath,* a research center in California's Santa Cruz mountains, say that when people replay an argument or traffic jam in their mind for five minutes, they experience erratic heart rhythms and reduced immune function, putting a strain on their entire body, even causing heart attack and sudden death.

Bunk?

Not according to Martin Sullivan, M.D., a cardiologist at Duke University Hospital in Durham, North Carolina. As quoted in March/April 1997 *Intuition Magazine*, "The science that they're doing is accurate," he says, "I've reviewed their methodology and it's pretty good."

The heart is much more than a blood pumping muscle, says Rollin McCraty, HeartMath director. "It is an intelligence system, crucial to determining the mental and emotional reactions that have an effect on health." McCraty says there is a "heart brain," a collection of neurons and nerves, which carry impulses from the heart to the brain and back again.

In essence, McCraty, is saying. "The heart provides initiatory control over the brain." This explains why we can become so irrational at time.

It's not the brain pacing the heart, say the California researchers, it's the massive electrical power of the heart setting the tempo. When we're angry, jealous or scared, our ability to analyze is temporarily shut off – and "all hell can break lose."

According to McCraty, "Anger and fear trigger a cardiac SOS signal to the brain, which tells our autonomic nervous system to put our bodies on full alert." When you're upset, even over a minor incident like waiting in a grocery store checkout line that is moving too slow, your heartbeat revs up, flooding your body with the stress hormones adrenaline and cortisol.

Untamed emotional reactions to stress present a more immediate risk of heart disease than smoking cigarettes or eating certain foods. Men who complain of high anxiety are up to six times more likely than other men to suffer sudden cardiac death, say HeartMath researchers.

According to McCraty, "a self induced state of emergency" has become chronic in our busy lives, and the physical effects are creating hormonal havoc." Drops in DHEA, precursor to forty other adrenal hormones, have been linked to many disorders, including heart attacks and heart disease. (See chapter 18, Hormones and the heart.)

Intuition reports that when 28 participants used HeartMath techniques for one month, they achieved a 100 percent increase in DHEA and a 23 percent decrease in cortisol. Yes, you can supplement DHEA, and/or you can let go of judgment, guilt, and past emotional trauma and thereby restore more youthful, beneficial hormone levels.

If we can believe the HeartMath findings – and at least one prominent cardiologist does – we can give up trying to tame, suppress or calm the mind. Instead, we can conscientiously listen to and nourish the intelligence and power of the heart. When that happens, the beat of the heart and the waves of the brain are "entrained."

In HeartMath terminology, we can experience the power of inner self-management:

"Our research shows that when we engage the heart and consciously shift to a positive emotion, our heart rhythms immediately shift. This change in the heart affects the brain, creating a favorable cascade of neural, hormonal and biochemical events that actually reverse the effects of stress, boosts cognitive function, and benefit the entire body. In other words, our research scientifically substantiates what we all intuitively know: That a change of heart literally changes everything, nourishing the body and mind to create optimal conditions for health, vitality, emotional stability and performance."

For more information about HeartMath programs, contact:

Institute of HeartMath   ph: 831-338-8500
14700 West Park Ave.   fax: 831-338-8504
Boulder Creek, CA 95006

Email: **info@heartmath.org**   **www.heartmath.org**

Resistance Is The Devil

When there is enough pressure of any kind – the stress hormones adrenaline and cortisol race through the blood, increasing blood sugar, insulin, and the fight or flight response. After too much stress - we can exhaust ourselves and "burn out."

Acceptance is "the lazy person's guide to enlightenment." Acceptance doesn't mean you have to like something; it just means you quit resisting something you can't control. If we refuse to accept something, we feel the pressure immediately. The struggle takes place within us where it causes the most harm.

Resistance is the devil. If you don't like your thoughts right now, don't try to change them - accept them. Accept whatever feelings you have. Accept all the things you did - but wish you didn't - and accept all the things you didn't do - but wish you did. Practice acceptance.

"Love yourself as much as you can" and then move on. Accepting our thoughts, including the negative ones, is a step in the right direction. Even if we do want to change or control something, acceptance is still the starting point. If we can replace *fight or flight* with *acceptance*, we might prevent a heart attack.

Acceptance inevitably leads to: Cooperation, courage, creative purpose, dignity, discernment, goodwill, honesty, joy, love, optimism, patience, peace, self-determination, self-respect, tolerance, wisdom, and unity.

Give and it will be given unto you is still the truth about life - when we let it.

For further study, look for *Sacred Healing*, the Curing Power of Energy and Spirituality, by C. Norman Shealy, M.D., Ph.D.

Or, *You Can't Afford The Luxury Of A Negative thought* by John-Roger and Peter McWilliams.

Chapter 3

-------- 🙶 --------

Homocysteine –not cholesterol – is to blame

To say that McCully's ideas were unwelcome at the cholesterol feast in the late 1970s would be a mammoth understatement.

Michelle Stacey, *NY Times Magazine*

In the late 1960s, Kilmer McCully, M.D., Harvard Medical School pathologist and researcher, discovered that the risk of heart attack and stroke were strongly associated with elevated levels of homocysteine, an amino acid produced in the body.

By 1969, McCully was ready to go public with his discovery. He published a paper in the *American Journal of Pathology* postulating that high blood levels of homocysteine could trigger plaque buildup and blood clots. Homocysteine – not cholesterol – he said, was the underlying cause of heart and vascular disease.

Dr. McCully's research found that elevated cholesterol and clogged arteries were secondary symptoms of heart disease – not causes. Instead, homocysteine was directly provoking arteriosclerosis – damaging artery cells and tissues.[1]

Vitamin deficiency was to blame, said McCully, not red meat. McCully's research included a simple solution: Excess homocysteine is quickly removed from the bloodstream by replacing refined foods with whole foods and supplementing with three common B-complex vitamins – folic acid, B-6, and B-12[2].

"After publication, I was astounded to find that research scientists around the world who had read the paper were asking me for reprints because they were looking for another explanation for the cause of arteriosclerosis," McCully said in a 1997 *NY Times* interview.[3]

> "The American Medical Association now considers high homocysteine levels in the blood to be an independent risk factor for heart disease. But while everyone – researchers, physicians, and drug companies – was figuring out ways to beat high cholesterol, the issue of homocysteine was essentially overlooked."
>
> Stephen L. DeFelice, M.D., *The Carnitine Defense*

McCully's finding that cholesterol buildup in the arteries was initiated by homocysteine challenged the prevailing hypothesis that cholesterol and saturated fat caused heart disease. McCully became a "loose lips sink ships" fall guy – and the diet-heart hypothesis was the titanic of cardiovascular research.

Casting doubt on the diet-heart hypothesis, McCully's paper was greeted with fear and even hostility. "Kilmer McCully's hypothesis seemed to challenge the cholesterol-heart hypothesis, which was riding high," said Irwin Rosenberg, director of the USDA Human Nutrition Research Center at Tufts University.[4]

"A lot of money had been funneled into studying cholesterol, and a sizeable number of scientists had based their careers upon it…. Many people had invested heavily in the cholesterol theory, and few wanted it challenged," wrote Michelle Stacey in her 1997 *New York Times* interview with McCully.[5]

"You couldn't get ideas funded that went in other directions than cholesterol," said Thomas N. James, cardiologist and president of the University of Texas Medical Branch, and president of the AHA in 1979 and 1980. "You were intentionally discouraged from pursuing alternative questions."[6]

Reflecting on the Heart Institute's insistence that the heart disease debate be limited to cholesterol, Dr. James says:

"It's the money that's a problem. Look at the colorful advertisements in general interest publications, explaining to grandfather that his grandchildren want him to stay alive using these drugs. The anti-cholesterol medications are multibillion-dollar industries now, and they have a huge stake in fanning the flames of the cholesterol mission"[7]

When McCully's National Institute of Health (NIH) funding was not renewed, his research assistants were reassigned, and he was asked to relocate to a basement office. Discouraged at every turn and faced with a drastically reduced income, McCully finally gave up his tenure and left Harvard.[8]

McCully had a hard time finding a new job. For two years, "poison phone calls" from Harvard made it difficult for McCully to get a second interview anywhere in the country. After seeking the assistance of a well-known Boston attorney, the poison phone calls stopped, and McCully landed a position at the Veterans Hospital in Providence, R.I.[9]

With two children in college, McCully and his family had faced two years of financial hardship and emotional upheaval. Meanwhile, throughout the 1980s, – out of reach of the powerful National Institutes of Health - scientists in Sweden, Norway, the Netherlands and Ireland were busy validating McCully's findings.

In the early 1990s, American science, led ironically by Harvard, was taking another look at homocysteine. Two ongoing long-term trials - the Physicians Health Study and Framingham - both turned up strong correlations between high homocysteine levels and the incidence of heart disease.

In 1992, Meir Stampfer, M.D., professor of epidemiology and nutrition at Harvard School of Public Health, surveyed homocysteine levels in the Physicians' Health Study, a survey of almost 15,000 doctors between the ages of 40 and 84. It had been 23 years since the publication of McCully's paper.

Dr. Stampfer and his researchers discovered that homocysteine levels were directly correlated to heart disease risk. Those with the very highest levels of homocysteine were three times more likely to have a heart attack than those with the lowest levels. But even mild elevated homocysteine levels increased the risk of heart disease.[10]

The Harvard study demonstrated that a high homocysteine level was not only an independent risk factor for heart disease, but also a much more predictive risk factor than cholesterol. "The majority of heart attacks occurred in individuals with 'normal' cholesterol," said Stampfer.[11]

Jacob Selhub, M.D., senior scientist at Tufts University, looking at Framingham data, found a strong association between homocysteine levels and insufficient levels of vitamins B-6, B-12 and folic acid. Selhub found that "the higher the homocysteine in the blood, the higher the prevalence of stenosis," the narrowing of the carotid artery leading to the brain.[12]

Shunned for two decades, McCully and homocysteine were back in the limelight. Even the Heart Institute's veteran diet-heart proponents had to acknowledge that homocysteine was, at minimum, "a very important issue." McCully was enjoying his redemption, saying, "I thought it was great that these big shots were paying attention to it."[13]

> *McCully quietly supports the follow-the-money explanation for what happened to him at Harvard: "People don't make a profit preventing disease," he says, "They make a profit through medicine – treating critically advanced stages of disease."[14]*

Nearing retirement today, McCully has received numerous belated awards for his research, including the 1998 Linus Pauling Functional Medicine Award.

Elevated homocysteine levels have been linked to all causes of death. In a long-term study of nearly 2,000 residents of western Jerusalem, trial participants with mild to moderately elevated homocysteine levels had a 30 to 50 percent higher risk of death than those with the lowest levels.[15]

In February 1998, Harvard's School of Public Health published the results of the Nurses' Health Study, a trial originally designed to prove that cholesterol was causing heart disease. Instead, among other findings, the researchers found that the nurses with the lowest consumption of folic acid and B-6 had the highest rates of heart attack and cardiovascular disease.[16]

In a 1995 meta-analysis of 38 homocysteine studies published in the *Journal of the American Medical Association* (*JAMA*), Carol J. Boushey, Ph.D., University of Washington, Seattle, clearly demonstrated that the higher the level of homocysteine, the greater the risk of cardiovascular disease. Boushey estimated that each 5-microgram increase in blood homocysteine was associated with a 60 percent increase (for men) and an 80 percent increase (for women) in CHD risk.[17]

In an English study published in the *Archives of Internal Medicine* in 1998, researchers compared the homocysteine levels of 229 men who died of heart disease with 1,126 healthy men. They found significantly higher homocysteine levels among the men who died of heart disease.[18]

Their results agreed with Dr. Stampfer's findings in the Physicians Health Study; the risk of heart disease was at least three times greater for people with the highest levels of homocysteine. The risk was linear. As homocysteine levels increased, the risk of heart disease and stroke increased as well.[19]

Homocysteine is a normal by-product of metabolizing methionine, an amino acid found in meat, milk and eggs. It is normally cleared rapidly from the bloodstream. Chronic elevated levels are a consequence of suboptimal levels of folic acid, B-6 and B-12. Also, according to McCully, aging, certain drugs, cigarette smoking, diabetes, high blood pressure, and hormonal changes such as meno-pause increase blood levels.[20]

Elevated in only 1 percent of the U.S. population, homocys-teine is elevated in 20 percent of heart disease patients and 33 percent of patients with peripheral vascular disease (cold hands and feet).[21] "High homocysteine is an almost uncanny alarm bell that signals an increased danger of vascular disease, whether coro-nary, peripheral, or cerebral," says Dr. Robert Atkins.[22]

According to Atkins, 10 percent of all heart disease deaths, at minimum, can be attributed directly to elevated homocysteine. Atkins estimates that between 1979 and 1994, at least 1.5 million Americans died needlessly of homocysteine-related vascular dis-ease. In most of these cases, larger than RDA amounts of folic acid, vitamin B-6 and vitamin B-12 would have reduced the risk.[23]

Doctors may be reluctant to test for homocysteine. When my friend, George, and brother, Jim, made their respective visits to the Veterans Administration Hospital in Minneapolis, and a hos-pital in rural Minnesota, neither of their assigned doctors wanted to do the test. My brother's doctor said, "Jim, if I got the number for you, I wouldn't know what to do with it."

It's not necessarily the doctors' fault. Early on, it was the prac-ticing medical doctors who resisted the idea that dietary choles-terol and saturated fat caused heart disease. But over their heads – the medical and political research elite – aligned themselves with the drug and food industries who wanted to make as much money as possible scaring the daylights out of people about cholesterol.

According to Dr. Atkins' grim but conservative calculations, they succeeded.

21-Day Plan key principle #3:

Remove elevated homocysteine with B-complex vitamins

Risk factor	optimum	risk	serious risk
homocysteine	< 8	8-12	>12

Homocysteine is an independent risk factor for heart disease – and high levels aggravate all other mechanisms involved in atherosclerosis. Ask your doctor to include a homocysteine test in your blood work (it may cost about $128.00), especially if you have a family history of premature heart disease.

A reading of 8 micromoles per liter or higher means increased risk of heart disease. Risk is linear; the higher your homocysteine, the greater the risk. If your levels are 12 or higher, B-complex supplements are required. Homocysteine levels above 14 can increase your risk of heart attack and stroke two to four times.

When elevated, homocysteine promotes clotting and is a serious risk factor for clotting not just in the coronary arteries but also in the veins and arteries in the legs and the carotid artery leading to the brain.[24]

Elevated homocysteine is even more dangerous when it's associated with other blood clotting risk factors, especially lipoprotein(a) and fibrinogen (see chapter 14). In combination, these risk factors may be especially dangerous for people who have recently undergone invasive vascular treatments, including heart bypass operations or balloon angioplasty.[25]

Whole foods and B-complex vitamin supplements remove excess homocysteine from the bloodstream. Supplements work fast, but, ultimately, according to McCully, your best option is to replace refined, enriched foods with whole foods, plant and animal.

- In combination, in most people, supplemental vitamin B-6 (50-100 mg), folic acid (800-2,000 mcg), and vitamin B-12 (1,000-2,000 mcg) quickly reduce elevated homocysteine. If these supplements do not reduce elevated homocysteine, also include supplements of choline and betaine.
- In the liver, choline and betaine convert homocysteine to methionine by a separate enzymatic pathway (according to McCully). Choline is abundant in eggs and betaine is abundant in beets.
- NOW Foods manufactures an "all-in-one" product called *Homocysteine Regulators* that includes vitamin B-6, folic acid, vitamin B-12 and trimethylglycine (betaine).
- Liver and other organ meats are the *absolute best sources* of folic acid, vitamin B-6 and vitamin B-12. Liver and organ meats from grass-fed beef are safe and excellent to eat on a regular basis. (See 21-Day Plan, chapter 17.)
- Food sources of vitamin B-6 include liver, fish, red meat, poultry, peas, nuts, broccoli, Brussels sprouts, lentils, kale, and properly prepared whole grains and beans.
- Food sources of vitamin B-12 include liver, fish, red meat, cheese, raw milk, clams, oysters and eggs. There are no reliable plant sources of B-12
- Excellent food sources of folic acid include liver and organ meats, green leafy vegetables, grapefruit, nuts, peas, and properly prepared whole grains and beans.
- More than 6 cups of coffee per day may increase homocysteine. Tea, which contains less caffeine, has little or no affect on homocysteine levels.

For more information about homocysteine, read *The Heart Revolution* by Kilmer McCully, M.D.

Chapter 4

-------- 🖎 --------

A look at the Multiple Risk Factor Intervention Trial (MRFIT)

Sadly, the drastic changes that the MRFIT trial participants made in their eating habits for years had little effect on the level of cholesterol in their blood…and had produced no measurable benefits.

Thomas J. Moore, *author of Heart Failure*

In 1971, two year's after rejecting McCully's findings on homocysteine, the Heart Institute convened the Task Force on Arteriosclerosis. Their goal: To design studies to prove that lowering dietary cholesterol and saturated fat would reduce blood cholesterol levels, which, in turn, would reduce the risk of coronary heart disease and extend lives.

Launched at 28 medical centers across the country, the $115 million dollar Multiple Risk Factor Intervention Trial (MRFIT) employed 250 full time researchers and took ten years to complete. MRFIT was directed by Jeremiah Stamler, M.D., a professor at Northwestern University Medical School in Chicago.

The researchers selected 12,855 middle-aged men (age 35-57) out of 361,662 applicants. Using the Framingham Study risk factor equations, MRFIT researchers set out to prove that by reducing high cholesterol, cigarette smoking, and high blood pressure, they could lower the risk of heart disease in high-risk study participants.

As a group, these men were not ready to run a marathon: Two-thirds smoked, their typical diet included more than twice the recommended amount of cholesterol, two-thirds already had high blood pressure, and 60 percent were obese.[1]

At the start of the trial, half of the men were assigned to the "usual care" control group. They received no advice; just an annual physical that was sent to their personal physician and a warning that they were at greater than average risk of heart disease.

The other half were assigned to the "special intervention" treatment group. Special intervention meant initially ten weekly group therapy sessions during which doctors, psychologists and other health professionals sought to motivate the participants into making dramatic, far-reaching changes in their daily lives.

Dietitians taught participants how to shop and gave classes in preparing low fat and low cholesterol meals. Participants were instructed to switch from cholesterol-laden lard and butter to vegetable fats like margarine and corn oil.

The men were able to cut dietary cholesterol 42 percent, saturated fat 28 percent, and total calories 21 percent. At the same time, they increased their consumption of polyunsaturated vegetable fats by 33 percent.[2]

Smokers in the treatment group responded positively to the intense anti-smoking message, which included "stern lectures from physicians," hypnosis, and even monetary rewards for not lighting up. After four years, most of the light smokers had quit and after seven years half of all smokers quit.[3]

In the treatment group, high blood pressure was treated energetically with drugs. According to Thomas Moore, 87 percent reduced their blood pressure to a moderate threshold while two-thirds reached normal levels during the study period.[4]

Disappointing Results:

In February 1982, the study results were tallied. Although the trial had succeeded in modifying the risk factors among treatment group participants, overall, the MRFIT trial failed.

After a seven year period, blood cholesterol levels in the treatment group had dropped no more than 6.7 percent. In the usual care control group, blood cholesterol had dropped almost as much, and at the end of the trial, there was little difference in blood cholesterol between the two groups.[5]

There was no significant difference in overall mortality; in fact, there were five more deaths in the treatment group - and a small difference in coronary heart disease (CHD) mortality that was not considered significant.[6]

Mortality	Treatment Group	Usual Care
Overall Deaths	265	260
CHD Deaths	115	124

Among those treated for high blood pressure, "special intervention" may have backfired. The drugs helped lower blood pressure, but also raised blood cholesterol by seven percent and may have increased the death rate among treatment group participants.[7]

The usual care untreated group left to their own devices had less heart disease than expected. Even without "special intervention," 29 percent had quit smoking. This reflected the overall decline in heart disease mortality throughout the 1970s as adult smokers in large numbers quit.

The percent of adult smokers declined from 42 percent in 1970 to 30 percent by 1996. As McCully points out in *The Heart Revolution*, smoking cessation, nutritional supplements, and emergency response, in combination, had finally reduced heart attack death rates.[8]

In spite of the disappointing results, MRFIT researchers declared success. By emphasizing a favorable outcome among a subgroup of treatment group participants who had quit smoking, the researchers improved their results. Sorting participants into subgroups was not part of the original study design, but it did reveal that smoking cessation was the only positive special intervention that had had any influence on the outcome of the trial.[9]

The failure of MRFIT was a divisive issue within the medical community but received little attention in the press. Dietary advice that was already being heavily promoted was not validated in a carefully controlled scientific trial. **After ten years and more than $100 million dollars, the MRFIT trial had only confirmed the already widespread belief that it's a good idea not to smoke.**

21-Day Plan key principle #4:

Use L-Carnitine to prevent heart attacks and promote weight loss

"Carnitine is a heart attack insurance policy. There is compelling evidence that high levels of carnitine in your system can minimize damage to the heart muscle that takes place during a heart attack. Carnitine supplements offer an effective one-two punch. They can help keep your heart healthy and protect it during a cardiac crises."

Stephen L. DeFelice, M.D., *The Carnitine Defense*

"Carnitine is the most important nutrient for naturally supporting the weight loss process, and the results you get if you take it in the right doses (1,000 mg and beyond) can be quite dramatic."

Robert Crayhon, M.S., *The Carnitine Miracle*

Do you need more energy? Do you want to lose weight? Are you under a lot of stress? Do you want to protect yourself from a heart attack? Have you had a heart attack already? If you answered "yes" to any of the above questions, you should consider supplementing with L-Carnitine and/or making sure that you're getting enough carnitine-rich foods in your diet.

As Robert Crayhon emphasizes in *The Carnitine Miracle*, the true measure of health is optimum cellular energy. Heart muscle cells need more energy than any other cell in the body. L-Carnitine strengthens the heart and increases cardiac output.

L-Carnitine is essential for energy production and fat metabolism. The key function of L-Carnitine is to shuttle fat into the mitochondria. Mitochondria are the tiny cell furnaces that burn fuel to create energy, known as ATP (adenosine triphosphate). L-Carnitine forklifts fat into cell furnaces throughout the body.

In the absence of L-Carnitine, fat isn't turned into energy. Since the heart is constantly at work and needs a lot of energy, L-Carnitine is of specific importance to the heart; sugar is only a backup fuel. Fat is the most concentrated source of energy available to the body and vital for optimum heart function.[10]

"Carnitine is the stroker, the molecule that shovels fuel into the engine. It makes cardiac energy possible. In a way, the onset of heart disease is a process of energy starvation. If your heart doesn't get enough high quality fuel, it can't produce enough energy to pump blood to the rest of your tissues as well as to sustain itself," writes Stephen L. DeFelice, M.D., in *The Carnitine Defense*.

Cells need abundant energy to prevent disease. When we provide our cells with enough carnitine, they are able to create a better defense against viruses and bacteria and to protect, maintain and regenerate critically important cell membrane structures throughout the body.

L-Carnitine is most abundant in red meat, especially mutton and lamb. Don't trim the fat or you'll lose most of the carnitine. Don't be afraid of the less expensive fatty cuts of supermarket lamb.

They are a good value – and high in carnitine. Pork, chicken, turkey and dairy products contain lesser amounts. Among plants, only avocados, asparagus, and tempeh (fermented soy) contain small amounts.

Food Source	Total content of L-Carnitine *
Mutton (over 1 year-old)	210
Lamb	78
Beef	64
Pork	30
Chicken	7.5

* (mg/100 grams of raw food)

Not an amino acid, L-Carnitine resembles choline, another B-vitamin-like nutrient found abundantly in egg yolk lecithin. L-Carnitine is technically not a vitamin because it can be produced in the body. A vegetarian diet is low in L-Carnitine and deficient in the nutrients the body uses to synthesize carnitine.

Cereal grains such as corn, wheat and rice are low in lysine and methionine, the amino acids needed by the body to produce carnitine. Lysine and methionine are found abundantly only in red meat. Vegetarians lack these amino acids. Other carnitine building blocks include niacin, vitamin B-6, vitamin C, and iron.

According to Robert Crayhon, for thousands of years, our predecessors consumed 500 to 2,000 mg of L-Carnitine per day. Our bodies need that much to function optimally. The "carnitine advantage," in Crayhon's words, is abundant energy.

Applications for Supplemental L-Carnitine

- Athletic performance
- Type II diabetes
- Heart attack prevention
- Inherited carnitine deficiency
- Weight loss
- Increase resistance to muscle fatigue
- Chronic fatigue syndrome
- Peripheral artery disease
- Prevent second heart attack
- Vegetarian diet deficiency
- With CoQ-10 for heart failure

L-Carnitine helps burn up elevated triglycerides – dangerous sugar made fats we discuss in chapter 10. Anything that lowers triglycerides increases protective HDL cholesterol. People with an adverse TG/HDL ratio (even 2:1 or higher), need supplemental L-Carnitine (and magnesium).

By lowering triglycerides and increasing protective HDL, carnitine promotes circulation and oxygen levels throughout the body. Carnitine creates a healthier balance of fats in the blood and in the cells of the body. Carnitine is one of the most important nutrients for any condition involving the heart.

L-Carnitine, combined with CoQ-10, is an effective remedy for congestive heart failure. Heart failure patients, with the assistance of their doctor, may be able to reduce their reliance on prescription drugs like digitalis (Lanoxin).

L-Carnitine is a safe, effective fat burner. To initiate and sustain weight loss, Crayhon recommends up to 4,000 mg of L-Carnitine daily. As you reach your weight loss goals, you can slowly reduce supplemental carnitine to 500 mg daily.

For best results, use L-Carnitine with omega-3 rich milled flaxseed or flaxseed oil. Omega-3 fats, supporting the action of L-

Carnitine, instruct the body to burn fat. Also, you must restrict carbohydrates, especially grains and starchy vegetables (see chapters 9).

The minimum dose to feel a difference is 500 mg. Some people will not see lowered triglycerides and weight loss until they take 2,000-4,000 mg daily. If you need to take larger amounts for therapeutic relief, back your dosage down slowly again as you reach your goals.

L-Carnitine is best early in the day on an empty stomach. One or two capsules one to three times a day in early morning and early afternoon works best. If taken late in the day, L-Carnitine may give you unwanted energy and delay sleep.

Carnitine is water-soluble and does not build up in the body. Several clinical studies, cited by Stephen L. DeFelice, M.D., show that L-Carnitine is safe and effective. Clinicians recommend both L-Carnitine tartrate and fumarate. *NOW Foods* makes a tasty (natural vanilla flavor) L-Carnitine in liquid form. Each tablespoon provides 500 mg.

Online, check out **www.nowfoods.com** or **www.nokobeach.com**. Also, you can find L-Carnitine at your local vitamin or natural foods grocery store.

The *Carnitine Defense* by Stephen L. DeFelice, M.D. provides a complete supplement program for the heart, featuring L-Carnitine.

The *Carnitine Miracle* by Robert Crayhon, M.S., clinical nutritionist, focuses on overall benefits of L-Carnitine, including weight loss and brain health.

Chapter 5

-------- 🐟 --------

A look at the Lipid Research Clinics - Coronary Primary Prevention Trial (LRC)

In the Alice-In-Wonderland atmosphere of the Lipid Research Clinics, nothing plus nothing conveniently equals something.

Uffe Ravnskov, M.D., Ph.D.

Launched by the Heart Institute around the same time as the MRFIT study, LRC (Lipid Research Clinics) was designed to prove that lowering blood cholesterol with a drug would reduce the risk of coronary heart disease and thereby extend the lives of the study participants.

To conduct the study, twelve new cholesterol-research laboratories were set up by the Heart Institute at large universities throughout the country, such as Baylor, Stanford, Johns Hopkins, and the University of Washington, Seattle.

The researchers selected 3,806 men (35 to 59 years old) out of a group of 480,000 applicants. LRC looked for men with extremely high blood cholesterol levels – only the upper 0.8 percent qualified. This meant that many of the participants had **familial hyper-cholesterolemia**, a rare genetic defect in cholesterol metabolism present in just 0.5 percent of the population.[1]

In a preliminary report LRC researchers announced that they would study two separate outcomes: Nonfatal heart attacks and CHD-related deaths. Note: LRC researchers emphasized that they would be satisfied with nothing less than the strongest statistical proof of their findings, meaning they would be "99 percent certain" that the results were not due to chance.[2]

The LRC researchers were looking for solid results. Over a seven-year period, they hoped to lower blood cholesterol 25 percent or more – something that hadn't been done before in a trial - and thereby reduce the risk of heart disease in the treatment group by 50 percent.

Among the drugs available in the early 1970s, the researchers chose cholestyramine (Questran), one of the older anti-cholesterol medications (bile acid resin). At that time, the newer statin drugs (such as Zocor, Mevacor) were not yet available.

In 1984, the disappointing results were tabulated. After 7.4 years, the cholesterol levels in the treatment group were only 6.7 percent lower than those in the control group. The drug had failed to lower cholesterol enough to prove that lowering cholesterol would reduce the risk of CHD.

Lipid Research Clinics After 7.4 years	Treatment Group (1,906 men)	Placebo Group (1,900 men)
Nonfatal heart attacks	130	158
Deaths from CHD	30	38
Deaths for all causes	68	71
Deaths from violence/ suicide	11	4

Treatment group participants had trouble taking their six packets of cholestyramine daily; and their livers may have compensated for the drug's action by stepping up cholesterol production. LRC researchers made a point of not emphasizing that there were 8 gastrointestinal cancer deaths in the treatment group (out of 21 cases) versus just one in the placebo group (out of 11 cases).[3]

The difference in nonfatal heart attacks was not statistically significant. In the treatment group, 130 participants (6.8 percent) had experienced a nonfatal heart attack versus 158 participants (8.3 percent) in the placebo group – a 1.5 percent net difference in actual risk after 7.4 years.[4]

The difference in CHD-related deaths was not statistically significant either. In the treatment group, 30 participants (1.6 percent) suffered a fatal heart attack, compared to 38 participants (2.0 percent) in the placebo group – a 0.4 percent net difference in actual risk after 7.4 years.[5]

Nonetheless, by using *relative risk* statistics (a percent of a percent), LRC researchers announced that they had reduced the risk of nonfatal heart attacks by 19 percent and CHD-related deaths by over 30 percent.[6]

To help reach their inflated numbers, LRC researchers *excluded* uncertain nonfatal heart attacks from the treatment group and *included* uncertain fatal heart attacks in the placebo group.[7]

> LRC researchers "Left no stone unturned in their manipulation of data so that insignificant results could be transformed into what appeared to be significant results," stated Howard H. Wayne M.D.[8]

Using the original 99 percent announced standard, the small favorable trend in either group could only be explained by chance, as defined by the researchers themselves. But by applying the less stringent 95 percent standard and by combining the two groups into one, LRC researchers declared success.

Statements released at the time claimed, "For the first time it had been proven that lowering cholesterol would reduce the mortality from heart disease and lower the risk of having a heart attack."[9] When other scientists voiced their objections to the study's design changes, the LRC directors simply denied that they had ever embraced the more stringent standard.[10]

Giving cholestyramine for over seven years to 1,906 middle age men – many with a genetic predisposition to atherosclerosis - had only saved the lives of eight, but the Heart Institute was now recommending that drug treatment be extended to patient groups that had not been part of the trial.

The results, the Heart Institute said, "Leave little doubt of the benefit of cholestyramine therapy." In January, 1984, The *Journal of the American Medical Association (JAMA)* dutifully reported:

"The trial's implications…could and should be extended to other age groups and women, and to others with more modest elevations of cholesterol levels. The benefits that could be expected from cholestyramine treatment are considerable.[11]

Now retired, George Mann, M.D., professor in medicine and biochemistry at Vanderbilt University, severely criticized the LRC directors and the trial's unsupportable results:

"The managers at the National Institutes of Health have used Madison Avenue hype to sell this failed trial in the way the media people sell an underarm deodorant…"

Doctors Vitale and Ross, in a critique of LRC at the time, said, "The whole story of the Lipid Research Clinic's Coronary Primary Prevention Trial is an impressive example of misconstrued research results."

Doctors Vitale and Ross could not fathom how trial results involving a high percentage of men with a genetic defect in cholesterol metabolism could be applied to other patients. "Any attempt to generalize the findings to the remainder of the population, to women, and especially children was not only unscientific but dishonest."[12]

"The contradictions in these studies made a lot of unsatisfied researchers start looking for alternative explanations of what exactly was going on in those arteries," wrote Thomas Yannios, M.D., in his book, *Heart Disease Breakthrough.*[13]

But the Heart Institute had now spent 60 percent of its $494 million clinical trials budget on MRFIT and LRC. Diet-heart promoters were ready to get on with treatment:

"Now we have proved that it is worthwhile to lower blood cholesterol; no more trials are necessary. Now is the time for treatment."[14]

21-Day Plan key principle #5:

Supplement with vitamin C and vitamin E

Vitamin C (ascorbic acid or ascorbate) is important for healthy blood vessels. The average American takes in about 60 mg of vitamin C daily, which is the recommend daily allowance and enough to prevent scurvy. But, is 60 mg a day enough to protect us from heart disease?

According to the late Linus Pauling, people with low blood levels of vitamin C have weakened blood vessels and a greater risk of heart disease. Vitamin C is required for the synthesis of collagen and elastin, which are used by the body to strengthen blood vessel walls. Animal experiments conducted by Pauling provide proof.

Guinea pigs, like us and other primates, have lost the ability to synthesize vitamin C. When Pauling placed laboratory guinea pigs on a low ascorbate diet, corresponding to the average human U.S. intake, they rapidly developed atherosclerotic plaques, similar to human plaques. When large amounts of ascorbate were restored to their diet, the plaque formations regressed.

Dogs do not die prematurely of coronary heart disease. Corrected for body weight, dogs synthesize between 3,000 and 18,000 mg of vitamin C per day. Apparently, large amounts of ascorbate keep dogs' blood vessels healthy and strong. Humans cannot synthesize vitamin C, and suboptimal dietary intake increases the risk of heart disease.

In chapter 14, you'll read about lipoprotein(a). Lipoprotein(a) has been called the "heart attack cholesterol" and for good reason. Lipoprotein(a) is LDL cholesterol with something that resembles a suction cup attached to it, a *glycoprotein* called "Apoprotein(a)."

Lipoprotein(a) is a sticky, bastard form of cholesterol. Lp(a) promotes clotting around atherosclerotic plaques and interferes with the body's efforts to break up those clots. Worse, it readily oxidizes (is damaged) and can migrate into the artery wall. Lp(a) is the blood fat you need to be most concerned about.

Pauling discovered that only animals that have lost the ability to synthesize vitamin C (guinea pigs, humans and other primates) produce lipoprotein(a). Low levels of vitamin C trigger lipoprotein(a) buildup in the bloodstream. Lp(a) is the body's fallback mechanism to plug blood vessels walls until adequate dietary ascorbate is restored.

Margarine increases Lp(a) and butter or saturated fats reduce it (chapter 14). In small amounts, Lp(a) performs important stop gap functions. Called upon too much, it has the ability to make matters dangerously worse. Avoiding margarine and all *partially hydrogenated* vegetable fats is a critically important part of the anti-lipoprotein(a) program. Supplementing with vitamin C (500 to 2,000 mg per day) is another.

Without sufficient vitamin C, its ruthless cousin, lipoprotein(a) takes over. According to a study in the *Journal of the American College of Nutrition* (1999; 18(5): 451-61), supplemental vitamin C keeps lipoprotein (a) at bay, and thereby protects LDL cholesterol from oxidation.

Optimum – not RDA – levels of vitamin C promote healthy collagen-based connective tissue throughout the body, including strong joint linings and capillary walls. Vitamin C is also instrumental in the formation of both red and white blood cells and provides water-soluble antioxidant protection to all the cells in your body.

Vitamin C in foods can be lost through cooking, heating, drying or any processing. Drying an herb, for example, will concentrate certain constituents and deplete others. Fresh peppers contains a lot of vitamin C; dried peppers have none.

Asparagus, broccoli, Brussels sprouts, cabbage, dark green leafy vegetables, tomatoes, red and green peppers, kiwi fruit, and oranges and grapefruit are excellent sources of vitamin C.

Though naturally occurring vitamins in food are best – they're disappearing. A recent German study noted that the vitamin C content of strawberries declined from 60 mg (per 100 grams of fruit) in 1985 to just 13 mg in 1996. In the same study, apples lost 80 percent of their vitamin C, and bananas lost 92 percent of their vitamin B-6 and 94 percent of their folic acid.[15]

In the German analysis, spinach had 58 percent less vitamin C and 59 percent less vitamin B-6. Where are the nutrients going? No one knows for sure, but recent USDA studies confirm that it takes more and more food to provide basic levels of required vitamins and minerals.

Supplemental vitamin C, in the range of 500 to 2,000 mg daily, is cheap insurance, especially if you have a family history of diabetes or cardiovascular disease. Supplementing with larger amounts of vitamin C – at least 2,000 mg per day – can help reduce plaque formation and clot-related activity (*Journal of Cardiovascular Pharmacology* 1999; 34 (5): 690-93).

Water soluble, vitamin C is not stored in the body. The mineral ascorbate form (ascorbic acid attached to a mineral) with bioflavonoids is much better and longer lasting than unbuffered ascorbic acid.

Supplemental vitamin C is synthetic. When discussing water-soluble vitamins (vitamin C and the B-complex), the issue isn't natural versus synthetic; it's dosage and formulation. Read the label. Make sure you are taking *mineral ascorbate*. Mineral ascorbate is slow release vitamin C. Also, mineral ascorbate should contain at least 200 mg or more of a mixed citrus bioflavonoid combination plus acerola powder, rose hips, and rutin.

Average person is a myth - not to be found. We are more different than alike. Our need for essential vitamins and minerals varies dramatically from person to person. *Recommended Daily Allowances* (RDAs) may prevent overt disease, but do little to promote optimum health. In *Biochemical Individuality*, Roger Williams, Ph.D., demonstrated that requirements for nutrients such as calcium and vitamin C vary by a factor of four or more.

Vitamin E

Vitamin E is the most important fat-soluble antioxidant. Together, natural vitamin E and mineral ascorbate vitamin C provide strong first line antioxidant defenses. While other antioxidants may even be more powerful, your body will not function optimally without sufficient vitamin C and vitamin E.

Early animal studies in the 1980s showed that both rodents and piglets with low vitamin E diets were prone to atherosclerosis. When the animals were given supplemental vitamin E, the plaques regressed. A University of Pittsburgh study published in 1998 found that mice given vitamin E for 16 weeks had 40 percent less artery plaque than the mice not given vitamin E.[16]

Careful, long term human studies are more persuasive. Eric Rimm, D.Sc., assistant professor of nutrition and epidemiology at the Harvard School of Public Health, monitored approximately 40,000 male physicians between the ages of 45 and 70 for several years. Rimm found that physicians who took 100 IU or more of vitamin E daily for at least two years had a 40 percent reduction in heart attack risk.[17]

Meir Stampfer, M.D., professor of epidemiology and nutrition at the Harvard School of Public Health, was one of the physicians involved in the Nurses' Health Study, a long term trial involving 85,000 female nurses who were between the ages of 34 and 59 when the study began in 1976. Dr. Stampfer and his associates found that nurses who took 200 IU of vitamin E daily for at least two years also enjoyed a 40 percent reduction in heart disease risk.[18]

Both Dr. Rimm's study and the Harvard Nurses study took into account other variables, including age, dietary differences, and exercise habits. Both studies demonstrated that it takes two years before the benefits of vitamin E supplementation can be measured in a trial, and that women need double the amount that protects men.[19]

Many other well-respected clinical studies support the findings of Rimm and Stampfer. "Whether the studies are cross-cultural, strictly observational, or clinical trials testing the effects of many supplements, the results have been the same: Vitamin E can lower your risk of heart disease."[20]

Vitamin E's greatest benefit is preventing the free radical oxidation of LDL cholesterol. Free radicals are chemically reactive molecules racing around with an unpaired electron. Vitamin E, which contains many hydrogen molecules, lends a hydrogen molecule to the free radical, diverting them away from LDL.

Vitamin E can enter artery walls, attach itself directly to LDL, and thereby prevent the merger of LDL with free radicals. Vitamin E also slows the clotting process by making platelets less sticky. More viscous, free flowing blood, in turn, reduces plaque formation. Vitamin E may also slow down smooth muscle growth in the artery wall.[21]

Vitamin E is destroyed when foods are processed and packaged. Milling wheat berries into white flour removes 80 percent of the vitamin E. Roasting nuts depletes 80 percent of the vitamin E. Oxygen, heat, light and freezing all destroy vitamin E.[22] For most people, supplements are the only practical way to ensure 400 IU per day.

Vitamin E, is a complex nutrient with eight active components. The most active and important component is alpha tocopherol, designated "d-alpha". If you see "dl-alpha" on the label, put the bottle back. It's synthetic – made from petroleum by-products - and in the case of fat-soluble vitamins, synthetic isn't even a second choice (unless you are allergic to natural vitamin E).

Three other tocopherols, beta, delta, and gamma, are part of the vitamin E family. These additional "mixed tocopherols" are added to d-alpha to form a superior vitamin E complex. While d-alpha is most active – and most important - the additional tocopherols enhance antioxidant defenses.

Tocotrienols are the least known component of the family. While the mixed tocopherols provide proven antioxidant protection, adding tocotrienols to your supplement or dietary plan will mean even greater protection, especially if you are fighting cancer (*Journal of Nutrition* 1997, vol. 127, no. 3, pp 544-48).

Most of us don't consume enough tocotrienols. The vitamin E in palm oil, a saturated tropical fat, consists largely of these missing tocotrienols. As you will read in chapter 13, these healthy tropical fats are no longer available in the U.S. In the 1960s, the U.S. edible oil industry in an effort to sell more domestic vegetable fats, smeared the good name of tropical oils in duplicitous public relations and advertising campaigns.

Palm oil and palm kernel oil are derived from palm trees. Palm oil comes from the fruit; palm kernel oil comes from the seeds. In Dr. Robert Atkins' words, both "are unbelievably rich in cancer-fighting antioxidants." Both oils contain beta carotene, alpha carotene, gamma carotene, and lycopene. In a study published ten years ago, a natural carotenoid extract of palm oil suppressed tumor cell proliferation 10 times better than beta carotene alone. (*Journal of* *the National Cancer In*stitute, vol. 81, 1989).

Until these healthy tropical fats are restored to our food supply, tocotrienol supplements can provide the missing vitamin E family members. *NOW Foods* has a *Tocotrienols and E Complex* that provides d-alpha tocopherol, beta, gamma and delta tocopherols, plus alpha and gamma tocotrienols from rice bran oil. Selenium (70 mcg) is added for synergistic antioxidant activity.

The RDA for vitamin E is only 40 IU, well below the minimum levels needed to reduce the risk of heart disease. Supplements easily and reliably boost vitamin E levels into the zone of protection. Natural vitamin E (d-alpha) with mixed tocopherols, made from soybean oil, is far superior to synthetic dl-alpha products made from petroleum by-product.

You will find natural vitamin E and mineral ascorbate vitamin C at your local vitamin or natural foods grocery store.

For comprehensive guidance on the use of nutritional supplements, read *Nutrition Made Simple* by Robert Crayhon, M.S., or Dr. Atkins' *Vita-Nutrient Solution*, by Robert C. Atkins, M.D.

The *Carnitine Defense* by Stephen L. DeFelice, M.D., provides a cardiovascular supplement program emphasizing: L-Carnitine, vitamin E, the B-Complex and magnesium.

Chapter 6

-------- ❧ --------

"War on Cholesterol"

This has got to be one of the most blatant health scams I've seen in my more than 40 years in medicine.

John R. Lee, M.D.

The diet-heart idea is the biggest scam in the history of medicine.

George Mann, M.D.,

I n 1985, acting on its considerable authority, not requiring approval from Congress or the White House, the National Heart Lung and Blood Institute (the Heart Institute), a division of the National Institutes of Health, launched the National Cholesterol Education Program (NCEP) – the largest medical intervention in American history.

First described in a 1982 AHA policy statement, the NCEP is the "poster child" of the diet-heart hypothesis. The Heart Institute and the AHA, pejoratively called "the Alliance" by Dr. Mann, administer more than 90 percent of all grants for cardiovascular research.

Still gloating over their high profile LRC media victory the year before, the alliance was now ready to launch their long awaited "War on Cholesterol." Major critics of the diet-heart hypothesis, like Kilmer McCully, M.D., had been run out of town, and the considerable resistance of some of the nation's outspoken medical doctors had finally died down to a whimper.

For the first time in history, like kids at the carnival, adults were lining up to have their cholesterol checked. Cholesterol travels in the blood stream as lipoprotein – bundles of fat particles and protein. The concentration of cholesterol in the blood is expressed as milligrams per deciliter (mg/dl).

Lucky for the drug companies, the NCEP had decreed that a cholesterol level above 200 was abnormal. People classified high, over 240 mg/dl, 25 percent of the adult population, were prescribed a strict, low fat diet or drugs for the rest of their lives.

People with average cholesterol, between 200 and 239, were classified "*borderline high.*" Those designated "borderline high" with one additional risk factor (two for women) were prescribed the same medical treatment as those classified high. Only people with cholesterol in the "desirable" range, below 200, were sent away untreated.

Unfortunately, laboratory performance at this time was notably poor. According to the Heart Institute's own documents, error rates in laboratories were as high as 9 percent. Someone whose actual blood cholesterol was 230 mg/dl could end up with a number as low as 187 or as high as 267.[1]

Walt Bogdanich, a reporter for the *Wall Street Journal*, sent blood to five different New York State laboratories. The results he got back placed him in all three categories – from desirable to high.[2] Cholesterol measurement is not an exact science. Sub-fractions of cholesterol must be calculated, and cholesterol levels may vary within a single sample.

And what were they testing? Many doctors, including Howard H. Wayne, M.D., author of *How to Protect Your Heart from Your Doctor*, say there is no such thing as a normal cholesterol level. Emotional stress, age, disease conditions, seasons of the year "cause extensive fluctuations in normal values."[3]

Thomas Yannios, M.D., states, "In fact, there is no such thing as 'normal' cholesterol, or a 'normal' lipid profile. Dr. Yannios recommends a complete set of tests (see chapter 21) in order to understand your risk of heart disease.[4] Cholesterol readings, by themselves, mean very little and can be highly inaccurate.

In the Framingham Study, as noted earlier, there was extensive heart disease among people with high cholesterol, and there was extensive heart disease among people with low and average cholesterol. In fact, the majority of people who died of heart disease had low or average levels. What sense, then, did the War on Cholesterol make – except to sell drugs to people who didn't need them.

In MRFIT, and LRC, we should have learned two things. First, the body sets cholesterol levels for itself and then goes to elaborate lengths to maintain them. Second, human response to diet is highly variable. Low fat diets may lower cholesterol levels in a small percentage of people, but raise them in many others.

Conclusive data from Framingham and other studies had already established the inability of low fat diets to lower cholesterol or extend lives. Putting people on low fat diets will reduce beneficial HDL cholesterol, increase LDL, and promote elevated triglycerides, the dangerous carbohydrate-induced blood fats we describe in chapter 10.

According to Dr. Yannios, "One of the problems associated with low-fat diets is their affects on HDL and LDL particles. Lack of fat and overabundance of carbohydrates are both independent and synergistic factors. On average, HDL levels drop 10 percent for every 10 percent rise in the amount of energy provided by carbohydrate rather than fat."[5]

The NCEP directors ignored the results of nine large-scale cholesterol lowering clinical trials that had already been conducted in Norway, Finland, Australia, England, and the U.S. After following over 11,000 people between 2 and 10 years, "There was an insignificant decrease in the incidence of coronary artery disease, and no effect on overall mortality of the people studied."[6]

In other words, lowering cholesterol with drugs or diet didn't prevent heart attacks or extend lives. Dr. Basil Rifkind, who had directed the LRC study, acknowledged in the *British Medical Journal* (301, 815, 1990) that, like all the other diet-heart studies, LRC had not reduced the number of deaths from coronary heart disease.[7]

In response to the launching of the NCEP, the late Russell Smith, Ph.D., author of two large scientific papers on the diet-heart hypothesis, said:

> "The current campaign to convince every American to change his or her diet, and in many cases, to initiate drug therapy for life is based on fabrications, erroneous interpretations and/or gross exaggerations of findings and, very importantly, the ignoring of massive amounts of unsupportive data…"

Beginning in 1956, before any studies had been conducted, the AHA had been warning the public about the "dangers of dietary cholesterol," urging Americans to replace animal fat with margarine and polyunsaturated vegetable oils.

"We know enough to call for altering some habits even before the final proof is nailed down," said Dr. Jeremiah Stamler, Northwestern University Medical School, AHA leader, and later director of MRFIT and other Heart Institute funded studies.

To their credit, doctors, too, had required some softening up. In a poll conducted by the Heart Institute in 1983, while two thirds of the general public believed that saturated fat had a "large effect" on coronary heart disease, only 28 percent of doctors saw saturated fat as a dietary hazard.[8]

In 1987, the American Medical Association (AMA) sent every practicing doctor the NCEP "consensus conclusions" on cholesterol, and a much more elaborate information kit was sent to 200,000 primary care physicians and cardiologists. In its letter to physicians in 1987, the AMA wrote, "The AMA's Campaign Against Cholesterol will use national and local television to tell the public about the risks of high blood cholesterol and the availability of cholesterol testing through your office." [9]

For rank and file medical doctors, cholesterol testing and office visits were potentially lucrative business – a way of getting reluctant adults (especially men) in to see them. The AMA had pulled the right strings – well-meaning skeptical American doctors reluctantly came around, and in 1987, the "War on Cholesterol" went public.

The AHA, the drug companies, cereal and vegetable oil manufactures, and the AMA launched their well-coordinated public relations and advertising campaigns.

Getting FDA approval in record time, Merck began aggressively marketing lovastatin (Mevacor), its new cholesterol-lowering drug. Unlike cholestyramine, lovastatin was easier to take and had fewer immediate side effects.

Cereal makers like Kellogg's were launching new heart-healthy cereals with catchy names like *Common Sense.* For a $2,500 fee, low fat high sugar food products could earn the AHA's Heart-Check Seal of Approval. *Pop-Tarts*, a qualifying product, was touted as a "low fat nourishing food you can enjoy as part of a healthy breakfast…"

The AHA was advising Americans to stay away from eggs for breakfast, but eating sugary Pop Tarts with 39 grams of carbohydrate (18 from sugar) was perfectly OK. Heavily promoted margarine and "cholesterol-free" polyunsaturated vegetable cooking oils – full of dangerous trans fatty acids (see chapter 14) - were flying off supermarket shelves.

Seventeen years later, without anything resembling scientific support, the National Cholesterol Education Program continues to influence heart disease research, education, and treatment. Jobs, prestige, and privilege – at the highest levels in medicine – have been placed ahead of the health of ordinary citizens.

To the detriment of the American people, the NCEP has slipped the truth about heart disease behind a door marked "experts-only." Working together to protect their economic self-interest, they following organizations have put selling drugs, cereal, and margarine ahead of the health of the patient:

- American Heart Association (AHA)
- American Medical Association (AMA)
- The drug companies
- National Heart, Lung and Blood Institute
- The National Institutes of Health (NIH)
- University nutrition/dietitian departments
- U.S. Food & Drug Administration (FDA)
- U.S. food-processing industry

In coming chapters, we'll carefully examine the consequences of this "War on Cholesterol" and see it for what it really is: questionable science selling a lot of sugar, cereal, margarine, doctors appointments, and drugs.

21-Day Plan key principle #6:

Avoid pasteurized milk. Attempt to replace low fat and powdered milk or nondairy products with whole raw milk.

What about milk?

For some people, milk is an emotional issue, and nutritionists have sent mixed signals for decades. Does milk do a body good – or not? There are many different milk issues and they are usually jumbled together. We know that infants need mother's milk, and most growing children benefit from milk.

When I've asked people why they use milk, most answered, "I put it in my cereal." My response has always been - why are you eating cereal? What kind of cereal do you eat? You can eliminate two harmful, highly processed foods right away by not buying commercial boxed cereals and pasteurized milk.

If you like and tolerate milk, there is no substitute for whole raw milk from grass-fed cows. Of course, this type of quality product is no longer available, and milk lovers must settle for skimmed, 2 percent, or whole pasteurized/homogenized milk – a risk you should consider very carefully.

"It boggles the mind to observe that ranking countries by their incidence and severity of osteoporosis produces the same list as countries ranked by the amount of milk their people drink," writes John R. Lee, M.D.[15] It just happens that the two highest countries in both respects, Finland and the U.S., also consume more coffee and sugar than anyone else.

Milk drinking increases the risk of diabetes, heart disease, and osteoporosis. But, let's note, the milk Finns and Americans are drinking today isn't the milk of old. It's been pasteurized, homogenized, and a lot of the naturally occurring healthy fats and fat-soluble vitamins have been removed.

Pasteurization and homogenization affect the quality of milk and milk products. The two-week-old milk you buy at the convenience store in 2002 is a far cry from the milk delivered to your door in 1910.

The value of pasteurization has been highly inflated. Shelf life and large-scale production methods, alone, support pasteurization. Raw milk contains lactic-acid producing bacteria that protect the raw milk against pathogens. Pasteurization destroys these helpful organisms and all the enzymes found naturally in milk.

Without enzymes, specifically lipase, it is more difficult to absorb minerals from milk, including calcium. Pasteurization alters proteins (amino acids), promotes rancidity of unsaturated fatty acids, and destroys 50 percent of the vitamin C and 100 percent of the vitamin B-12.

Homogenization, straining fat particles through tiny pores under tremendous pressure, is another insult to milk. Homogenization suspends the fat throughout the milk, and renders the fat and cholesterol more susceptible to oxidation. Pure cholesterol is healthy, oxidized cholesterol is harmful.

Milk contains something called xanthine oxidase (XO), particularly in the fat droplets. Homogenization breaks these droplets down into much smaller particles. These tiny particles of oxidized fat can go right into the bloodstream – undigested. Studies show that drinking homogenized milk results in detectable levels of XO, and XO concentrations in the arteries are highest where there is plaque.[14]

Pasteurization and homogenization ruin a healthy food – and even worse - put a legal barrier between the farmer and the consumer. It prevents the farmer from selling directly to the consumer – which is the way milk ought to be sold.

As Sally Fallon points out, "Getting rid of pasteurization laws is, I believe, key to opening the door to prosperity for our farms and ultimately the entire populace." Raw milk is only sold in stores in California and a few other states.

Even raw milk may be difficult for some people to digest. If you lack intestinal lactase, an enzyme that digests lactose or milk sugar, you may want to avoid milk altogether – even pasture-raised raw milk. Some people continue to produce lactase and do OK with milk. All mammalian infants are born with lactase, but production of the enzyme declines over time.

Some people are allergic to milk protein, called casein, a difficult protein for the body to digest. If milk and milk products have been used for centuries in a human group, they will, through natural selection, digest milk sugar and milk protein better than other populations.

According to Sally Fallon in *Nourishing Traditions*, the practice of fermenting and souring milk is found in all traditional groups that herd cows. Fermenting or souring breaks down lactose and predigests casein. As a result, homemade yogurt, kefir and clabber are often well tolerated and provide superior nutrition as well.

Butter and cream (fat) contain little lactose or casein and are usually well tolerated by almost everyone. Nonetheless, soured butter and cream are even more digestible. Traditionally, in America, the milk fat was highly valued and the "skimmed milk" was fed to the hogs.

Cheese is highly concentrated casein. Some people do well with cheese and others must avoid it. Cheeses made from raw milk contain a full complement of enzymes and are therefore more easily digested. Natural cheese should be eaten unheated. Processed cheeses should be strictly avoided – trans fats and all.

My grandfather's Guernsey cows produced 4,000 to 5,000 pounds of milk per year. Today's genetically engineered overactive pituitary Holsteins produce 20,000 to 30,000 pounds annually.

The freak-pituitary modern cow is prone to many diseases and almost always secretes pus into the milk. While my grandfather's cows ate grass and hay, today's Holsteins are fed high protein soy pellets to increase milk production. No one knows for sure what this does to the quality of milk. We do know that it dramatically shortens the life of the cow.[10]

While some people are genetically equipped to handle milk in all its forms, supermarket milk is bad for everyone. Since the early 1990s milk has contained a higher level of bovine growth hormone injected into cows to increase milk production.

There is a big difference, too, between the milk of grass- and grain-fed cows. Approximately 85-95 percent of the cows in American dairies are now raised in confinement and are fed a grain-based diet. Grain feeding greatly diminishes the nutrient content of cow's milk.[11]

Milk from grass-fed cows has an ideal 1:1 ratio of omega-6 and omega-3 fatty acids (see chapter 16). Milk from grain-fed cows has an adverse 5:1 ratio of omega-6 to omega-3. As we will discuss throughout this book, Americans today are consuming excess omega-6 and not enough omega-3.

Grain-fed dairy cows – like grain-fed beef - are adding to the essential fat imbalances in the American diet, and almost all supermarket milk has this unhealthy 5:1 ratio of omega-6 to omega-3.

Certified organic milk is better quality since the grains are pesticide free, and these herds usually spend time in the pasture eating grass. Grain-feeding, however, whether organic or not, increases the omega-6 and reduces the omega-3.[12]

Milk from grass-fed cows offers many other nutritional benefits, including higher amounts of conjugated linoleic acid (CLA), beta carotene, vitamin A, and vitamin E. Cows on grass produce less milk than their grain-fed counterparts. As a result, their smaller milk volume translates into a higher concentration of vitamins per glass.[13]

While it may be difficult at this time to obtain high quality milk from grass-fed cows, we must at least recognize that anything but 1910-style milk is not health-promoting. Grain-fed pasteurized reduced fat milk is a health risk for the following reasons:

- Grain-fed milk and meat contain unbalanced omega fats; excess omega-6 and not enough omega-3.

- Pasteurized milk has no enzymes; it's difficult to digest. The fats and proteins have been altered, and the minerals are hard to absorb.

- Skim and 2 percent milk are high in lactose (milk sugar) and low in fat. Reduced fat milk has too much carbohydrate and not enough fat.

- For flavor, highly oxidized dry milk powder is added back to skim and 2 percent milk.

- Added synthetic vitamin D is inferior to the natural vitamin D that has been removed. Like any synthetic fat-soluble vitamin, synthetic vitamin D is harmful. Synthetic D-2 was quietly removed from milk recently because of evidence that it promotes calcium migration into soft tissue (like arteries). Hard-to-absorb synthetic D-3 has replaced D-2.

Go to **www.realmilk.com** for a listing of good quality milk and milk products or **www.westonaprice.org**.

PART II

The role of carbohydrates

Chapter 7

-------- 🕊 --------

Sugar – it's not so sweet

If the NCEP was truly concerned about your health, they would be mounting a vigorous nationwide campaign to reduce the American addiction to sugar and refined carbohydrates, which are the real culprits in causing low HDL cholesterol and oxidized LDL cholesterol.

John R. Lee, M.D.

Personal sugar consumption has soared in the last hundred years, increasing from about 10 pounds per person in 1910 to 160 pounds per person in 1996. People today, according to USDA statistics, are averaging at least 13 pounds of sugar per month, representing over 20 percent of daily calories.[1]

Refined sugar includes barley malt, brown sugar, corn syrup, dextrose, fructose, glucose, high fructose corn syrup, honey, maltose, maple sugar, rice syrup, and sucrose. All of these are simple sugars. Refined white sugar (sucrose) is a combination of glucose and fructose.[2]

In its affect on the body, says Nancy Appleton, author of *Lick The Sugar Habit*, refined sugar is more like a pharmaceutical drug than a food. She offers plenty of evidence that our bodies are not equipped to safely metabolize large amounts of sugar. Appleton states, "If you have sugar cravings, sugar is already at work destroying your body."[3]

According to Appleton, our bodies, at any given time, only need two teaspoons of blood sugar to function properly. As little as two teaspoons of refined sugar can throw blood chemistry out of balance. Typical soft drinks like *Coke* contain 9 to 10 teaspoons of sugar, and the average person today consumes 53 gallons a year – double that of the mid-1970s.[4]

Refined sugar has no nutritional value and no fiber. Refined sugar is 99.7 percent pure calories – no vitamins, minerals, or proteins. Even worse, to safely metabolize sugar, your body must give up minerals, especially magnesium, chromium and zinc, which have been removed in the refining process.[5]

In the 1960s, British Physician John Yudkin was one of the first researchers to notice a relationship between sugar and heart disease. Dr. Yudkin discovered that the average daily sugar intake of patients with heart disease was much higher when compared to the control group of healthy subjects.

In 1964, in the British medical journal *Lancet*, Yudkin showed that a person consuming 120 grams (8 tablespoons) of sugar a day is five times more likely to develop CHD as a person consuming fewer than 60 grams. Elevated sugar levels elevate *thromboxane*, one of the body's blood clot triggering compounds.[6]

It doesn't take long for people on low fat diets to go over 60 grams a day. There's an enormous amount of sugar in most processed foods. Just two Cokes a day (78 grams) puts you into the zone of increased risk.

Many products, especially in fast food restaurants, contain hidden sugar. The bun, hamburger, poultry and sauces may all contain sugar. Sugar can be found in dry-roasted nuts, *Jif* and *Skippy* peanut butter, bouillon cubes, egg substitutes, canned fruits, luncheon meats, and in virtually all commercial breakfast cereals.

Yudkin was among the first to express concern about fructose, made from corn, which, he wrote, "magnifies nearly all of the effects found with sucrose." While fructose does not trigger as steep a rise in blood sugar, it nonetheless promotes insulin resis-

Food Product	Grams of Sugar	Grams of Carbohydrates
One Pop-Tart	18	39
One cup Cocoa Blasts cereal	16	29
One Toaster Strudel	10	26
One scoop of Slim-Fast	17	24
One can of Coke	39	39
8 oz concentrated Grape Juice	28	28
One Body Smarts crunch bar	20	23
Two Life Savers	4	5

tance and blood sugar disorders just as sugar does.[7]

Since the mid-1980s, corn sweeteners, especially high fructose corn syrup (HFCS), have replaced as much as one half of the sugar added to commercial food products. For food processors, high fructose corn syrup is less expensive than sugar, easier to use, and has even longer shelf life![8]

Sugar consumption data doesn't always include corn sweetener. HFCS is found in soft drinks, catsup, breakfast bars and most processed, packaged foods, including cereals promoted to children (*Rice Krispies*) and cereals promoted to adults (*Special K*). Both also contain sugar.

Nancy Appleton says high fructose corn syrup is especially damaging to growing children. Appleton has found that "fructose causes white blood cells of the immune system to become 'sleepy' and unable to defend against harmful foreign invaders."[9]

Sugar and corn syrup are staple ingredients in products aimed at children, like Keebler's *Honey Grahams* and Quaker's *Cocoa Blasts.* Both also contain "partially hydrogenated cottonseed oil," trans fatty acids that reduce the ability of red blood cells to carry insulin.[10] *Cocoa Blasts* also contain artificial chocolate flavor, Yellow #6, Red 40, and last on the list – a paltry amount of the B vitamin folic acid.

In combination, *Honey Grahams* ™ and *Cocoa Blasts*™ contain ingredients that may predispose you and your children to diabetes. Sugar, corn syrup, enriched flour, and partially hydrogenated cottonseed oil render these products "high glycemic" (see glycemic index, chapter 9) and nutrient-depleting.

Since the Fortification Act of 1942, a few synthetic B vitamins and synthetic iron have been added to refined, enriched flour. Don't let "fortification" mislead you into believing this is good for you. By adding a tiny amount of folic acid to flour – less than the food colors - the government is saying, in effect, eat a lot of sugar to get a little folic acid.

Refined flour and sugar concoctions are still missing a wide range of essential nutrients, such as vitamins B-6 and B-12, found abundantly only in animal foods. Your body cannot fully utilize the fortified synthetic B vitamins without the entire B-complex. In this manner, excess sugar and sweeteners trip up body chemistry and cause nutrient deficiencies and imbalances.

> *"Sugar is atherogenic – that is, it causes heart disease. In addition to increasing levels of blood fats, such as blood triglycerides and the LDL to HDL ratio, sugar actually makes blood platelet cells...stickier and more likely to clump together."*
>
> Burton Berkson, M.D., *Syndrome X*

Dr. William Philpott found that the aortas of people who die of coronary heart disease have "no detectable amount of chromium," leached from the body to metabolize sugar.[11] Minerals are needed in relatively small amounts, but like B-complex vitamins, they only function in relation to each other. If there is a shortage or overload of just one mineral, imbalances and disruptions will occur.

Excess sugar and phosphoric acid found in soft drinks can disrupt the body's balance of calcium and phosphorus, ideally 10:4.

If dietary calcium is low, calcium will then be leached from the bone to help restore the proper ratio to phosphorus and to neutralize acid conditions caused by a high sugar diet.[12]

Calcium, leached from the skeleton, out of relationship to phosphorus, becomes dysfunctional and even toxic. This excess dysfunctional calcium can replace magnesium in soft tissues, causing bone spurs, cataracts, hardening of the arteries (plaque), kidney stones, and large calcium deposits.[13]

Magnesium is also needed to safely metabolize sugar. As calcium is leached from the bone, magnesium is drawn from muscle tissues. While the body easily gives up magnesium via the kidneys, excess leached calcium will migrate into the soft tissue vacated by magnesium.

In this manner, excess dietary sugar can cause both a bone calcium deficiency and calcium overload in the heart and arteries. Calcium and magnesium have a complementary and antagonistic relationship. In balance, they support cardiovascular health. But too much dietary or dysfunctional calcium and not enough magnesium is a prescription for heart attacks, diabetes, and osteoporosis.

The typical American diet already contains more calcium than magnesium. Sugary breakfast cereals and flour-based snacks like *Honey Grahams* are fortified with calcium. Milk contains a lot of calcium. A lot of us ingest too much calcium and not enough magnesium. As we age, excess calcium coupled with magnesium deficiency leads to calcification of muscular artery walls and irregular heartbeats.

The latest method of diagnosing coronary heart disease is using high technology imaging to measure calcification. According to *Heartscan Minnesota,* their new $1.6 million Electron Beam CT is used "to screen for coronary calcification, essential in aiding the *early detection* of heart disease."[14]

"Coronary calcification means that a patient has atherosclerosis or plaque on the arterial wall lining of the coronary arteries," says *Heartscan*. By accurate visualization of the coronary arteries, the Electron Beam CT precisely calculates the patients' calcium levels. Exposure speeds are 10 to 20 times faster than conventional CT scanning.[15]

While *Heartscan* may call this "early detection," in truth, it's already too late. Calcification represents advanced atherosclerosis – injury that's been developing for many years, even decades. From the patient's point of view, a yearly $22.00 fasting blood sugar test – carefully considered - would provide an earlier and more cost effective warning of impending heart disease.

But most doctors aren't even asking patients with "high normal" blood sugar what they're eating, and patients have been advised to eat high carbohydrate diets that promote calcification. Focused only on cholesterol, doctors are not paying close enough attention to early stage blood sugar disorders.

This is the most important health issue aging Americans face today. Stress of all kinds – especially blood sugar stress - lowers the concentration of magnesium in the muscles of the heart and arteries and increases calcium. The older and the more stressed we are, the more calcium will predominate over magnesium in the heart and circulatory system.

Not a normal consequence of aging, calcification is *accelerated aging* - caused in large part by excess dietary sugars that disrupt metabolism and critically important mineral relationships. Only a medical system that has chosen to ignore the role of sugar in heart disease would find the Electron Beam CT an important breakthrough.

To date, at least 57 Electron Beam CT's have been installed in the U.S. at a cost of $1.6 million each – for a total of almost $100 million dollars. Willing to spend big bucks measuring calcification, the medical establishment is unwilling to spend any money preventing it.

Why, I ask?

Warning: These products contains trans fatty acids and a lot of sugar.

Quaker Cocoa Blasts™

Ingredients:

Sugar
Corn Flour
Partially hydrogenated cottonseed oil
Cocoa (Processed with Alkali)
Salt
Natural and artificial chocolate flavor
Caramel color
Disodium phosphate
Yellow 6
Calcium carbonate
Sodium ascorbate (a vitamin C source)
Niacinamide
Red 40
Reduced iron
Zinc oxide
Vitamin A (palmitate)
BHT (preservative)
Blue 1
Thiamin mononitrate
Pyridoxine hydrochloride
Riboflavin
Folic acid, (a B-vitamin)

Keebler Honey Grahams™

Ingredients:

Enriched flour (with synthetic iron
- and three B-vitamins)
Sugar
Partially hydrogenated soybean
- and/or cottonseed oil
Graham Flour
Molasses
Honey
Corn Syrup
High Fructose Corn Syrup
Calcium Carbonate (2% or less)
Salt
Leavening
Soy Lecithin
Artificial Flavor

High fructose corn syrup has no fiber or nutrients. While fructose doesn't raise blood sugar as fast as sugar, fructose raises triglycerides and actually increases insulin resistance, the root cause of Type II diabetes. *Journal of Nutrition*, 1997, vol. 127.

21-Day Plan key principle #7:

If you supplement with just one mineral, make it magnesium

Magnesium – not calcium – is the most common mineral deficiency in the U.S. (zinc and iron are second and third). Magnesium deficiency is especially common among the elderly and among people with diabetes, heart disease, and osteoporosis.

In *Heart Healthy Magnesium,* James B. Pierce, Ph.D., says magnesium helps:

- Control blood pressure.
- Soothes muscles and prevents cramps.
- Suppresses the formation of kidney stones.
- Inhibits the formation of clots in the blood vessels.
- Increases blood flow without increasing blood pressure.
- Helps to keep the heart beating with a normal rhythm.
- Prevents spasms of the muscles and blood vessels.
- Protects muscles cells from being injured by calcium.
- Controls the correct balance of electrolytes.
- Reduces the risk of angina.
- Greatly reduces the risk of heart attack and stroke.

Don't let the doctor tell you, "Your magnesium is fine." She doesn't know. Ordinary blood tests do not reveal *intracellular* levels. Magnesium functions predominantly within the energy centers (mitochondria) of muscle cells and only one percent is found in the blood.

You can be deficient in intracellular magnesium and still maintain "normal" blood levels. No correlation exists between tissue and blood levels. The measurement of magnesium in blood serum has limited medical significance, but tissue levels reflect what is happening within the cells of the body.

In the past, assessing intracellular magnesium status required an inconvenient, time consuming magnesium-loading test. More recently, *Intracellular Diagnostics* has introduced *Exatest*, a noninvasive tool for doctors to quickly assess the intracellular status of magnesium, calcium, potassium, phosphorus, sodium and chloride. *Intracellular Diagnostics* can be found online at **www.exatest.com** or have your doctor call **650-349-5233.**

If you're not ready for testing, it's safe to begin magnesium supplementation as a precautionary measure. Robert C. Atkins, M.D., who tests all new heart disease and diabetes patients, has found that nine out of ten have insufficient tissue levels of magnesium.

Involved in more than 300 different enzyme reactions (enzymes depend on minerals to function), magnesium is the second most abundant *intracellular* mineral after potassium. A key function of magnesium is regulating the balance of all other mineral electrolytes, including potassium, sodium, chloride and calcium.

Electrolytes, minerals that have an electrical charge, control many things, including osmosis (water movement), acid-base balance, and our ability to respond to stress. Magnesium deficiency, as you can see, can easily lead to a wide range of critically impaired bodily functions.

Angina, congestive heart failure, fading memory, heart attacks, high blood pressure, insomnia, irregular heartbeats, low HDL cholesterol, stage fright, and stiff, aching painful muscles are all associated with magnesium deficiency. Without sufficient magnesium, it's hard to absorb other minerals, control blood sugar, digest food, or detoxify the body.

Good blood sugar control and nutrient absorption depend on adequate magnesium. Your body gives up magnesium and other minerals to metabolize sugar and refined carbohydrates. Poor blood sugar control increases magnesium excretion, which, in turn, further impedes blood sugar control.

Magnesium regulates heartbeat. While magnesium has a relaxing effect on muscle cells and artery walls, calcium makes them more rigid. In balance, magnesium and calcium complement each other but become antagonistic when out of balance.

Excess calcium easily leads to a variety of cardiovascular problems. Finland has the highest ratio of calcium to magnesium intake (7:1) and has the highest rates of coronary heart disease in the world. (J Am College Nutrition 13: 429-46, 1994.)

> **Food Sources of Magnesium (alphabetical order):**
> Avocados, almonds, beef, blackstrap molasses, beet greens, brown rice, corn, dark green leafy vegetables, fermented soy (miso, tempeh), legumes, millet, peanuts, sardines, seeds (flaxseed and sunflower), sea vegetables (kelp and wakame), and tuna.

The body will store calcium and give up magnesium. Many things cause magnesium losses, including extreme exercise, excess dietary calcium, high sugar diets, diuretic drugs, driving in rush hour traffic, fear, guilt, pessimism, prejudice, and sweating in the heat or shivering in the cold.

Minerals function in the body only in teamwork fashion. You need them all in relatively small amounts. Supplementing with individual minerals is potentially hazardous. Eating a wide variety of wholesome natural foods – especially from the sea – is your best source of balanced mineral nutrition.

ConcenTrace Mineral Drops, produced by the Trace Mineral Research Company of Ogden, Utah, is liquid magnesium and trace minerals harvested from the Great Salt Lake. Solar evaporation is used to remove sodium and concentrate all other minerals.

Forty (40) drops (1/2 teaspoon) diluted in a quart or liter of water provides 250 mg of ionic (ready to absorb) magnesium. You can use ten drops at a time diluted in 8-10 oz. of water or tea. Some people re-mineralize a gallon of water with 1-2 teaspoons.

Adding a pinch of lemon provides flavor, superior hydration, and it's good for the liver.

Other recommended forms of magnesium include citrate, aspartate, and orotate. Typically, these do not provide trace minerals. Read the label carefully and make sure you understand how many capsules or tablets you must take to reach 400 mg daily.

Do not rely on multiple vitamin products for your magnesium requirement. Most multiples contain poor quality magnesium oxide. Under the most ideal conditions, only 40 percent is absorbed. The elderly and those with impaired digestion absorb far less.

If your multiple vitamin contains more calcium than magnesium – and most do - consider replacing it or using *ConcenTrace* to balance the excess calcium. We need as much magnesium as calcium. If you supplement with just one mineral, make it magnesium. Because it contains ionic magnesium and trace minerals from the sea, *ConcenTrace* is best – in liquid or tablet form.

For more information about *ConcenTrace,* click on **www.nokobeach.com** or **www.traceminerals.com**. Ask your local vitamin or natural foods grocery store to carry ConcenTrace liquid minerals or ConcenTrace mineral tablets.

For further information about magnesium, read *Heart Healthy Magnesium* by James B. Pierce, Ph.D. (Some of the information about fats is out of date.)

Or, read *The Healing Power of Minerals* by Paul Bergner, clinical nutritionist and instructor of therapeutic herbalism.

Chapter 8

-------- ✸ --------

Cleve's Rule of Twenty Years

Members of the medical establishment who continue to recommend sugar-laden cereal as heart healthy should perhaps be consulting with their attorneys.

Robert Atkins, M.D.

In 1975, T.L. Cleave, surgeon-captain in the Royal Navy, former director of medical research at the Institute of Naval Medicine in England, published a book called *The Saccharine Disease* (now, out of print).

Dr. Cleave conducted a study in third world countries, mainly in Africa, to try and learn why they were not suffering from our modern western diseases. Studying hospital records, he was struck by the fact that colon cancer, diabetes, gallstones, heart disease and obesity were nonexistent.[1]

Cleve concluded that the absence of sugar and refined carbohydrates in traditional diets protected the natives from 20th century illnesses. His colleague, Dr. Dennis Burkitt, looking at the same data, concluded that the protective feature of traditional diets was their high dietary fiber intake.

Cleve demonstrated that about 20 years after introducing modern western foods to the diet – replacing the native whole foods – diabetes, high blood pressure, and heart disease appear. Cleve became know for his "Rule of Twenty Years." Within 40

years, said Cleave, diabetes and heart disease would be widespread
– as they are today in the United States.[2]

Jews who lived in Yemen, for example, consuming their natural, unrefined whole foods diet, were thought to be almost "genetically free" of diabetes. In 1977, after consuming refined carbohydrates and vegetable oils in Israel for twenty-five years, 11.8
percent of Yemenite Jews were suffering with Type II diabetes.[3]

In Saudi Arabia, before 1970, there was virtually no diabetes.
After the introduction of highly processed western foods, Saudi
Arabia has one of the highest rates of diabetes in the world: In
urban areas, 12 percent of men and 14 percent of women; in rural
areas, 7 percent of men and 7.7 percent of women.[4]

Worldwide, the dietary acceptance of refined carbohydrates
and highly processed vegetable oils (see chapter 14) is causing a
global epidemic of diabetes. Cleave's rule is coming true today in
many other countries, such as Japan, where, once a minor specialty, cardiologists are now in high demand.[5]

Native and pioneer Americans ate mostly whole, unprocessed
carbohydrates. Wheat berries were milled at home and immediately made into bread. Porridges and casseroles were made from
whole grains soaked overnight. Prepared and processed at home,
grains and legumes provided plenty of nutrition and fiber.

In 1910, people ate just as much or more carbohydrates as
today, but only a small percentage were refined. They consumed
sugar, but more often as unrefined molasses, a rich source of iron
and important B-vitamins. As the century progressed, however, an
increasingly large percentage of our carbohydrates were milled,
refined, and canned.

Stripped of their vitamins, minerals, and fiber, refined carbohydrates can exhaust the body's nutrient reserves. The body gives
up chromium, cobalt, copper, magnesium, manganese, zinc and
B-complex vitamins to metabolize sugar and refined carbohydrates
– the same nutrients – along with fiber - that are removed in the
refining process.

Nutrient Loss During Food Processing

Whole Food	Refined	B-6 Loss	Folic Acid Loss
Brown Rice	White Rice	69%	---
Brown Rice	Instant	94%	---
Fresh Tuna	Canned	50%	---
Fresh Meat	Luncheon Meat	77%	---
Wheat Berries	Flour	82%	79%
Lima Beans	Canned	---	62%
Beets	Canned	---	83%

The majority of minerals are processed out of whole foods. Up to 85 percent of the major minerals and 88 percent of the trace minerals are lost when wheat is milled into flour. Milling also removes approximately 70 percent of the chromium, cobalt, copper, and zinc.[8]

By reducing the body's mineral and vitamin stores, refined carbohydrates cause enzyme and nutritional deficiencies, which, in turn, further impede the body's carbohydrate metabolizing ability. These multiple deficiencies and mineral imbalances create blood sugar problems that lead inexorably to diabetes.

John Lee, M.D., refers to diabetes as a "magnesium deficiency disease." Magnesium deficiency is common but generally unrecognized in the U.S. Supplementing with magnesium and trace minerals is key principle #7 in the 21-Day Plan.

Also, whole, unrefined carbohydrates have potassium to sodium ratios above 4:1. As foods are processed, they lose potassium and gain sodium. When made into apple pie, the potassium/sodium ratio of an apple goes from 150:1 to 1:3.7.[9] Processed foods increase the risk of high blood pressure by disrupting mineral relationships.

Sugar and starch, stripped of nutrition and fiber, enter the bloodstream in a rush. The pancreas, adrenals, thyroid and other glands kick in, flooding the bloodstream with insulin and other blood sugar regulating hormones.

A lot of us cannot metabolize excess refined carbohydrates and still maintain optimum blood sugar control. Adapted to the whole foods our ancestors ate for thousands of years, our intricate blood sugar regulating mechanisms go on the fritz if we eat a lot of sugar, flour, white rice, pasta, deserts and other processed sugars and starches.

According to the U.S. Centers for Disease Control (CDC), new cases of diabetes, among adults aged 30 to 39, increased more than 70 percent between 1990 and 1998, and the overall incidence of Type II diabetes has tripled in the last 30 years.[10]

The majority of the 800,000 newly diagnosed diabetics each year have had impaired blood sugar metabolism for 10 years – and half are already experiencing blood vessel injuries.[11] Even before most cases of Type II diabetes are diagnosed, coronary heart disease is underway.

Diabetes is the most expensive of all chronic diseases. In the coming decades, the human and economic costs of Type II diabetes could go through the Medicare ceiling. In 1997, alone, diabetes permanently disabled 75,000 workers, and an estimated $98 billion was spent for treatment and productivity losses.[12]

Dr. Cleave's rule is hitting us in the 40-year teeth. This unprecedented increase in diabetes is reaching epidemic proportions. World wide, blood sugar disorders are becoming the model of 21st century accelerated aging. Waves of heart attack and heart failure are sure to follow.

21-Day Plan key principle #8:

Monitor your fasting blood sugar

Often the first sign of diabetes is a heart attack. The cheapest and easiest test of all is fasting blood sugar.

Thomas Yannios, M.D.

Risk factor	optimum	risk	serious risk
fasting glucose	87.1	100-109	>110

Ask your doctor to include fasting glucose (blood sugar) in your lipid evaluation. Any yearly physical should include a test for fasting glucose even if other lipids are not tested. Remember, you must fast for 12 hours before blood is drawn. You can drink water - but no coffee, tea or food.

Optimum fasting glucose is 87.1. Readings between 70 and 109 mg/dl are considered "normal." "High normal" levels (between 100 and 109), however, signal the likelihood that early stages of Type II diabetes and CHD are already underway.

You must forget "normal," says Dr. Atkins. He warns that "If your fasting glucose is in the upper range of normal (100-109), you have a substantially higher risk of death from heart disease than someone at the lower end of normal."[13]

Studies of older Americans reveal that high fasting glucose is an independent risk factor for mortality (death). Blood sugar in the "normal range" has predictive significance. The higher your fasting blood sugar, the greater your risk of CHD. If your doctor says your "fasting glucose" is normal, ask for the number.

Impaired glucose tolerance is diagnosed when fasting glucose levels go above 110 – and Type II diabetes is diagnosed when there is a history of readings above 125. A glycosylated hemoglobin test (GHb), also referred to as the HbA1c test, measures the average blood sugar you have been running for several consecutive months.

If you have fasting blood sugar above 100, unexplained weight gain, fatigue, food cravings and mood swings, you may want to request an oral glucose tolerance test (GTT). This test more accurately diagnoses insulin resistance and unstable blood sugar in response to food.

Again, you must fast at least 12 hours. You are given an oral dose of glucose (75 grams) and then blood is drawn periodically (two to eight hours). The GTT measures both the rise and fall of glucose levels over time.

In a healthy person, glucose levels increase a little, decrease slowly, and then plateau. Abnormalities can be seen as glucose rises too high (over 160 mg/dl) or falls off too quickly - more than 50 points in an hour. A doctor can diagnose insulin resistance with a symptom questionnaire and by looking at your glucose curve.[14]

A normal two-hour postprandial (after a meal) reading is generally below 139 mg/dl. (A physician might also draw blood to specifically measure insulin levels, though this is not commonly done.)[15] Only carbohydrates raise blood sugar. The more carbohydrates we eat, the more insulin the pancreas puts out to prevent blood glucose from climbing too high.

People sensitive to carbohydrates are the first to experience insulin resistance, meaning their cells are resisting the action of insulin, the blood sugar regulating hormone secreted by the pancreas. As your cells resist insulin, both blood sugar and insulin levels increase.

The pancreas puts out even more insulin in response to chronic elevated glucose. Chronic high insulin is called hyperinsulinism. Insulin resistance and hyperinsulinism are early stages of Type II diabetes – and the beginning of a cluster of blood fat abnormalities called Syndrome X (see chapter 10).

If you are diagnosed with Type II diabetes, you get a prescription for a home blood sugar monitor. By the time you get a monitor, however, you already have blood vessel damage and some degree of CHD. Because prediabetes is easier to reverse than Type II diabetes, tracking blood sugar in your lipid evaluation is very important.

- If your fasting glucose is above 100, strictly limit grains, legumes and all other high glycemic carbohydrates (see next chapter). Emphasize low glycemic index vegetables.
- Make sure your diet emphasizes high quality protein and natural fat at each meal (see chapter 17). Use milled flaxseed or flaxseed oil at least twice a day (see chapter 16).
- Supplement with magnesium and trace minerals. *Concen-Trace Mineral Drops* are best (see 21-Day Plan, chapter 7).
- Supplement with L-Carnitine or eat foods rich in carnitine, which would include grass-fed beef, lamb and wild game.
- Olive leaf extract (up to four 500 mg capsules per day) reduces blood sugar levels quickly in a carbohydrate-restricted diet.
- Walk the family dog.

Iron Status and Cardiovascular Health

Iron is a common deficiency in the U.S., especially affecting adolescent girls and women of child bearing age. Even a mild iron deficiency leads to learning disabilities, impaired immune function, decreased energy, and anemia. Symptoms of iron deficiency include headaches, shortness of breath, weakness, heart palpitations, intolerance to cold, and a sore tongue.

Hereditary hemochromatosis, a rare genetic condition, is now showing up in a larger percentage of adults. Hemochromatosis is iron overload or excess iron storage in the body. Symptoms include weight loss, weakness, fatigue, skin color changes, abdominal pain, decreased sex drive and onset of diabetes.

Robert C. Atkins, M.D., feels that "ill-conceived food fortification" has worsened the problem. By law (the Fortification Act of 1942), ferrous sulfate (iron) is added to all enriched foods. Breakfast cereals, bagels, supermarket bread, hamburger buns, pancake mixes, white flour, macaroni, pasta, cakes, crackers, cookies, and donuts all contain poorly metabolized synthetic iron.

There's your iron overload!

In Sweden, synthetic iron in cereals has been blamed for causing, among men, a rate of hemochromatosis 10 times higher than expected. In Belgium, Germany, France, Italy, and the Netherlands, food-processing companies are now prohibited from adding iron to their flours.

Dr. Atkins points out that alcohol accelerates iron absorption. People who consume fortified foods and drink alcohol on a regular basis are at greater risk of iron overload, especially men. A recent Finnish study found a much higher risk of heart attack in men who had elevated serum ferritin levels (blood iron).

Iron added to white flour (non-heme synthetic iron) is not the same iron found in red meat (heme iron). Clearly, no one needs iron from both sources. Because high quality red meat provides a wide range of nutrients – including iron – it's the preferred food over synthetically fortified, highly processed grains.

If you have symptoms of iron deficiency or iron overload, see your doctor. Adequate iron is vital for optimum health, and excess iron in highly processed foods is easily avoided.

Unless you have hemochromatosis, the small amount of iron in high quality multiple vitamin products will not increase your risk of heart disease. The iron in enriched foods (ferrous sulfate), combined with excess alcohol, however, will increase iron stores and your risk of heart disease.

Chapter 9

-------- 🐛 --------

The glycemic index

Unknown millions of heart attacks have been caused by the failure of insulin, the body's "sugar cop," to do its job. This means that for tens of millions of people, cholesterol is not the underlying problem leading to heart disease.

Gerald Reaven, M.D.

Although excess refined carbohydrates deplete the body's mineral and nutrient reserves, all carbohydrates – including the more nutritious whole carbohydrates - raise blood sugar (glucose) levels. The glycemic index (GI) ranks carbohydrates according to how fast they raise blood glucose.

Originally developed in 1981 by professor David Jenkins at the University of Toronto, the glycemic index only rates carbohydrates. Dietary protein and fat have no direct influence on glucose levels. The glycemic index is based on either glucose (100) or white bread (100) as the standard against which other carbohydrate foods are measured.

Foods that break down quickly during digestion score highest on the glycemic index and are referred to as "high glycemic." When you eat these foods, blood sugar increases rapidly. Even some healthy-sounding carbohydrates break down quickly and have high glycemic values.

The glucose-based index rates baked potatoes at 98, parsnips at 97, and cooked carrots at 92. Although these numbers vary a little from index to index, starchy carbohydrates raise blood sugar much more quickly than low glycemic carbohydrates like broccoli and cauliflower (rated under 40).

A moderately glycemic sweet potato, rated at 51, releases sugar more slowly than a baked potato (98) – and is more nutritious. Old-fashioned Irish oatmeal, rated at 49, is a better choice than Cream of Wheat, rated at 70. Both are better than highly processed sugary, boxed cereals, which are hard to digest – and typically have high glycemic values.[1]

Among fruits, dried dates (103) raise sugar faster than bananas (62), which raise sugar faster than apples (39), grapefruit (26), or cherries (23). While whole fruits vary in how fast they release sugar, they are better than highly concentrated fruit juices, which contain excess sugar and excess carbohydrates.

The more a carbohydrate is processed, the higher your body's glucose and insulin response. An apple is better than applesauce, which is better than apple juice, which is better than apple juice concentrate. Fiber slows glucose entry into the bloodstream – and equally important, has important nutritional effects.[2]

The GI has complicating factors. Different types of potatoes and different processing or harvesting methods can influence the glycemic value. Cooked carrots, for example, raise blood sugar faster than raw carrots. The exact glycemic value of a banana can depend on how ripe it is. Canned beans release sugar faster than soaked beans prepared at home.

In spite of this, the GI is a useful guide, especially helpful to people who are insulin resistant, diabetic or overweight. The GI would suggest to the carbohydrate sensitive that they avoid starchy vegetables and potatoes most of the time and eat their carrots raw – if at all.

Bread, bagels, and muffins, whether made with whole-wheat flour or white flour, have high glycemic values. The fiber in any flour is no longer intact. Whole-wheat flour found in bread and cereals breaks down quickly and raises blood sugar just as fast or faster than white flour products. Starchy foods have higher glycemic values than sugar, but foods that contain both sugar and starch are always high glycemic.

The GI is just one way of assessing carbohydrates. Carbohydrate density, the number of carbohydrate grams a food contains, must be considered too. Carbohydrate dense beans may have moderate glycemic values, but require a longer period of insulin release. Beans, even with moderate GI's, are too much carbohydrate for some people.

Nutritional value is equally important. Refined white sugar may not raise glucose levels as fast as figs or dates, but as we have learned, in the long run, sugar robs the body of vitamins and minerals while dates or figs have redeeming nutritional value. Don't let the lower glycemic rating of sugar overshadow the fact that it has no nutritional value.

The more whole grains, starchy vegetables and legumes you eat, the higher your overall insulin response. To spare insulin, carbohydrate sensitive individuals should emphasize low glycemic carbohydrates. They cause minimal rises in glucose, spare insulin, and have fewer digestible carbohydrates. Rated below 40, broccoli, cauliflower, chick-peas, lentils, Lima beans, summer squash, and zucchini are slow releasers.

For most people most of the time, low glycemic carbohydrates have advantages over high glycemic foods. Carbohydrates – especially refined and high glycemic index carbohydrates – put pressure on blood sugar and promote higher insulin levels. High glucose and high insulin promote elevated triglycerides, a blood fat we will discuss in the next chapter.

While dietary protein has no effect, dietary fats brake rising blood sugar in two significant ways. Fat is digested much more slowly than carbohydrates. Eating natural fats and protein at each meal helps control blood sugar by reducing the amount of carbohydrate eaten and by lowering the glycemic value of the meal.

Butter on bread, butter and sour cream on baked potato, or butter and milled flaxseed in oatmeal will slow the sugar release of the meal. If carbohydrates make you tired or fat, emphasize fat and protein. A bagel will raise your blood sugar, a handful of almonds won't. Pizza causes problems, a Caesar salad won't.

Restrict potatoes and eat California avocados. Any boxed cereal will raise insulin, an egg, lamb chop, or herring won't. To curb weight gain and obesity, restrict high glycemic carbohydrates. It's that simple.

21-Day Plan key principle #9:

Select low glycemic index carbohydrates

The glycemic index (GI) ranks foods on how fast they increase blood sugar or blood glucose levels. An apple is rated at 39. Two apples are still 39. Eating extra portions increases the amount of carbohydrate you're eating, but the speed of the sugar-release stays the same.

Scientists so far have measured the GI's of about 300 foods, including some specific food products, like *Rice Krispies* at 82 and *Total* cereal at 74. The GI numbers are percentages with respect to a reference food –whether it's glucose or white bread, both rated at 100.

The 21-Day glycemic index arbitrarily uses glucose as the reference index. You can convert a *white bread* index number to the *glucose* standard by multiplying the white bread GI number by 0.7: Corn Flakes are 119 on the white bread index; 83 on the glucose index (0.7 times 119 = 83).

Not only do researchers use different references standards, they frequently come up with different numbers for the same food. Bananas, for example, vary between 54 and 62 – depending on how ripe they are. Different varieties of potatoes and different processing and cooking methods will produce different numbers for the same item.

Don't get too hung up on specific GI numbers. When different people test the same foods at different times, different numbers may result. The importance of the glycemic index, however, is not diminished by the small variation in GI numbers for the same food.

It's the relative value that counts. While some potatoes are slower releasers than others, all potatoes are starchy and will release sugar faster than Lima beans, yogurt, or green leafy vegetables. If you are experiencing insulin resistance, weight gain, obesity, diabetes, or heart disease, emphasize low glycemic index carbohydrates.

The following GI's are compiled from various sources, including *Syndrome X* (by Jack Challem, Burton Berkson, MD, and Melissa Diane Smith); *Dr. Atkins Age-Defying Diet Revolution; Genetic Nutritioneering* by Jeffrey S. Bland, Ph.D.; and Glycemic Index Lists at **www.mendosa.com**. For a complete online listing, check out **www.glycemicindex.com**.

High-Glycemic Foods

- Whole wheat & white bread
- Boxed breakfast cereals (most)
- Instant/quick cooking cereals and grains
- Grain-based snack foods/chips
- Honey and table sugar
- Cookies, cakes & candy bars
- Potatoes, especially baked
- Dates/other dried fruits
- Brown & white Rice
- Cooked carrots
- Pizza
- Waffles, donuts
  Crackers

Moderate-Glycemic Foods

- Yams and sweet potatoes
- Kidney beans (canned)
- Slow cooking oatmeal
- Pinto and navy beans
- Green peas
- Bananas
- Beets
  Sweet corn

Low-Glycemic Foods

- Asparagus, Broccoli and cauliflower
- Chinese cabbage (bok choy)
- Celery, cucumber
- Green and red cabbage soybeans
- Chick peas
- Lentils, black-eyed peas
- Fresh-cooked kidney beans
- Yellow and green beans
- Peppers
- Milk/yogurt
- Salad greens of all types
- Peanuts
- Spinach
- Zucchini and summer squash
- Garlic, onions
- Mushrooms
- Tomato, tomato soup
- Lima beans
- Peaches, grapes, cherries
  Apple, plums, and grapefruit

Glycemic Index of Commonly Eaten Foods

Dates	103	Sweet corn	55
Glucose	100	Popcorn	55
Baked potato	85-98	Spaghetti durum	55
Parsnips	97	Oatmeal (slow cook)	49-55
French baguette	95	Green peas	51
Carrots (cooked)	92	Sweet potato	51
White bread, gluten free	90	Grapes	45
Instant white rice	90	Orange	44
Honey	87	Apple	39
Corn Flakes	83	Plum	25-39
Rice Krispies	82	Tomato	38
Pretzels	81	Pears	34-37
Rice Cakes	77	Chick-peas	36
Total Cereal	76	Lima beans	36
Waffles	76	Yogurt	36
French fries	75	Pears	34
Graham Crackers	74	Skim milk	32
Cheerios	74	Kidney beans	29
Corn Chips	74	Lentils	29
Bagel (white)	72	Whole milk	27
Whole wheat bread	72	Grapefruit	26
Watermelon	72	Cherries	23
White rice (low amylose)	72	Peanuts	13
White bread	71		
Potato (new) boiled	70		
Cream of wheat	70		
Taco Shells	68		
Shredded wheat	67		
Brown rice	55-66		
Raisins	64		
Beets	64		
Macaroni & cheese	64		
Bananas	54-62		

FOODS TO AVOID GUIDELINES :
From Warner-Lambert (a drug company):

<u>Foods To Avoid</u>	<u>Comment</u>
Limit egg yolks to two per week	They recommends egg substitutes (which contain sugar) or egg whites ("use freely"), which are harmful – protein without fat.
Coconut	They're deathly afraid of this antimicrobial saturated fat, even though it has nourished people in the South Pacific for centuries.
Avocados	Why would you want to avoid one of the most nutritious vegetables on the planet – providing healthy fats, vitamin E, and L-Carnitine?
Organ meats	Best sources of folic acid, vitamin B-6. and vitamin B-12 needed to lower homocysteine. Do they know about homocysteine?
Nuts	They're just plain nuts! Properly prepared (soaking, etc.) nuts are an excellent source of protein and unsaturated fatty acids.
Fatty fowl	Duck and goose contain mostly unsaturated fatty acids and complete protein.
Whole milk/products	Whole raw milk nourished Americans for hundreds of years.

Chapter 10

-------- 🖎 --------

Syndrome X
diabetes-related heart disease

Until the 1950s, cholesterol was considered the primary culprit in heart disease. But Yale University scientists challenged this notion late in that decade, when they showed that patients who had suffered heart attacks were more likely to have high triglycerides than they were to have elevated cholesterol levels. Despite the Yale University researchers' very persuasive evidence, the medical community was not ready to accept this new idea.

Gerald Reaven, M.D.

Gerald Reaven, M.D., professor emeritus, Stanford University Medical School, estimates that 25 to 30 percent of us must restrict carbohydrates - even whole carbohydrates. Depending on ethnic background, genes, nutritional status and how we handle stress, we have varying sensitivity to carbohydrates,

If bread makes you gain weight or if diabetes or heart disease "runs in your family," you must pay particular attention to your carbohydrate intake. People who consume excess refined carbohydrates, or more carbohydrates than their metabolism can handle, are developing insulin resistance and a related cluster of risk factors called *"Syndrome X."*

Syndrome X is prediabetes – high blood sugar accompanied by high circulating insulin. Dr. Reaven estimates that 60-75 million Americans have Syndrome X. "The Syndrome X culprit isn't red meat or butter, it's carbohydrates," says Dr. Reaven.[1] Syndrome X is caused principally by the over consumption of carbohydrates – and is corrected by the restriction of carbohydrates.

In his book, *Age-Defying Diet Revolution*, New York physician Robert C. Atkins, M.D., estimates that there are 15 million type II diabetics in the U.S. and at least 60 million – or four times more – pre-diabetics.

Dr. Reaven's 60-75 million Syndrome X Americans and doctor Dr. Atkins' 60 million pre-diabetics are one and the same. For all of these people, the low fat high carbohydrate diet can be deadly.

A cardiologist (Yale) and family doctor with decades of *clinical experience*, Dr. Atkins describes how Type II diabetes inflicts blood vessel damage as it progresses through five stages. The first stage, insulin resistance, is the beginning of both Syndrome X and Type II diabetes.

In carbohydrate sensitive individuals, in response to eating excess carbohydrates - especially high glycemic carbohydrates - body cells become resistant or insensitive to the action of insulin. Insulin is the powerful blood sugar regulating hormone secreted by the pancreas.

Insulin carries glucose from the blood into cells where it is burned for energy. The more a food or meal raises blood sugar, the more insulin is needed to escort and manage glucose. When body cells resist insulin, blood glucose levels start to increase.

According to Dr. Atkins, insulin resistance is a consequence of the intracellular vitamin and mineral deficiencies referred to in chapters 7 and 8, especially magnesium, chromium, and zinc, plus a host of trace minerals and B-complex vitamins. Without the nutritional fuel to process energy, cells refuse insulin and it's glucose load.

In most people, excess breakfast bars, breads, cereals, cookies, doughnuts, muffins, pasta, rolls, and soft drinks easily raise glucose and insulin to unhealthy levels. In carbohydrate sensitive people, even excess whole grains, legumes, and starchy carbohydrates promote insulin resistance.

Stage Two is referred to as "hyperinsulinism." The pancreas, responding to chronic high glucose, floods the bloodstream with insulin. An overload of insulin forces some glucose into the nutritionally deficient cells. Like elevated homocysteine, elevated insulin is atherogenic – it causes direct damage to the *endothelial* cells, which line artery walls.[2]

In *Stage Three,* unstable blood sugar is causing overt symptoms, such as carbohydrate cravings, fatigue, moodiness, and irritability that is brought on by hunger - and relieved by food. At this stage, a glucose tolerance test (GTT), mapping your "glucose curve," is the best method for diagnosing insulin resistance. An oral dose of glucose is given and blood is drawn to measure the rise and fall of glucose over time.

Stage Four is diagnosable Type II diabetes. Stages three and four are a continuum. Insulin resistance and hyperinsulinism rule, but in Stage Four blood sugar remains elevated throughout the day. You have recognizable Type II diabetes when there is a history of fasting blood sugar readings above 125.

When the overworked pancreas finally craps out, you have reached the final stage of Type II diabetes. Only at this stage are Type II and Type I diabetes similar. In Type II, the pancreas initially puts out *too much* insulin and then stops. In Type I, a congenital autoimmune disease, the pancreas puts out little or no insulin.

Throughout the development of Type II diabetes, blood vessel damage, sticky clot-prone blood, and the risk of heart attack are steadily increasing. If an alert doctor and knowledgeable patient diagnose insulin resistance (stage one) before it progresses any further, both diabetes and coronary heart disease can be prevented.

If not, the cluster of blood fat abnormalities called Syndrome X takes hold. In the liver, excess glucose is converted into a hard, body-made saturated fat called triglycerides (blood fats). These tiny fat particles travel in the bloodstream oxidizing cholesterol, promoting plaque buildup and blood clots - sharply increasing the risk of a heart attack.

Chronic, elevated triglycerides are a direct consequence of an excessive release of insulin in response to eating excess carbohydrates. Elevated triglycerides thicken your blood and promote clotting. The higher your triglycerides, the greater your chances of a heart attack. According to Dr. Atkins, if your triglycerides go above 100 mg/dl, your risk of heart attack starts to increase.[4]

Atkins and a growing number of medical doctors are challenging the medical establishment's reluctance to acknowledge that high triglycerides are an independent risk factor for heart disease. Triglycerides as high as 199 mg/dl are considered "normal." Directed to focus on lowering cholesterol, doctors are overlooking the danger of high triglycerides.

Excess triglycerides increase the size and number of fat cells and increase the ratio of fat cells to muscle cells. As fat cells increase, glucose-burning muscle cells decrease, adding to insulin resistance, weight gain and obesity.[3]

Men have a greater proportion of glucose-burning muscle cells than women. Men, in general, may be able to handle carbohydrates more efficiently and safely than women. There are also different degrees of insulin resistance; we don't all respond exactly alike to blood sugar disorders. You can develop insulin resistance and not gain weight. But if you eat excess carbohydrates, your body will produce excess triglycerides.

For women, elevated triglycerides are a particularly good predictor of CHD - while serum cholesterol never is. Approximately 75 percent of all heart attacks that women get are associated with elevated triglycerides.[5] Women with high triglycerides have a 70 percent higher risk of breast cancer than women with low levels.

Elevated triglycerides apparently trigger a rise in levels of circulating estrogen, a risk factor for breast cancer.[6]

Triglycerides within the so-called normal range have "predictive significance;" that is, the higher the triglycerides, the greater the risk, especially for women. This is not true of cholesterol, which, we have seen, has very little predictive significance.

"Normal" seldom applies to blood work. Like most heart disease risk factors, people with "high normal" triglycerides are at greater risk than those who are "low normal." Risk is linear - the higher the number, the greater the risk.

Like an old-fashioned teeter-totter, as triglycerides go up, HDL cholesterol goes down. Elevated triglycerides are strongly associated with depressed levels of protective HDL cholesterol (high-density lipoprotein). HDL, so-called "good" cholesterol, protects LDL from oxidation and clumping.

HDL is "reverse transport" - removing LDL away from artery walls and plaque and transporting it back to the liver for recycling. We want as much HDL cholesterol as possible. HDL levels of 60 mg/dl or more (70 for women) protect the heart.

- In a major Finnish study, men in the lowest HDL quartile were three times as likely to develop heart disease as men in the upper quartile.[7]
- In Harvard University's Physicians' Health Study, participants who developed heart attacks had the lowest HDL levels, while their total cholesterol values were the same as those in the healthy control group.
- In the Framingham Study, people who developed heart disease had HDL averages of 43 (men) and 53 (women), both classified "normal" by most doctors – but well below the protective levels of 60 and 70, respectively.[8]

The ratios of other blood components to HDL are important predictors of future coronary health. The ratio of triglycerides to HDL is most important, ideally 1:1. A TG/HDL ratio of 2:1 or higher represents increased risk of CHD, especially if triglycerides are over 100. A ratio of 4:1 or higher (TG = 200 and HDL = 50) calls for immediate action.[9]

A 1997 Harvard study, conducted by J.M. Gaziano, M.D., published in *Circulation* 1997; 96: 2520-25, found that participants in the highest quartile (highest triglycerides and lowest HDL) were sixteen times more likely to have a heart attack than those in the lowest quartile. Participants with triglycerides below 100 and HDL over 60 were least likely to suffer a heart attack.[10]

Reporting on the Harvard study, Dr. Robert Atkins said, "*No ratio has ever come close to being so predictive of heart disease.*" [11] The participants' total cholesterol was not predictive; the ratio of triglycerides to HDL was. In at least 25-30 percent of people, a low fat high carbohydrate diet raises triglycerides and lowers HDL cholesterol.

There is no shortage of studies documenting how high triglycerides, low HDL, high blood sugar, and high insulin cluster together. These blood fat abnormalities cause blood platelet cells – the cells that form blood clots – to become stickier and more likely to clump together (platelet aggregation). Blood clots, in turn, dramatically increase the risk of a heart attack.

Diabetes complications - like kidney failure, nerve damage, and blindness - are a consequence of abnormal blood fats and blood clots that get their start from high sugar and high insulin. According to Dr. Reaven, "The large amounts of blood sugar affect tissues and organs all over the body."[12]

At least fifty percent of hypertension can be linked to Syndrome X, says Reaven. "Several studies have made it clear that insulin resistance and compensatory hyperinsulinemia, the hallmarks of Syndrome X, tend to raise blood pressure." High insulin elevates blood pressure, in part, by increasing sodium retention and promoting sticky, clot-prone blood.

High insulin raises blood pressure, speeds up the heart, and increases the release of the stress hormone, cortisol, which, in turn, constricts or squeezes blood vessels. Chronic high levels of cortisol, in turn, reduce DHEA, the most abundant hormone in the body.[14] Less DHEA means less muscle mass and a further reduction of glucose-burning muscle cells.

Your adrenal glands manufacture DHEA from cholesterol. If your doctor is lowering your cholesterol with a drug, he is also compromising your body's ability to produce DHEA – at the same time that high insulin levels may be suppressing DHEA. Low DHEA, says Dr. Atkins, is a much better predictor of heart attacks than cholesterol.[15]

To put it bluntly, the lower your DHEA, the more likely you are going to suffer with cancer, diabetes, heart disease, osteoporosis, and lowered immunity. Conversely, high levels of DHEA will help protect you from these diseases. You can test your DHEA level and supplement to restore beneficial levels. See 21-Day Plan, key principle #19.

Excess highly processed foods and nutritional deficiencies promote insulin resistance. Insulin resistance leads to hyperinsulinism. Hyperinsulinism is an early stage of diabetes. Early stages of diabetes provoke coronary heart disease and a wide range of metabolic and hormonal disorders that shorten your life.

Avocado is high in oleic acid, the same type of fat found in olive oil, sesame oil, poultry and high quality lard. Avocados are one of the few plant sources of L-Carnitine, a potent fat burner found abundantly in red meat, especially lamb. Avocados are also rich in vitamins A, C, and E plus lecithin.

"People with insulin resistance or Type II diabetes should cultivate a special fondness for avocados. Besides cutting the risk of heart disease, the uncommon fruit guards against after eating increases in blood sugar."

Robert C. Atkins, M.D.

21-Day Plan key principle #10:

Monitor and reduce elevated triglycerides.

Promote HDL cholesterol.

Risk factor	optimum	risk	serious risk
Triglycerides	<100	100-199	>200
HDL (men)	>60	<60	<40
HDL (women)	>70	<70	<50

Most doctors believe the misinformation they were taught in medical school – that triglycerides levels of 250 to 500 mg/dl are perfectly normal. They're wrong, and their ignorance could kill you. Even 200 mg/dl is too high. As a matter of fact, you need to worry about your heart health when your triglycerides are anything above 100 mg/dl."

Robert C. Atkins, M.D.

"People with very high triglycerides levels and very low HDL levels – another pattern characteristic of Syndrome X – are 16 times more likely than normal people to have a heart attack."

Burton Berkson, M.D., *Syndrome X*

Long ignored by the medical establishment, elevated triglycerides have become a leading predictor of heart disease. The higher your triglycerides, the greater your risk of a heart attack. As triglycerides go up, protective HDL cholesterol goes down.

The problem starts when the liver converts excess glucose into triglycerides, body made saturated fats. Triglycerides not needed for energy are eventually deposited in fat or adipose tissue. Our

21-Day Plan objective: Triglycerides under 100 and HDL over 60 for men and over 70 for women.

The 21-Day key principles, taken together, reduce blood sugar, spare insulin, lower triglycerides, boost HDL, promote healthy blood vessels, reduce the risk of deadly blood clots, and extend life. Drugs and low fat diets can't do that.

- Eating eggs for breakfast, instead of cereal, will prevent blood sugar elevations, spare insulin, lower triglycerides and boost HDL. Eggs are a complete protein and provide a wide range of naturally occurring vitamins and minerals.

- Untamed emotional stress increases blood sugar, insulin, stress hormones and triglycerides – and lowers protective HDL and DHEA. Low DHEA is associated with diabetes and heart disease.

- Replacing refined foods with whole unprocessed low glycemic carbohydrates and properly raised animal foods will reduce homocysteine and triglycerides while promoting HDL cholesterol.

- In both supplement form and food (lamb and beef), L-Carnitine will lower triglycerides and promote beneficial HDL cholesterol. L-Carnitine burns fat and provides optimum energy for the heart and muscle tissues.

- Vitamins C and E are the base of the antioxidant pyramid. Antioxidants work in team fashion to strengthen blood vessel walls and prevent LDL cholesterol from oxidation. Alpha Lipoic Acid, Grape Seed Extract, Green Tea, NAC (n-acetyl-l-cysteine), and Pycnogenol further enhance antioxidant defenses.

- Pasteurized low fat milk contains oxidized dry milk powder and homogenized milk contains oxidized fragmented fat particles (xanthine oxidase) that damage arteries and increase the chance of deadly blood clots.

- Magnesium and trace minerals promote the generation of

energy in the mitochondrial cell furnaces throughout the body, enhancing the uptake of insulin, lowering triglycerides and increasing protective HDL.

- Fasting blood sugar near optimum (87.1) is associated with reduced triglycerides (below 100) and protective levels of HDL cholesterol (above 60 for men and above 70 for women).

- Excess carbohydrates produce elevated triglycerides. Elevated triglycerides reduce HDL cholesterol. Low levels of HDL cholesterol are one of the most significant warnings of a future heart attack.

- Activity, exercise and relaxation lower triglycerides and promote HDL cholesterol and healthy hormone levels. Extreme exercise causes heart attacks and CHD.

- The grain-based Food Guide Pyramid promotes high trigly-cerides and low HDL. The Pyramid recommends that all of us consume 6 to 11 servings of grain each day. This dietary advice is an underlying explanation for the explosive growth of Syndrome X and diabetes during the last 20 to 30 years.

- Regular use of herbs like cayenne, ginger, garlic, onion, hawthorn, American ginseng, Siberian ginseng, gotu kola, and valerian root stimulate, cleanse and nutritionally support healthy blood circulation, reducing fibrinogen and the chance that a deadly blot clot will block blood flow in a coronary artery.

- Excess omega-6 fats found in commercial vegetable oils, margarine, partially hydrogenated fat, vegetable shortening, meat from grain-fed cattle, and eggs from grain-fed chicken: Inflame arterial tissue, promote blood clots, increase blood pressure and arterial tension, and reduce the ability of red blood cells to carry insulin.

- The traditional, healthy cooking fats - butter, coconut butter, lard, olive oil, palm oil and palm kernel oil - raise protective

HDL cholesterol and reduce triglycerides. They are heat-stable and safe for cooking and baking.

- Omega-3 rich milled flaxseed is nutritionally dense – an excellent source of minerals, fiber, and cancer-fighting plant lignans. Milled flaxseed promotes HDL cholesterol and lowers triglycerides. Daily flaxseed helps promote a favorable 1:1 or 2:1 balance of omega-6 and omega-3 essential fats.

- Protein, especially protein from pasture raised grass-fed animals, promotes HDL cholesterol and reduces triglycerides.

- Balanced and physiologically beneficial levels of DHEA, Progesterone and Pregnenolone promote optimum body functioning and extend longevity.

- Small amounts (no more than two glasses a day) of high quality red wine boosts HDL levels. A glass or two of beer also has a beneficial effect on HDL. Excess alcohol stresses the liver and impairs blood sugar metabolism. Replacing excess coffee with antioxidant rich green tea, the national beverage of Japan, will reduce triglycerides and promote beneficial HDL cholesterol.

Chapter 11

-------- 🐟 --------

Anti-Aging:
Good blood sugar control

Basically, diabetics get old faster than non-diabetics, and it is reasonable to assume that people with elevated glucose, insulin resistance and Syndrome X also age much faster than people without these conditions.

Burton Berkson, M.D., *Syndrome X*

An epidemiological study published in the *Journal of the American Medical Association* (*JAMA*), February 25, 1998, provides strong evidence that good blood sugar control, exercise, and staying involved in social activities are all associated with living a longer life.

The purpose of the Cardiovascular Health Study was to learn what factors "jointly predict mortality in community dwelling men and women age 65 years or older." Basically, who lives longer and why? To this end, 5,201 men and women from four U.S. communities were carefully monitored, and after five years, 646 people (12 percent) had died.

Elevated fasting glucose (high blood sugar) was one of the factors "significantly and independently associated with mortality." High blood cholesterol was not. In fact, as reported in *The Felix Letter*, people with higher LDL cholesterol (more than 153 mg/dl) had just two thirds of the mortality risk of those with levels of less than 96 mg/dl – the supposedly desirable levels.[1] This study, Framingham and many other studies suggest that higher levels of cholesterol seem to protect older adults.

Other factors that increased mortality included cigarette smoking, male sex, narrowing of the aorta and carotid arteries, major abnormality on electrocardiograph, and congestive heart failure. Use of diuretic drugs was associated with a 67 percent higher risk of mortality.[2]

People who scored high on a cognitive functioning test had nearly half the risk of mortality as those with low scores. Also, those who exercised lived longer. In *The Felix Letter*, Clara Felix writes, "Exercise – mental and physical – promotes growth of new neurons in the brain, those responsible for learning and memory! Yes, in the elderly too."[3]

Dr. Atkins reports that the Cardiovascular Health Study confirmed his own view that impaired blood sugar control damages blood vessels and accelerates aging. "Nearly half of all adults…by the age of fifty will demonstrate at least some instability in their blood sugar and at least some insulin resistance," says Atkins, who has reviewed more than 45,000 glucose tolerance tests.[4]

"Most of today's premature aging comes from heart-damaging atherosclerosis," writes Atkins, which he blames on the preponderance of carbohydrates in our diet, especially the refined products with most of their original nutrient content discarded. "Excessive insulin, prediabetes, and refined carbohydrates have an awfully strong connection with shortening human life spans."

Harvard University's ongoing New England Centenarian Study provides strong additional evidence that Dr. Atkins is right. Only six of the 169 study participants - people over age 100 - have Type II diabetes.[5] Excess sugar not only provokes higher insulin and triglycerides levels but also directly damages cells, tissues, glands, and organs

Sharp-edged sticky glucose molecules can attach themselves to the more than 50,000 proteins in our body. These abnormal "cross-linked" proteins are called Advanced Glycosylation End Products, or AGEs.[6] Glycation (or glycosylation) is a glucose-protein reaction. When protein and sugar bind together, new dangerous chemical structures are formed.

Anthony Cerami, Ph.D., Rockefeller University, New York City, is the U.S. pioneer in glycation research. Dr. Cerami noticed the relationship between sugar and aging as he observed diabetics who were aging rapidly.[7] Sugar is sticky – and it's particularly dangerous in aging blood vessels.

Over time, when incorporated into body tissues, AGEs do enormous damage. Glycation alters the structure and function of proteins – keeping them from doing what they're supposed to do. Collagen is one of the first proteins to be affected. Collagen is the tough, flexible connective tissue that holds the skeleton together.

Collagen attaches muscles to bones, and is the primary building block of blood vessels, skin, lungs and cartilage. When collagen is "glycosylated," collagen's flexibility is destroyed. Blood vessels stiffen, skin wrinkles, and joints ache. Your muscles weaken, and, as you age, skeletal fragility may make you more susceptible to fractures. (*Bone* 2001; 28(2) 195-201.)[8]

AGEs cloud the proteins in the lenses of the eye and cause cataracts. "Sticky AGEs tend to form clumps of cross-linked proteins that are very similar to the tangles and plaques found in the brains of Alzheimer's patients. In fact, AGEs have been found in these plaques at about three times the level of normal brains."[9]

Glucose can attach to tiny protein molecules called peptides that circulate in the blood. These AGE-modified peptides latch onto LDL cholesterol. Your body can no longer recognize this new cross-linked substance as LDL and fails to clear it from the bloodstream. Once glycated, LDL is more susceptible to oxidation.[10]

Glycated cholesterol explains why diabetics often have high levels of serum LDL. The extra sugar in their blood leads to high levels of circulating AGEs. This is the "bad" oxidized cholesterol the medical establishment has been slow to warn you about.[11]

A test for Type II diabetes, glycosylated hemoglobin (GHb), is a measure of the glycosylation of hemoglobin (red blood cells) in your blood. GHb provides a history of the blood sugar readings you have been running for 120 days. GHb documents the accumulated damage done by sugar-induced glycosylation. (GHb is also referred to as HbA1c.)

AGEs cause heart disease in a couple of ways. As mentioned above, they oxidize LDL cholesterol. Also, they create cross-links in the collagen in blood vessel walls, which age those walls and make them less flexible. Also, high carbohydrate diets generate large numbers of free radicals, highly reactive out of balance molecules which damage cells and increase the production of AGEs.[12]

High levels of glucose accelerate the production of both free radicals and AGEs. Together with AGEs, free radicals deliver the deadly one-two punches that cause us to age prematurely and die agonizingly slowly of cancer and heart failure. In Dr. Atkins' words, "Avoiding, minimizing, and counteracting the damaging effects of free radicals must be the fundamental principle of any age-defying program."[13]

Extreme exercise produces a lot of free radicals. It's not uncommon for highly conditioned athletes and marathon runners to be plagued with colds and infections.[14] Worse, extreme exercise is like running a car with gas but no oil. You may get there in a hurry, but you run the risk of blowing the engine.

William Campbell Douglass, M.D.:

- "In fact, the leading cause of exercise-related deaths even in well-trained athletes is coronary heart disease."
- "Severe coronary atherosclerosis is the most common cause of death in marathon runners."
- "A compelling argument can be made that over-exercising can cause atherosclerosis and coronary heart disease."[15]

21-Day Plan key principle #11:

Don't be a couch potato and don't over-exercise

"Everybody has a story of a neighbor or co-worker who worked out everyday and was nonetheless felled by a heart attack."

Stephen L. DeFelice, M.D., *The Carnitine Defense*

Dr. William Campbell Douglass' *Real Health* newsletter documents the danger of extreme exercise. The standard medical advice, "exercise and eat a low fat diet" is doubly dangerous if you have serious unrecognized heart disease. While there is evidence that both mental and physical exercise prolong life (Cardiovascular Health Study), there is also evidence that extreme exercise causes coronary heart disease.

For thirty years now, I have had one or more dogs, including three German Shepherds. Annie, who will be 14 on May 7, 2002, is still ready for a daily W-A-L-K. In order to prevent joyous thrashing about in the house, we must spell out our plans. As you dog lovers already know, dogs love to walk.

Theodore, a mix of shepherd, lab, retriever, and coonhound, is the most persistent let's-take-a-walk lobbyist I've ever seen. "No walk," he says, then "no reading or watching the news either." With high pitched guttural noises and persistent nudging, Theodore will hound you - cold, bitter Minnesota weather notwithstanding - into a walk.

Walking is the best exercise for the heart.

Like a dog, be sensible. Just go out your door, if possible, and walk around a block or two. Any walk is better than no walk. In adverse weather, walking indoors on a small trampoline, or walk-ing the floors of an indoor shopping mall are options to consider. Some people have special needs, but most of us benefit right away by simply walking.

Walking may be the best exercise for the heart, but gardening, hobbies, and any activity that gets you off the coach and hopefully out of the house counts as exercise too. Most of us should aim for 15 to 30 minutes of moderate daily exercise.

Your body and mind benefit much more from regulation and balance than from swinging back and forth from one extreme to another. Mild daily exercise - walking and stretching – benefit your heart the most. If more demanding exercise interests you, get into it gradually as you become more relaxed, stretched, and toned.[16]

A relaxed body is less likely to be injured than a tense body. Like any other muscle, the heart benefits from plentiful exercise as long as its not worked beyond its capacity. As Dr. Douglass points out, "Any kind of aerobic exercise, if done more than moderately, can induce atherosclerosis and consequent heart disease."[17]

"Heart pounding" exercise can enlarge, stress, and stop the heart. As reported in *Real Health*, *The American Journal of Cardiology* published a study on five runners who died of heart attacks after a run. None had evidence of heart disease before starting to run.[18]

Marvin Moser, M.D., professor of medicine at New York Medi-cal College, a hypertension expert, says, "There are no convincing data that systematic exercise, even if performed vigorously three to four times a week, has resulted in significant lowering of blood pressure.[19]

High blood pressure causes the heart to enlarge and reduces life expectancy. Controlling your blood pressure with drugs may lead to heart failure, says Robert C. Atkins, M.D., and less than 43 percent of those taking drugs actually get their blood pressure down to acceptable levels.[20]

If you have high blood pressure, first learn how to breathe deeply. Deep, slow breathing is a simple, immediate way to reduce pressure and improve circulation. Shallow breathing reduces circulation, causing cold hands and feet, fatigue, and the loss of mental concentration and clarity.

It's possible to conduct heart-pounding aerobic exercise and still not breath properly. Good breathing practices will improve circulation without moving a muscle. Good circulation is vital, but like breathing, it happens automatically and it's easy to take for granted.

Learn to relax during all phases of your life. "Relaxing is something that happens to the body and mind simultaneously," writes Meir Schneider, in *The Handbook of Self-Healing.* "When you relax, the flow of blood throughout your blood vessels, down to the smallest capillary, is automatically increased without any extra work by the heart."[21]

If you have high blood pressure, start exercising, consider a Yoga or meditation class, see an acupuncturist, get a message, consider a colonic, take liver and colon cleaning herbs, and supplement or eat cayenne, garlic, hawthorn, flaxseed, magnesium, trace minerals, and the amino acids arginine and carnitine.

The advice that all of us should "Exercise and eat a low fat diet," however, is a prescription for disaster. We know that up to 75 million people (Syndrome X) must avoid a low fat diet, and exercise, in the face of nutritional deficiency, may be dangerous – especially when pushed too far.

If your have elevated blood pressure and you're still following a low fat high carbohydrate diet – change your diet! Gerald Reaven, M.D., who has conducted more than 20 years of research into carbohydrate-related heart disease, says, 50 percent of hypertension is related to excess carbohydrates in the diet. Following current low fat medical advise often leads to heart disease.

Dr. Douglass warns women, in particular, to be careful about vigorous sport and provides several examples that are detailed in the book, *The Exercise Myth*, written by Dr. Henry Solomon (out of print). The female pelvis, designed for the delivery of babies, says Douglass, is proportionately wider than the males. This causes the thighbone to angle inward where they meet with the knees:

"So stress put on the female knee has quite a different effect from that on the male knee. Add to this the facts that female musculature is not as firm or strong (ounce for ounce) as male musculature and that female joints are more mobile due to delicate and supple ligaments, all adds up to a recipe for knee dislocations, sprains, and torn ligaments."

As controversial as Douglass's statement may be - given the seemingly beneficial aspects of greatly expanded women's sports - he is at least alerting us to some basic physiological differences between women and men. When I consider that both of my sisters and two close female friends have had knee surgery, I realize that Dr. Douglass may be on to something.

Tennis and elevated triglycerides, for example, both represent a greater threat to women than men, just as men, in general, may be much less able to discuss their feelings and express their emotions – holding everything in. When we're talking about heart health and longevity, there are differences between men and women that ought to be looked at more carefully.

In his *Real Health* newsletter, Dr. Douglass provides references to studies linking strenuous exercise with the development of coronary heart disease and sudden death episodes. It would behoove the people who exercise strenuously to take a closer look:

- Solomon, Henry, M.D., *The Exercise Myth*, (out of print - try amazon.com)
- Chapman, et. al. *American Journal of Public Health* 1957; 47: 33-43
- Malhotra, et. al. *British Heart Journal* 1967: 895-905
- Punsar, et. al. *Advances in Cardiology* 1976; 18: 196-207
- Wilhelmsen, et. al. *Preventive Medicine* 1975; 4: 491-508
- Rechnitzer, et. al. *American Journal of Cardiology* 1981; 47: 419
- Rosenman, *Annals of the New York Academy of Sciences* 1977; 301: 627-641
- Moser, *Primary Cardiology* 1980; 6(4): 11
- Allison et. al. *Journal of Cardiac Rehabilitation* 1981; 1(4): 257-265
- Lees, et. al. *New England Journal of Medicine* 1982; 306: 1,546-1,548
- Thompson, et. al. *Journal of the American Medical Asso.* 1982; 247: 2,535-2,569

For compelling commentary on health and nutrition, subscribe to Dr. William Campbell Douglass' *Real Health* newsletter. Write to *Real Health*, 819 N Charles St., Baltimore, MD 21201 or call 978-514-7851.

For developing your own deep breathing, exercising, and fitness program, read *The Handbook of Self Healing* by Meir Schneider (with Maureen Larkin and D. Schneider). The information on fat is out of date.

Chapter 12

-------- 🖎 --------

Grainy Goodness

"Boxed breakfast cereals are made by the extrusion process, in which flakes and shapes are formed at high temperatures and pressures. Extrusion processing destroys many valuable nutrients in grains, causes fragile oils to become rancid, and renders certain proteins toxic."

Sally Fallon, *Nourishing Traditions*

Somewhere between ten thousand and five thousand years ago, the shortage of large game animals forced most human groups into farming. Graphing it on paper, the 2.6 million year Paleolithic period would stretch 236 miles. Agriculture on the same graph would span one inch.

While grains and agriculture allowed for more people, they were not always healthier people. Less robust than the meat eaters who preceded them, grain eaters were shorter, had weaker bones, and suffered from more tooth decay. Our distant ancestors "were taller and stronger than we are today!"[1]

Many of us do poorly on grains. Relatively new to the human gut, eating grains can make us feel tired, weak, and bloated. Almost everyone is telling us to eat more whole grains, but in truth, most Americans couldn't tell the difference between a bushel of wheat, barley, rye, or buckwheat.

I know I would fail the test, and most people who tell you to eat whole grains would fail the test too. Whole grains, fruits, and vegetables are the good guys in American nutrition. Everyone is telling us to eat more fruits and vegetables – and the USDA Food Guide Pyramid says to eat six to eleven servings of bread, cereal, and grain every day.

While this advice may be well meaning, it doesn't mean much. Fruits, vegetables, and grains are all carbohydrates but their similarity ends there. There are big differences among fruits, vegetables, and grains. To lump them all together and then tell us to emphasize these foods is simply bad advice.

Black bears eat fruit to fatten up for winter. A lot of us simply can't eat a lot of fruit without gaining weight. Eating a banana may be too much for someone who is insulin resistant. A glass of orange juice and a banana – both fruits - can bump up blood sugar and insulin, as will healthy-sounding but high glycemic cooked carrots, parsnips, and potatoes.

As noted in chapter 9, there is a big difference between eating potatoes on a regular basis and eating vegetables like broccoli, Brussels sprouts, cauliflower and cabbage. While the cruciferous vegetables are always healthy choices, starchy vegetables and fruits have the potential to raise blood sugar and cause harm.

> **Carbohydrates**, especially starches, if eaten in excess, cause cancer. In a study reported in *Lancet*, women who ate large amounts of pasta, rice, white bread, and other starches had a 39 percent increased risk of breast cancer.
>
> *Lancet*, 1996, vol. 347

Some people should avoid grains all together. Enriched grain products have been stripped of most of their nutritional value and then have been fortified with a few synthetic B-vitamins and a form of iron that is best avoided (ferrous sulfate). Fortified simply means the product has extended shelf life.

Refined grains deplete the body of nutrients and raise blood sugar. Even in small amounts, highly processed boxed breakfast cereals – refined or whole grain – cause harm. If you like grains and can handle them, avoid high processed grains in every form: bread, cereal, chips, muffins, and snacks.[2]

The next time someone says eat more whole grains, ask them for a recipe. Without preparation techniques that have been largely forgotten, whole grains are not health promoting. In moderation and properly prepared, whole grains are of benefit to some people – but not everyone.

While some of our ancestors ate whole grains, they knew how to prepare them. My grandmother didn't make bread with packaged flour. She milled the grains and made the bread every week from scratch. "Grains quickly go rancid after grinding, and optimum health benefits are obtained from freshly ground flour," states Sally Fallon, author of *Nourishing Traditions*.[3]

"Porridge is the mother of us all," says a Russian proverb, and old-fashioned porridges are still one of the best ways to eat whole grains. *Nourishing Traditions*, has recipes for porridges that are soaked overnight and cooked in the morning. Fallon recommends adding the final nutritional touch: Butter, cream or raw milk to help absorb the minerals in the grain. Also, try adding omega-3 rich milled flaxseed or flaxseed oil to your breakfast.

Nourishing Traditions cookbook provides extensive information on preparing and eating whole and sprouted grains, including several porridge, casserole and bread recipes. It's the only cookbook you'll ever need. According to Fallon, our ancestors – and most pre-industrial people – soaked or fermented their grains before making them into porridge, breads, or casseroles.

In fact, around the world today, grain preparation is still the rule where people eat traditional foods. In India, rice and lentils are fermented for at least two days. In Africa, people soak coarsely ground corn overnight before adding it to soups and stews. Mexican corn cakes, called *pozol*, are fermented for several days (and for as long as two weeks) in banana leaves.[4]

All grains contain phytic acid in the outer layer or bran. In the intestinal tract, untreated phytic acid can combine with calcium, magnesium, copper, iron, and especially zinc and block their absorption.[5] Though grains contain a lot of valuable nutrients, you must soak or sprout them in order to neutralize the anti-nutrients. Soaking or sprouting also leaves the protein easier to digest.

As little as seven hours of soaking in warm water will neutralize a large portion of the phytic acid. "The simple practice of soaking cracked or rolled cereal grains overnight will vastly improve their nutritional benefits," says Fallon. Proteins in grains, especially gluten, are hard for most people to digest. A diet high in improperly prepared whole grains, especially high-gluten grains like wheat, puts a big strain on the digestive system.

During the process of soaking and fermenting, gluten and other difficult to digest proteins are partially broken down into simpler components that are more readily available for absorption. Soaking in warm water, says Fallon, also neutralizes enzyme inhibitors and promotes the growth of other beneficial enzymes.

Oats are low in hard to digest gluten, but contain more phytic acid than almost any other grain. Whole oats are nutritious, containing B-vitamins, calcium, iron, magnesium, phosphorus and potassium, but they must be soaked overnight for best results. Instead of buying quick refined oats, try old-fashioned whole oat groats or lightly processed oat flakes. You can find them at your natural foods grocery, preferably in an airtight package.

Miso is a fermented soybean paste. Fermentation removes the phytates and neutralizes the enzyme inhibitors. Miso (and tempeh) are the only beneficial soy products. Miso is rich in omega-3 fatty acids and is a complete protein because it is made with grains and soybeans.

Miso Porridge, a *Nourishing Traditions* recipe, shows how to prepare rolled or cracked oats to neutralize the phytates and enzyme inhibitors found in the oats. The recipe calls for 1 cup of rolled or cracked oats, 2 cups of filtered water, and two table-spoons of fermented light miso.

> In the evening, cook oatmeal in water for 5-10 minutes or until all water is absorbed. Allow to cool and mix in miso. Cover and leave the mixture at room temperature overnight. In the morning, reheat gently without bringing to a boil.

Adding milled faxseed and butter to the oats in the morning helps promote mineral absorption and reduces the glycemic value of the breakfast.

Oats, rye, barley and especially wheat contain gluten and re-quire preparation before they can be safely eaten. Buckwheat, rice, and millet do not contain gluten, do not require soaking, and are tolerated by more people. In *Nourishing Traditions*, Fallon recom-mends that rice and millet be "steamed for two hours in a high mineral gelatinous broth."

Slow steaming in broth neutralizes the small amount of phytic acid, provides additional minerals, and greatly facilitates nutrient absorption.[6] If properly prepared, rice is an excellent choice for people who are allergic to other cereal grains. Try adding milled flaxseed, flaxseed oil, or olive oil to your steamed rice.

Fallon does not recommend granola or any processed boxed cereals. These grains have been subjected to high heat and high pressure. Like fats, modern processing methods destroy many valu-able nutrients in grains, causing the oils to go rancid and render-ing the product hard to digest.[7]

Native Americans traditionally cooked corn with lime. Like grains, traditional recipes call for soaking corn or corn flour. Lime releases niacin (vitamin B-3) that otherwise remains bound up in the corn. In combination, traditionally prepared corn and beans were a staple of native peoples in Central America. The benefit of these nutritious foods, however, depends on knowledge that has been passed down for centuries.

Ethnic and genetic considerations are paramount. No Food Guide Pyramid can apply to all Americans – especially if we disregard the traditional food preparation wisdom of the past. Asians, for example, have proportionately longer intestinal tracks, larger pancreas and larger salivary glands than Europeans. These traits make the Chinese and Japanese more suited to a grain-based diet.

Because of rancidity problems, Fallon recommends that we buy brown rice and grains that have been rolled or cracked in airtight packaging. While that may go against the grain of the bulk is always better mentality, rancid rolled oats will contain harmful oxidized omega-6 fat.

To incorporate whole grains into your diet, you need a cookbook – either *Nourishing Traditions* by Sally Fallon - or a used cookbook printed before 1920.

USDA Food Guide Pyramid

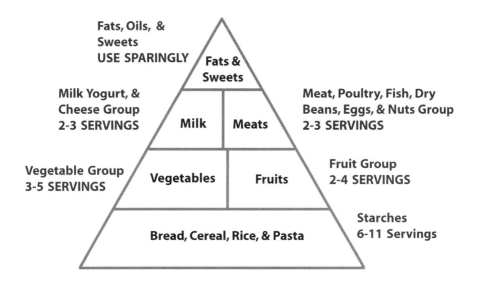

The USDA Food Guide Pyramid emphasizes grains and recommends that everyone eat 6-11 servings of starch every day.

21-Day Plan key principle #12:

If you eat grains, eat whole grains that have been properly prepared.

Ignore the USDA Food Guide Pyramid recommendation to eat 6-11 servings of grain everyday.

Problems with the pyramid:

1. The pyramid recommends that everyone eat six to eleven (6-11) servings of grain daily. This is wrong for a lot of people. According to Gerald Reaven, M.D., it's wrong for 60-75 million people who are sensitive to carbohydrates and easily become resistant to the action of insulin. Plenty of research, cited in this book, including Dr. Reaven's extensive research at Stanford University Medical School, documents that excess carbohydrates increase the risk of heart disease. This pyramid recommendation ignores the blood sugar sensitivity of up to 75 million people.

2. The food pyramid does not acknowledge that all grains contain phytic acid in the outer layer or bran. Untreated, phytates block mineral absorption, especially calcium, copper, iron, magnesium, and zinc. In *The Carnitine Miracle*, Robert Crayhon writes, "Grains also contain a compound called pyridoxine glucoside which can block vitamin B-6 absorption by up to 80 percent." The pyramid is wrong to emphasize a grain-based diet for everyone without educating people about the antinutrients and enzyme inhibitors found in untreated whole grains.

3. The food pyramid makes no distinction between refined grain products and properly prepared whole grains. There is a big difference between properly prepared rolled oats soaked overnight, for example, and eating sugary *Cheerios* and other boxed cereals. Yet, the pyramid fails to mention that there are qualitative differences among grain products. Why not a warning to avoid "highly refined carbohydrates."

4. The food pyramid recommends 2-4 fruit servings daily for everyone. Again, the pyramid is ignoring the carbohydrate sensitivity of 75 million people. Insulin resistant people may have to limit fruit to one serving a day. Among fruits, there are some that raise blood sugar and contain more carbohydrates than others. An apple, for example, releases sugar slower than a banana and contains less carbohydrate. Also, the pyramid makes no mention of seasons of the year. While summer may be a good time for additional fruit in a northern climate, too much fruit in the winter may cool the body. The pyramid makes no mention of eating a wide range of varying foods in order to maximize nutrition and minimize the chance of food allergies.

5. The food pyramid emphasizes grains, fruits, and vegetables and minimizes the need for adequate daily protein. The section that includes meat, poultry and fish also includes beans. Beans are a high carbohydrate food. While fresh, properly prepared beans may be good for a lot of people, they represent a threat to optimum blood sugar control in up to 75 million people. Beans or legumes should be included in the grain group and have a recommendation of zero to five servings per day.

6. The pyramid says to eat fat sparingly and places fats in the same category as "sweets." This is not helpful at all. We need generous amounts of high quality fat from both plant and animal sources. Also, the pyramid ignores critical issues concerning fats, such as degree of processing and the need for balanced intake. No mention is made of the critically important "essen-

tial fatty acids" or the dangerous "trans fatty acids." In the U.S. today, we are consuming excess omega-6 and not getting enough omega-3 (see chapter 16). Ideally, the ratio of omega-6 to omega-3 is no more than 3:1. Today, our ratio is 20:1. We are consuming excess omega-6 and excess heat-damaged omega-6 in the form of partially hydrogenated vegetable oils, which contain trans fatty acids (TFAs).

7. The pyramid makes no qualitative distinctions in any of the food groupings. Just as there are excessively refined carbohydrates, there are excessively refined vegetable fats and there are meat products that contain oxidized cholesterol, nitrates, nitrites, and even sugar. Among meat and poultry, there should be a distinction between grain-fed cattle and pasture raised grass-fed cattle, and between battery chickens and free range foraging chickens. Grain-fed beef and grain-fed battery chickens contain excess omega-6 and are deficient in omega-3. Grass-fed animals and eggs from foraging chickens contain a favorable balance of omega-6 and omega-3, but all of this is missing from the USDA recommendations.

8. The USDA pyramid ignores differences in quality, differences in people, and differences in needs of people. Two or three servings of dairy are recommended without considering dairy allergies or difficulty breaking down casein, milk protein. Because all milk has to be pasteurized, Americans are not even given the option of obtaining enzyme-rich raw milk, which would be much better for growing children and for adults who tolerate and digest milk efficiently.

Nourishing Traditions - Cookbook

Sally Fallon combines a background in nutrition with training in French and Mediterranean cooking. Fallon has studied gourmet culinary techniques in both Paris and the U.S. and has devoted many years to researching genuine versions of traditional cooking methods. *Nourishing Traditions* was written with Mary G. Enig, Ph.D., lipid biochemist, researcher, and consultant.

- *Nourishing Traditions* is "The Cookbook that Challenges Politically Correct Nutrition." It contains over 700 recipes, many that your grandmother's mother knew by heart, including hard-to-find information on whole grains and soup stocks.

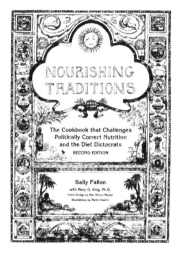

- *Nourishing Traditions* unites the traditional culinary wisdom of the past with the latest independent accurate scientific research. The result: A lot of clearly written, detailed recipes and consumer food and nutrition information you can trust.

- *Nourishing Traditions* reintroduces food preparation techniques that most of us never learned or have forgotten. Fallon's kitchen skills will help you get much more nutrition out of the money you are now spending on food.

In 1999, Fallon founded the Weston A. Price Foundation in Washington, D.C. The foundation is dedicated to education, research and activism in the field of nutrition and food preparation. The foundation can be found online at **www.westonaprice.org** or by writing to the foundation at PMB #106-380, 4200 Wisconsin Ave. NW, Washington, D.C., 20016.

Food for Life Breads: Different from most breads today, Food for Life Bread is made from freshly sprouted live grains and contains absolutely no flour. Water is added to whole organically grown grains. Beneficial enzymes are activated which cause the grains to sprout and become a living food. For more information online, go to **www.food-for-life.com** or call **800-797-5090**.

French Meadow Bakery: Sourdough Bread composed simply of organic stoneground flours, unrefined sea salt, and pure water. For more information online, go to **www.frenchmeadow.com** or call **612-870-4740** for store locations or to make a mail order purchase.

SPROUTED 16 GRAIN & SEED BREAD

Organic Sprouted Wheat, Organic Oat Groats, Organic Sunflower Seeds, Organic Flaxseeds, Organic Sprouted Barley, Organic Sprouted Rye Berries, Organic Sprouted Millet, Organic Sesame Seeds, Organic Sprouted Whole Corn, Organic Sprouted Soybeans, Organic Sprouted Triticale, Organic Sprouted Spelt, Organic Sprouted Kamut, Malted Barley, Organic Short Grain Brown Rice, Organic Sprouted Quinoa, Organic Sprouted Amaranth, Organic Wheat Germ, Organic Sprouted Spelt, Honey Organic Wheat Germ, Yeast, Poppy Seeds, Unrefined Sea Salt

Compare the ingredients in this bread to the bread you typically find at the supermarket. For more information on bread like this, check out **www.rainiernaturalbakery.com** or call **253-833-4369**.

PART III

The role of fat and protein

Chapter 13

-------- 🖛 --------

Fat of the land

The claim that saturated fat leads to heart disease is simply false. This claim was initiated as a marketing tool to sell oils and margarine (in competition to butter, lard and tallow). Eventually the idea became dogma as it was repeated year after year.

Mary Enig, Ph.D., *Know Your Fats*

Beginning around 1956, the AHA said limit fat - fat is *bad*. From the mid-1960s through the 1980s, it was eat *good* polyunsaturated fat and limit *bad* saturated fat.

In the mid-1990s, when the *Mediterranean diet* was rediscovered - and the bad news about commercial trans fatty acids (TFAs) could no longer be concealed - it became *good* fats (olive oil, fish) versus *bad* fats (saturated, trans fats).

Today, most health writers, nutrition reporters, and college professors remain almost comically afraid of saying anything good about *saturated fat*. Saturated fat is to blame for just about everything, the dietary scapegoat, the least loved nutrient in the high carbohydrate dietary kingdom.

Food writers and pundits, in books and articles, are even reinventing the Paleolithic or Stone Age diets, suggesting they were "lean." Bestselling author Jean Carper's version of a *Stone Age Salad* includes "mixed greens, garbanzo beans, and *skinless* chicken breasts."[1]

Repeatedly, we are told to remove chicken skin in the mistaken belief that because it's animal fat – it's saturated. This is far from the truth. Chicken fat is 70 percent unsaturated, particularly the skin. Vilifying saturated fats is one thing – not knowing what they are is another.

The Paleolithic diet didn't include beans or grains – and it wasn't lean. Hunter-gatherers ate meat and fat from every kind of animal – including the skin and brains - and consumed a diverse variety of nuts, seeds, wild plants, fruits, insects, worms and occasionally eggs.

Moose, elk, caribou, deer, antelope, bear, and the buffalo were staples of many Native American diets. They ate the entire animal - not just the muscle meat – and used every bit of fat. In *The Ways of my Grandmothers*, Beverly Hungry Wolf describes how "All the insides, such as heart, kidneys and liver, were prepared and eaten,

Dietary Fat Intake In The U.S. Food Supply 1909 – 1993

1909 – Average American ate less than 2 grams of liquid vegetable oil.

1910 – Butter consumption: 18 pounds per person annually

1910 – Proportion of animal fats in diet: 83 percent

1911 – Crisco (a partially hydrogenated shortening) went on sale

1930 – Heart attack deaths: 3,000

1940 – Hydrogenated margarines introduced

1950 – Butter consumption: 10 pounds per person annually

1950 – Margarine consumption: 8 pounds per person annually

1960 – Heart attack deaths: 500,000

1970 – Proportion of animal fats in diet: 62 percent

1970 – Butter consumption: 4 pounds per person annually

1993 – Average American ate more than 30 grams of liquid vegetable oil.

(Derived from Atkins, Enig and others)

roasted or baked or laid out in the sun to dry." The brains were eaten raw.[2]

Most highly prized was the internal kidney fat of ruminant (grass-eating) animals. Natives learned to value what lipid biochemists have just discovered - that ruminant animal fat contains conjugated linoleic acid (CLA), a fat-burning anti-cancer fatty acid.[3] Grain-fed animals have virtually none (see chapter 17).

CLA has been studied extensively since it was discovered a decade ago. A study published in *Diabetes* magazine found that CLA actually improves insulin activity in animals, resulting in improved glucose tolerance and enhanced insulin uptake. CLA's ability to optimize insulin function explains why it can help the body burn fat. Supplements are now available – or you can eat meat from pasture-raised animals.

Hungry Wolf describes how all of the foods considered important for reproduction and all of the foods considered sacred were animal foods rich in fat. "Boiled tongue was an ancient delicacy," she says, "served as the food of communion at the Sun Dance."[4]

Native Americans who lived on the fat of the land had broad faces, high cheekbones, straight teeth, and fine physiques. Early explorers consistently described the natives as strong and well formed. "The men could run after a deer for an entire day without resting and without apparent fatigue…" wrote the explorer, Cabeza De Vaca.[5]

No longer Paleolithic or Native American, the 1910 American diet nonetheless contained mineral-rich organic vegetables, wild berries, whole carbohydrates processed in the home, pasture raised grass-fed animals, and up to 40 percent of calories from traditional saturated fats.

In 1910, one third of the population lived on farms, and Americans ate more cholesterol and saturated fat than they do today. People cooked with fat rendered from beef, poultry, chicken and pork. Butter, cream, and "drippings" were highly valued.[6]

Fat in the American diet has always ranged from 30 to 43 percent of calories.[7] Both numbers are well within the range of the desert nomads (10 percent fat) and Greenland Eskimos (50 percent fat) – who have little or no heart disease.

You can put your calculators away. There is no one right amount of fat. Depending on genes, your job, activities, the season of the year and the climate you live in, Americans have lived for thousands of years on a wide range of fat – but always *a wide range of minimally processed natural fats.*

In 1910, animal fats comprised 83 percent of fat calories. Per capita butter consumption was approximately 18 pounds. By 1970, the proportion of animal fats had declined to 62 percent of fat calories, and per capita butter consumption had fallen to about 4 pounds. During the same period, dietary cholesterol intake stayed about the same, while our consumption of vegetable fats increased 400 percent and our consumption of sugar and refined foods increased 60 percent.[8]

Dietary fat consumption during the period 1930 to 1985 increased from 124 grams to 164 grams per day. Most of the 40 gram increase came in the form of highly processed polyunsaturated vegetable fats like margarine and shortening.[9]

Trans fatty acids (TFAs) are created when, for baking and cooking purposes, vegetable seed oils are "partially hydrogenated," turned from a liquid to a more solid fat. Margarine and shortening, made from corn and soybean oils, are "partially hydrogenated fats." During the hydrogenation process, says Mary Enig, Ph.D., up to 50 percent of the fatty acids convert from the natural cis-configuration to the not found in nature trans-configuration.

During the last 40 years, the federal government, American Heart Association, and other organizations have prodded us into giving up healthy traditional animal and tropical fats for cooking, replacing them with the new, untested commercial vegetable oils and partially hydrogenated fats. We have been intentionally misled into thinking that saturated tropical fats are bad.

Coconut, palm, and palm kernel fat, nourishing healthy populations for centuries, are heat-stable and ideal for baking and cooking. Coconut fat is the best source of 12-carbon lauric acid, a medium chain anti-microbial fat found only in tropical oils, butter, and human milk. Lauric acid, used by the body to kill pathogenic viruses and bacteria, is readily burned for energy – and not stored as body fat.[10]

Joining the anti-saturated fat campaign in 1986, the *Center For Science in the Public Interest (CSPI)* – along with the soybean oil industry - spearheaded an intense anti-saturated fat, anti-tropical fat campaign. In 1986, the CSPI petitioned the FDA to introduce legislation requiring "singularly pejorative anti-tropical oils labeling."

Although the effort failed, the CSPI book, *The Saturated Fat Attack*, spewed out enough disinformation to deliver the final, fatal blow to the U.S. tropical oil business.[11] As a result, fast food restaurants, commercial bakeries, and movie theatres across the country replaced the healthy, tropical saturates with the not so healthy partially hydrogenated soybean oils.

Substituting partially hydrogenated soybean oil in French fries, baked goods, and popcorn meant an increase in fat calories consumed and a substantial increase in *trans fats* in the American diet.[12]

In their *Nutrition Action Newsletter*, CSPI states that they "advocate honest food labeling and advertising, safer and more nutritious foods, and pro-health alcohol policies." If trashing healthy tropical oils and increasing the American people's intake of harmful trans fatty acids constitutes honest, pro-health policies, I'll need a tall glass of Irish whiskey with my French fries, please!

Birds of a feather flock together. *Nutrition Action Newsletter* has won awards from the National Cholesterol Education Program, the U.S. Food and Drug Administration, and the American

Medical Writers Association. That's why it's hard to trust anything any of them say.

Among CSPI's scientific advisory board sits Jeramiah Stamler, M.D., director of the ill-fated MRFIT study and the staunch diet-heart advocate who recommended the switch from traditional animal fats to the new commercial vegetable fats even "before the final proof is nailed down."[13]

Forty years later, the only thing nailed down for sure are the nails on the coffins of the people who consumed too much partially hydrogenated fat and trans fatty acids. Lucky for the anti-saturated fat lobby – the people who have died prematurely, and their families, never knew what hit them.

Throughout the 70s, 80s, and 90s, in one persistent voice, the Heart Institute, the AHA, and organizations like CSPI, said eat margarine and corn oil – avoid all saturated fats. Now, today, all of a sudden, like the cat who ate the canary, they are coyly backpedaling – starting to warn us about these mysterious, new fangled trans fatty acids.

Like their recent born-again anti-trans fat conversion, the campaign trumped up in the 1960s by the government and U.S. edible oil industry to discredit animal fats is deceitful. It was simply their way of scaring the public into buying more margarine and partially hydrogenated fats – both of which contain trans fatty acids.

And fifty years later… what, if anything, has changed?

In his popular *8 Weeks to Optimum Health*, Andrew Weil, M.D., ignoring Framingham and stacks of scientific data, states that butter is *"clearly implicated in atherosclerosis,"* and goes on to suggest that we dip our bread in olive oil or eat it dry!

Has it really come to that? Dry toast? My grandfather, I'm sure, would finally roll over in his grave. Olive oil is 100 percent fat. Butter is 80 percent fat (20 percent water). Dipping your sourdough into olive oil - instead of a thin even spread of butter - will increase your fat intake 2 to 3 times.

Butter, according to Mary Enig, Ph.D., is "one of the most complex natural fats in existence," containing a large number of short-, medium-, and odd-chain fatty acids. Butter is 50 percent saturated fat and 28 percent oleic acid, the type of fat found abundantly (71 percent) in olive oil.[14]

While a higher fat intake is not inherently bad, it's better to load up on butter than olive oil. Containing predominantly long chain-18 carbon oleic acid, olive oil in excess, gets stored in adipose tissue (fat cells). In a word, olive oil is "fattening."

Butter, on the other hand, is about 15 percent short- and medium-chain fatty acids. Biologically important and readily burned, they are shuttled via the portal vein directly to the liver. Short chain fats in butter inhibit the growth of pathogenic fungi, and medium chain lauric acid kills or disables many pathogenic viruses and other organisms.

Butter – not olive oil – is an excellent source of these antimicrobial fats. Eaten for thousands of years, butter provides small but balanced amounts of omega-3 and omega-6. Butter is rich in lecithin, choline, and many trace minerals, including selenium, manganese, zinc, chromium and iodine.

Don't get me wrong. Use both. They have different flavors and culinary characteristics. Olive oil (extra virgin) and butter (grass fed cows) are both healthy natural fats with laudable roles to play in cooking and nutrition.

What we don't need, however, is a misplaced unscientific campaign against traditional, healthy saturated fats. The smear campaign has hurt patients and producers alike. After all, it's the refined vegetable oils and "plastic" trans fats that have led us on this road to ruin - tilting things in favor of chronic degenerative disease.

Please, pass the butter!

21-Day Plan key principle #13:

Use herbs to stimulate, cleanse and nutritionally support healthy blood circulation

An herb can be a bark, flower, fruit, leaf, root, seed, stem, or any other plant part used for medicinal purposes. Herbs contain naturally occurring chemicals that have biological activity. Herbs, as a rule, are gentle and take time to provide therapeutic benefit.

Herbs are excellent as tea (simple infusion), liquid extracts (tinctures), or as dried powdered herbs in capsules. Herb extracts – whether liquid or powder - are concentrated; whole herbs are used as is. Leafy materials like ginkgo biloba are often more effective in extract form. Many herbs, especially good quality berries and roots, are just as therapeutic in whole form.

Some herbs are used periodically – like goldenseal to fight infection – and others, are beneficial taken on a daily, regular basis. Daily use herbs can be called "tonic," they are safe and effective when used long term.

The eight cardiovascular herbs described below are cardiovascular tonics. In combination, they help promote blood flow to the heart and extremities and provide direct nourishment to the heart and arteries. No combination of eight prescription drugs can do that.

Eight Cardiovascular Herbs: cayenne, ginger, garlic, onion, gotu kola, hawthorn, Siberian ginseng, and valerian root.

Cayenne (the hotter the better) stimulates blood flow, strengthening the heart and metabolism. Cayenne is also a general tonic, helpful specifically for the circulatory, digestive, and eliminative systems. Cayenne increases stomach secretions and peristaltic action in the colon. Dried cayenne is high in beta carotene, cobalt, essential fats, niacin, and zinc.

In *Scientific Validation of Herbal Medicine*, Daniel Mowrey, Ph.D., recommends cayenne for circulatory stimulation, blood purification, detoxification, and fatigue. Dr. Mowrey documents cayenne's ability to inhibit the tendency of blood clots to stick together (platelet aggregation) and form clots.

Cayenne increases fibrinolytic activity; that is, ingesting cayenne with a meal prevents fibrin – which forms blood clots or blood stickiness – from building up in the blood. Taking small amounts of cayenne on a daily basis keeps fibrinolysis at a more of less consistently high level.

In **Left For Dead**, Dick Quinn described how cayenne pepper extended his life after a heart attack and failed coronary bypass surgery. In 1993, Dick and Al Watson cofounded the Cayenne Trading Company, home of "Quinn's Blend" formulas.

Like exercise, cayenne must be taken on a regular basis to protect you from heart disease. Get in the habit of using cayenne (and exercising) everyday. Cayenne only promotes fibrinolysis while it's in the system. Cayenne also lowers elevated triglycerides, helping to keep blood flowing freely and smoothly through arteries and veins.

Cayenne is the purest and most certain stimulant known. High heat cayenne – about 100,000 heat units - contains larger amounts of capsaicin and is more therapeutic than supermarket red pepper (40,000 heat units). Cayenne can be sprinkled into chili, soup, and tomato juice. Liquid tinctures and cayenne in capsules or bulk powder are available online from **www.nokobeach.com** or by calling Nokomis Nutrition, **800-641-6802**.

Ginger is the most widely cultivated spice in the world. Ginger, like cayenne, is a circulatory and digestive stimulant. A more diffuse stimulant, ginger promotes return blood flow through the veins back to the heart. In *Ginger*, Paul Schulick points out that ginger has 180 times the protein-digesting enzymes as papaya.

In combination, cayenne and ginger stimulate circulation throughout the body. Ginger has anti-coagulant (blood thinning) activity similar to aspirin. As a catalyst, ginger combines well with other herbs, helping the body digest the more pungent cayenne.

According to Schulick, ginger is a powerful antioxidant with at least twelve constituents that help neutralize cell and tissue destroying free radicals. Ginger's antioxidant nutrients counter inflammation and provide strong immune system support.

Ginger, endorsed by Confucius 2,500 years ago, is safe. In *Ginger*, Schulick cites hundreds of scientific references from current international medical research. Excellent ginger comes from Jamaica, Nigeria, and China (non-sulfite). Ginger comes in whole root, tea, tincture, and capsules. Ginger is excellent in all forms – fresh or dry – or added to hot bath water.

Garlic/Onion are close relatives, complement each other, and are excellent in combination. Garlic and onion, like cayenne and ginger, are beneficial fresh or dry. In combination, cayenne, ginger, garlic and onion lower triglycerides (blood fats) and promote more viscous, free flowing blood. You can have a baby aspirin everyday or you can power up with the incredible healing power of herbs – it's your choice.

In *The Healing Benefits of Garlic*, John Heinerman, Ph.D., explains why garlic is so effective: Over 30 sulfur compounds, 17 amino acids, plus chromium, selenium, and germanium. Garlic, an underground bulb, contains volatile oils that are readily transported throughout the body, nurturing the circulatory, digestive, respiratory, and urinary tracts.

Gotu Kola is a traditional blood purifier, tonic herb, and diuretic, grown in Pakistan, India, Malaysia, and East Africa. Mowrey refers to gotu kola (centella asiatica) as an excellent neural tonic, which "slowly builds mental stamina and neural health." Gotu Kola has been valued for centuries in India for improving memory and extending longevity.

Mowrey compares the action of gotu kola to ginseng; a slow, steady increase in resistance to stress and fatigue. He cites gotu kola's proven ability to promote blood flow through the veins back to the heart. According to Mowrey, "Centella strengthens and repairs connective tissues, decreases capillary fragility, and nutritively supports the cells of the vein. Gotu kola can help promote circulation to the extremities, including the lower limbs and the brain.

Hawthorn berries, flowers, and leaves contain flavonoids (plant chemicals) that have an affinity for the heart muscle. Hawthorn provides direct nourishment to the heart and, over time, helps dilate the coronary arteries. Hawthorn is a gentle heart tonic. You must use hawthorn several months to achieve therapeutic benefit.

In Europe, hawthorn liquid extracts are mainstream medicine – used clinically for a number of heart-related conditions. Hawthorn, in German scientific research, has been found to lower high blood pressure, increase the contractibility of the heart muscle, increase blood flow to the heart, and decrease heart rate.

James Green, author of *Male Herbal*, calls hawthorn "the best tonic for the heart and circulatory system. Mowrey writes about the combination of cayenne and hawthorn: "Cayenne and hawthorn in a single capsule produces a special kind of synergism that augments the cardiotonic activity of both." In *The Green Pharmacy*, James A. Duke, Ph.D., says "Extensive research has demonstrated that hawthorn extracts improve heart function by opening up the coronary arteries."

Siberian ginseng (Eleuthero) is considered one of the best "adaptogenic" herbs, increasing the body's ability to respond to stress. Technically not a member of the ginseng family, Eleuthero root, heavily researched in the former Soviet Union, has a growing reputation for increasing immune response and improving mental and physical performance.

Eleuthero acts as an MAO inhibitor, according to Dr. Duke, helping to improve mood in people suffering with depression. In the German government's official *Commission E* reference for herbs, eleuthero – and the other ginsengs – are endorsed "as a tonic to combat feelings of lassitude and debility, lack of energy and ability to concentrate, and during convalescence."

For fatigue, Dr. Mowrey recommends cayenne, Siberian ginseng, gotu kola, and ginger root. In his formula, which includes other herbs, Mowrey names Siberian ginseng as "the number one tonic herb in the world." Siberian ginseng works with the adrenal gland to help prevent the cumulative effect of different types of daily stresses.

Valerian, since ancient times, has been one of the most widely used medicinal herbs. Valerian is a safe nighttime sleep aid. Valerian helps relieve anxiety by calming activity in the brain and spinal column. Valerian, a nervine, improves sleep quality and shortens the time needed to fall asleep.

Known for its sedative and sleep-enhancing qualities, valerian is also excellent for stress-related high blood pressure and heart rhythm problems. Valerian has other heart benefits as well, says Dr. Duke. "Valerian lowers blood pressure, increases blood flow to the heart, and improves the heart's pumping ability."

Good quality valerian stinks like dirty socks. Valerian tea, as you might expect, would not taste good. Valerian is best in powdered capsules or liquid tincture. Valerian is particularly good combined with hawthorn. Although a well-respected nervine, valerian has a mild stimulating effect in some people. Most people appreciate the muscle tension relieving properties of valerian.

Oysters: Vitamin A to Zinc:

Oysters are the best-known and highest source of zinc – providing 150 mg per gram. Second on the list is ginger root (7 mg per gram), followed by beef, fish, lamb, and shellfish. Most vegetables do not provide zinc, and phytic acid in grains and beans binds up zinc – making it difficult to absorb.

Oysters are important for men and women. Zinc is required for many enzymes (enzymes are mineral dependent) that support reproduction and mental function. Pregnancy increases the body's need for zinc – and zinc is not stored in the body. Excess alcohol reduces our capacity to absorb zinc.

Raw oysters quickly restore zinc and also supply iron, selenium, fat-soluble vitamin A and D, and omega-3 EPA and DHA. Non-fish-eating vegetarians must eat a lot of cheese (cheddar, Swiss) or fermented soy (miso, tempeh) to get their zinc. People consuming unfermented soy (tofu, soy milk) and excess whole grains are most susceptible to zinc deficiency.

For more information about herbs of all kinds, read *The Green Pharmacy* by James A. Duke, Ph.D. Contains A-Z entries that includes over 120 health conditions

Or, look for *Scientific Validation of Herbal Medicine* by Daniel B. Mowrey, Ph.D. Dr. Mowrey's book focuses on combination formulas and is based on his extensive personal research.

Men would like the herbal and other information found in *The Male Herbal* by James Green, herbalist.

Chapter 14

-------- 🐛 --------

Funny fats, margarine, and trans fatty acids

The presence of the trans fatty acids in the diet today are causing shifts in favor of chronic disease.

Mary Enig, Ph.D., *Know Your Fats*

For decades, Americans have been replacing heat-stable saturated fats like butter, lard and tropical oils with large amounts of highly refined polyunsaturated and partially hydrogenated vegetable oils – *trans fats* - consumed since Crisco shortening was introduced in 1911.

The great increase in the use of commercial vegetable oils and trans fats has exactly paralleled the great increase in heart disease and cancer in the United States. During the same period, as we have seen, the consumption of saturated fats, especially butter, lard, and tropical fats, declined dramatically.

Intended to replace butter, margarine is the worst of all fats. It is a fabricated food formed by taking an already rancid vegetable fat, such as soybean oil, stripping off the fragile essential fats, and bombarding what's left with hydrogen and nickel to make it solid at room temperature.[1]

Hydrogenation artificially saturates unsaturated fats - increasing shelf life. Once hydrogenated, a percentage of the unsaturated fatty acids are transformed from the natural cis-configuration to a not-found-in-nature trans-configuration. Hydrogenated fats contain up to 50 percent *trans fats*.[2]

Trans fatty acids (TFAs) are not listed on food labels; you find them indirectly in the ingredients list as "*partially hydrogenated vegetable oil*." TFAs are found abundantly in margarine, shortening, baked goods and in 70 percent of all highly processed foods – breakfast bars and cereals, imitation cheese, prepared dinners, salad dressings, snack chips, and candy bars.[3]

To a large extent, TFAs have displaced natural saturated fats in the U.S. diet. According to Mary Enig, Ph.D., biochemist, internationally known researcher and author of *Know Your Fats*, 11 percent of the fat intake of Americans is in the form of trans fats. That works out to about 4 percent of the average American's total daily calories.[4]

Based on results from Harvard's Nurse's Health Study, your risk of a heart attack is nearly double the average if you get just 2 percent of your calories from trans fats. [5] Attempting to steer clear of saturated fats, Americans, unknowingly, are loading up on deadly "plastic fats."

Molecular misfits, TFAs disrupt cellular function and compromise the integrity of delicate membrane systems. They alter enzymes that neutralize carcinogens, and increase enzymes that potentiate carcinogens.[6] They interfere with many body processes, including the conversion of the essential fatty acids (linoleic and alpha linolenic acid) to their elongated forms. (See Essential omega-3, chapter 16.)

TFAs decrease insulin binding. Dr. Enig warns that people who have a tendency to develop diabetes - 60-75 million people - should strictly avoid trans fats. When monkeys are fed trans fat-containing margarine in their diets, their red blood cells do not bind insulin as well as when they are not fed the trans fats.[7]

In human studies cited by Enig, trans fats increased blood stickiness and blood platelet aggregation, raised blood sugar levels, and caused people to weigh several kilograms (many pounds) more than people consuming the same amount of fat that is not hydrogenated."[8]

In a study published in the August 1990 *New England Journal of Medicine,* trans fats not only lowered protective HDL cholesterol, they also raised LDL and total cholesterol. According to Enig, trans fats will lower protective HDL and raise LDL in a dose-response manner.[9]

Trans fats also convert LDL into a dangerous, sticky particle called lipoprotein(a). "Feeding trans fatty acids from partially hydrogenated vegetable oils to adult humans lowers HDL cholesterol and raises lipoprotein(a)," says Enig, especially in people who already have elevated lipoprotein(a) levels.[10]

Lipoprotein(a) is a sticky protein that attaches to LDL cholesterol in the bloodstream. Lp(a) is LDL plus a super adhesive protein - Apoprotein(a) – surrounding it. Lipoprotein(a), in Dr. Atkins' words, "is a blood fat to take very seriously."

Called the "heart attack cholesterol," lipoprotein(a) accumulates around arterial lesions and promotes blood clots. Lp(a) can interfere with fibrinolysis, the body's own clot-dissolving process.[11] One third of CHD patients have elevated lipoprotein(a), which carries a 250 to 300 percent increased risk of heart attack, especially when accompanied by other blood fat abnormalities, such as elevated homocysteine and fibrinogen.[12]

Fibrinogen is a blood protein that promotes clotting and thickens blood. Elevated fibrinogen increases the lethalness of any other heart disease risk factor, especially lipoprotein(a). People with chronic high levels of fibrinogen, especially women, have a much greater risk of CHD. Levels above 350 mg/dl double the risk of heart disease.[13]

Lipoprotein(a) can be detected in a blood test and, like homocysteine, is a leading predictor or marker for heart disease. Dr. Atkins recommends keeping Lp(a) below 20 mg/dl. Anything above 20 indicates increased risk; levels of 30 or more require immediate attention. According to Atkins, lipoprotein(a) levels are set by genes, but can be influenced by the nutritional choices we make, including eliminating all processed foods and trans fats from your diet.[14]

A major cause of high lipoprotein(a) levels is eating large amounts of hydrogenated and partially hydrogenated fats. "If you throw out the margarine and switch to butter, you're making a good start on lowering your lipoprotein(a) level," says Atkins.[15]

In normal amounts, lipoprotein(a) helps keep blood vessels strong and in good repair. Linus Pauling and Matthias Rath, M.D., have theorized that our bodies produce lipoprotein(a) as a "fallback mechanism" to compensate for vitamin C deficiency. Chronic ingestion of trans fats and less than optimum intake of vitamin C and other nutrients can promote unhealthy levels of lipoprotein(a).

Optimum levels of vitamin C (500 mg to 2000 mg) and avoiding trans fatty acids found in highly processed foods will help keep lipoprotein(a) in check. Most fast foods contain a high percentage of TFAs. French fries, onion rings, and deep fried chicken are almost always prepared in trans fat, usually in partially hydrogenated soybean oil.

According to Enig, one large order of French fries easily contains 8-9 grams of trans fat. Chicken nuggets, heavily promoted to children, provide 12 or more grams of trans fats (order of six). One tablespoon of a "very popular margarine" has 4.6 grams of trans fat.[16]

Croissants made with butter contain less than ½ gram of natural trans fats; croissants made with partially hydrogenated vegetable oil contain 5 or 6 grams of man-made TFAs. Two ounces of natural American cheese has less than ½ gram of natural trans fat; two ounces of imitation American cheese has 8 grams of man-made TFAs.[17]

Although in widespread use for decades, TFAs are not identified separately on food labels. Enig estimates that the hidden TFA fat component of commercial cookies, crackers, donuts, cakes, breading, frostings, and pudding is between 25 and 50 percent *trans fat.*

Early on, the FDA recognized that these man made TFAs would not function as essential fats and did not allow food manufactures to classify them as *polyunsaturated* or in the case of canola, *monounsaturated*. Instead, they were added to the "total fat." TFAs have remained invisible – uncounted in government databases and in private company fat composition tables.

> **Low fat diets** are associated with greater feelings of anger, hostility, irritability and depression. These mood changes appear to be biological consequences of inadequate dietary fat in the central nervous system.
>
> *British Journal of Nutrition*, 1998, vol. 79

Although they are grouped together as "bad fats," don't confuse nutrient dense natural saturated fats with unnatural, heat-damaged TFAs. Because trans fats have no benefit, it's best to avoid them altogether. Although they function in a similar manner for food manufacturing purposes, trans fats and saturated fats are biologically dissimilar.

There are natural trans fats found in tiny amounts in ruminant animals – antelope, cow, deer, goat and sheep. These natural trans fats are a precursor to conjugated linoleic acid (CLA), a fatty acid with many health-promoting benefits. Natural trans fats found in ruminant animals and TFAs found in highly processed foods are not equivalent.[18]

Consumers will not see "TFA" on any food label. The edible oil industry has resisted separate labeling for trans fats. More than willing to smear the tropical oil industry and run down saturated fats, they are apparently unwilling to let consumers know how much "funny fat" is in their food.

As I write this, the FDA is still taking its time considering regulations that would require food processors to label "trans fats." For reasons that hopefully are now clear to the reader, powerful forces in the edible oil industries have opposed fair labeling and honest disclosure for decades.

Until a new fair labeling law is put in place, boycott fried fast foods and any processed products that contain partially hydrogenated or hydrogenated fat. You can safely assume that 70 percent of all processed, packaged food items contain up to 50 percent trans fat.

But, if you find yourself reading too many labels, you're in the wrong supermarket aisle. If you get concerned enough about the danger of trans fats and the industry's shenanigans to keep them invisible, join the organization that is doing something about it: Weston A. Price Foundation – online at **www.westonaprice.org**.

TFA Cover-up

Since the 1960s, various researchers warned the medical community and the public about the danger of consuming trans fatty acids found in partially hydrogenated vegetable fats. Each time, the edible oil industry enlisted the following organizations to write "cover-up" pieces – white papers to suppress information about the danger of trans fatty acids:

- Margarine Manufacturers Association
- Institute of Shortening and Edible Oils
- Grocery Manufacturers Association
- International Food Information Council (IFIC)
- American Soybean Association
- American Heart Association
- Center for the Science in the Public Interest (CSPI)

Don't buy products that contain partially hydrogenated vegetable fat. Up to 50 percent of the fat is trans fat. The majority of processed, packaged foods contain these harmful fats.

21-Day Plan key principle #14:

Do not eat margarine or hydrogenated or partially hydrogenated fats

Risk factor	optimum	risk	serious risk
Lipoprotein(a)	<20	>25	>30

"Lp(a) is thought to be mainly under genetic control but trans fatty acids in the diet increase its levels, and saturated fatty acids in the diet decrease its levels."

Mary Enig, Ph.D., *Know Your Fats*

"One-third of coronary artery disease patients have elevated Lp(a), and such elevations carry a 250 to 300 percent increased risk."

Thomas Yannios, M.D., *The Heart Disease Breakthrough*

"Margarine correlates with the risk of heart disease more strongly than any other food, including butter."

Lancet, 1993, vol. 341

High in trans fatty acids, stick margarine elevates lipoprotein (a), the sticky, dangerous form of LDL cholesterol. Butter, in contrast, lowers Lp(a).

New England Journal of Medicine,
1999, vol. 340

Trans fatty acids (TFAs) found in most margarine, shortening, and in 70 percent of all processed, packaged foods (hydrogenated or partially hydrogenated fats) increase blood levels of lipoprotein(a), referred to as Lp(a).

Lp(a) is a sticky, bastard form of LDL that causes blood clots. Lp(a) accumulates in plaque. If a plaque ruptures, Lp(a) attracts blood clotting factors, like fibrinogen, to the site of the rupture.

Trans fatty acids increase Lp(a); saturated fats decrease Lp(a). Just by switching from margarine to butter, you can reduce Lp(a) levels. Trans fats are especially dangerous if your Lp(a) levels are genetically high.

Lp(a) levels over 20 – but especially over 30 – signal the presence of sticky LDL. Sticky LDL is ten times more likely to oxidize than non-sticky LDL. Hence, ingesting trans fatty acids increases Lp(a) and oxidizes LDL cholesterol.

Trans fats lower HDL cholesterol in a dose-response manner. The more partially hydrogenated fats you ingest, the more downward pressure on HDL. This is a serious matter. We want HDL as high as possible.

Anything that lowers HDL doesn't belong in your cupboard. But trans fatty acids do more than lower HDL. Trans fatty acids raise blood sugar levels by making red blood cells less willing to carry insulin. It gets worse.

If a lactating mother consumes trans fatty acids, she is passing the plastic fats to her baby. When researchers examined the fat in milk that mothers are producing, they found up to 17 percent of the fatty acids as trans fats.

When they measured the levels in mothers who were not ingesting trans fatty acids, the levels of trans fats were less than 1 percent. When these same researchers examined the visual acuity of the babies receiving trans fats at 14 months, they had significantly lower visual acuity.[19]

Because trans fats are not clearly identified on food labels, look under ingredients for *partially hydrogenated vegetable oil* . You can avoid most trans fats by shopping only the outer isle at the grocery store.

When we eat hydrogenated foods and feed them to our children, we are increasing our risk of heart disease and predisposing our children to diabetes and other chronic illnesses.

Benefits of butter from Nourishing Traditions:

- **Fat Soluble Vitamins:** True retinol vitamin A, vitamin D, Vitamin K, and vitamin E – as wells as their naturally occurring cofactors. The fat-soluble vitamins survive pasteurization.

- **The Wulzen Factor:** Present in raw butter, cream, and whole milk – and destroyed by pasteurization. Researcher Rosalind Wulzen discovered that this substance protects humans and animals from calcification of the joints. It also protects against hardening of the arteries, cataracts, and calcification of the pineal gland.

- **Activator X:** Activator X is a powerful catalyst, which, like vitamins A and D, helps the body absorb and utilize minerals. It is found in organ meats from grazing animals and in some sea food. Activator X is not destroyed by pasteurization.

- **Arachidonic Acid:** Found in small amounts in animal fats. Arachidonic Acid plays a role in brain function, is a vital component of cell membranes, and is an immediate precursor to eicosanoid hormones (see chapter 16).

- **Short and Medium Chain Fats:** Butter is 12-15 percent short- and medium-chain fatty acids. These fats are sent directly to the liver from the small intestine via the portal vein. Short and medium chain fats provide quick energy and the have antimicrobial, antitumor, and immune system supporting properties – especially 12-carbon lauric acid, a medium-chain fat not found in any other animal fat.

- **Omega-6 and Omega-3:** The two essential fats occur in butter in small but balanced amounts.

- **Conjugated Linoleic Acid (CLA):** Butter from grass-fed cows contains CLA. CLA encourages the buildup of muscle and prevents weight gain. CLA disappears when cows are fed dry hay or grain.

- **Lecithin:** Lecithin is a natural component of butter that assists in the proper assimilation and metabolization of cholesterol and other fat constituents.

- **Cholesterol:** Butter contains pure, undamaged cholesterol.

- **Trace Minerals:** Butter is especially rich in selenium and contains many other trace minerals, including manganese, zinc, chromium and iodine.

Henri's Fat Free Honey Mustard Dressing
Ingredients: Contains 5 grams of sugar per tablespoon!

Vinegar
Water
High fructose corn syrup
Sugar
Honey
Corn syrup

4 of the top 6 ingredients are refined sugar

Prepared Mustard
Dijon Mustard
Modified food starch
Spice
Salt
Malto-Dextrin
Onion Powder
Yellow 5, Yellow 6
Propylene Glycol Alginate
Xanthan gum
Sodium benzoate
Calcium disodium EDTA
Natural flavor

Chapter 15

-------- 🖎 --------

Introduction to fats

"The much maligned saturated fats – which Americans are trying to avoid – are not the cause of our modern diseases. In fact, they play many important roles in the body chemistry…. They play a vital role in the health of our bones. For calcium to be effectively incorporated into the skeletal structure, at least 50 percent of the dietary fats should be saturated."

Sally Fallon, *Nourishing Traditions*

Fats (solid at room temperature) and oils (liquid at room temperature) are technically called *lipids*. Fatty acids are chains of carbon atoms (1-24 long) joined together by single or double chemical bonds.

The more double bonds a fat has, the more it will react to heat, light and oxygen. Stearic acid in beef, a saturated fat, has no double bonds. Monounsaturated fats, such as oleic acid in olive or sesame oil, have one double bond. Polyunsaturated linoleic acid in corn or soybeans has several double bonds.

With no reactive double bonds, saturated fats are the most heat stable. The tropical fats, coconut and palm, are among the most highly saturated of all fats and are ideal for high temperature cooking and baking. Monounsaturated olive oil has one double bond and is relatively stable – good for moderate heat cooking.

With several double bonds, polyunsaturated fats are highly reactive and chemically unstable and should never be used for cooking, frying, or baking. Of all substances ingested by the body, chemically unstable polyunsaturated fats are most easily rendered dangerous by food processing.

Commercial refined vegetable oils made from corn, canola, safflower, sunflower and soybean are not safe to cook with. They are obtained from their seed source using high temperature processing methods and usually harsh chemical solvents like hexane.[1]

Reactive to heat, light, and oxygen, they are derived from their source with heat, light, and oxygen. When you cook with these oils, you generate more heat, light and oxygen. Sitting in clear plastic or light colored bottles, these highly refined oils have no place in your kitchen.

Degree of processing is a key consideration when selecting fats or oils. "Cholesterol-free" oils have been degummed, dewaxed, bleached and deodorized. Over-processed and heat damaged, you don't want to put them in your mouth. Highly processed oils no longer contain their natural protective antioxidants like vitamin E and are swarming with dangerous, tissue damaging free radicals.

We should embrace the entire spectrum of healthy natural fats: saturated, monounsaturated and polyunsaturated. Native Americans were careful about this. All fat was highly valued. This is a lesson for us today: Include a balanced amount of saturated and unsaturated fats in your diet that have been minimally processed.

Omega is a designation for unsaturated fats. Omega-3 and omega-6 are polyunsaturated fats that are considered essential – they must come from the diet. Omega 9, such as oleic acid in olive oil, is a monounsaturated fat that our bodies can manufacture from other fatty acids.

All fats are combinations of saturated and unsaturated fatty acids. The most saturated fats (such as coconut) contain polyunsaturated fatty acids, and the most polyunsaturated fats (like flaxseed) contain saturated fats. It is a misnomer, for example, to refer to lard as an "artery clogging saturated fat."

Fatty Acid Families

Mostly Saturated
Coconut
Dairy Fats
Palm
Tallow

Mostly Monounsaturated
Canola*
Chicken fat
Duck fat
Goose fat
Lard+
Macadamia
Olive
Peanut
Safflower (hybrid)
Sunflower (hybrid)

Mostly Polyunsaturated

N-6 Linoleic
Corn+
Cotton Seed*
Soybean*
Safflower+
Sunflower+
(trans fatty acids/shortenings/margarines)

N-6 GLA
Black Currant
Borage Seed
Evening Primrose

N-3 Alpha Linolenic
Flaxseed
Pumpkin Seed

N-3 EPA/DHA
Deep Sea Fish

* usually partially hydrogenated
+ sometimes partially hydrogenated
Adapted from *Know Your Fats*, Mary G. Enig, Ph.D.

The not so well informed equate animal fat with saturated fat and quake in fear when offered "skin-on" chicken breasts. Little do they know, however, that chicken fat is about 70 percent unsaturated, and, the skin of the chicken is mostly polyunsaturated. (Chicken fat is about 31 percent saturated, 49 percent monounsaturated and 20 percent polyunsaturated.)[2]

Lard, the rendered fat from a pig, has an equally undeserved bad reputation. Lard contains more unsaturated fat (60 percent) than saturated fat (40 percent). Lard is 48 percent monounsaturated, and, like olive oil, should be referred to as a monounsaturated fat.

In China, parts of Europe, and in the U.S. until Crisco was introduced in 1911, lard has been a major food fat for centuries. Lard is a stable, excellent fat for baking and occasional frying, and is one of the best possible sources of vitamin D.[3]

In 1910, Americans were still cooking in lard, butter, coconut fat, and tallow – all relatively high in *saturated* and *monounsaturated* fats. These stable, traditional cooking fats have a relatively high melting point and will withstand high temperatures and remain chemically stable.

"Basic fatty acids are the same molecules regardless of whether they came from plants or animals," writes Enig in *Know Your Fats*:

> "It should be noted that the fatty acid oleic acid is the same oleic acid whether it comes from olive oil (or any other plant oil) or dairy fat (or any other animal fat). The same holds true for any of the saturated fatty acids or polyunsaturated fatty acids."[4]

Your body doesn't know the difference between the monounsaturated fat in lard (48 percent) and the monounsaturated fat in olive oil (71 percent). While lard contains more saturated fatty acids, both olive oil and lard contain 12 percent polyunsaturated fats. Used for centuries, olive oil and lard are healthy natural fats. One isn't better than the other. An experienced cook would have priorities for each.

Degree of processing is the critical issue; both olive oil and lard can be obtained from their source without damaging the fat. For centuries, lard was rendered right on the farm, and olive oil is one of the oldest known oils. Fully ripened olives are crushed between stone or steel rollers, and the oil is pressed from the pulp.

The first pressing yields the top grade "extra virgin" oil. Virgin oil is cloudy, darker in color, contains more flavor; and is richest in naturally occurring antioxidants. Olive oil is time tested – the safest vegetable oil you can use. But, as Sally Fallon points out, "The longer chain fatty acids found in olive oil are more likely to contribute to the buildup of body fat than the short- and medium-chain fatty acids found in butter, coconut oil, or palm kernel oil."[5]

Fats come in different chain lengths. Longer chain fats (14-24) can be saturated, monounsaturated, or polyunsaturated. Stearic acid in beef and oleic acid in olive oil are both 18-carbon chain fats. These long chain saturated and monounsaturated fats metabolize slowly and are more likely to end up stored in adipose tissue.

Short and medium chain fats (3-12) are a type of saturated fat found in butter, coconut oil, and palm kernel oil. They have lower melting points, do not produce as many calories, and are shuttled quickly to the liver where they are burned for energy.

Also used for centuries, sesame oil contains an equal percentage (42-43 percent) of monounsaturated oleic acid and less stable polyunsaturated fat. A less processed darker version of sesame is excellent for occasional stir-fry. Purchase the highest quality in small opaque bottles and keep refrigerated. Peanut oil, similar to sesame, can be healthy if stored properly and used in moderation.[6]

Solid at room temperature, tropical vegetable fats such as coconut and palm oil have all but disappeared from our grocery shelves. Vilified by the U.S. edible oil industry, highly saturated tropical oils have nourished South Pacific populations for thousands of years.

Coconut oil is very stable and can be stored for a long time without going rancid. Approximately 49 percent of coconut fat is medium chain (12-carbon) lauric acid, an important anti-microbial fat. "Antimicrobial fatty acids are those that the body uses to kill or disable pathogenic viruses, bacteria, and protozoa," says Enig.

Far from being an inert food component like sugar or starch, fats are dynamic biochemicals with important metabolic roles to play in protecting our health and welfare. Lauric acid from coconut fat, added to baby formulas, plays a critical role worldwide in infant nutrition.[7] Found in butter, human milk, and coconut fat, lauric acid is a "smart fat" labeled as a "bad fat" by those friendly folks who wanted to sell us their TFA-laden partially hydrogenated soybean oil.

Fats do things. They're not just something to sit on – padding for our organs and nervous system. Fats are cellular gatekeepers, chemical police, good guys and gals to have around. Lipids control the flow of life-giving chemicals in and out of the many gates and doorways of our trillions of cells and protect the integrity of cell and organelle (inside the cell) membranes throughout the body

It's easy to argue that fats are the most important of all dietary constituents. After water, they are required in high levels throughout the body. Fatty acid deficiency, alteration, oxidation or imbalance is now related to a wide range of chronic degenerative conditions, including the major killers, heart disease and cancer.

Heart disease and cancer were rare before 1910 when Americans cooked with their traditional saturated fats. It's the commercial vegetable fats that have tipped things in favor of serious degenerative disease. Sugar plays a role, but it's the partially hydrogenated vegetable fats, trans fatty acids, and the imbalance created by these fats that is the greatest threat to the health and welfare of the American people.

In 1910, only one in thirty people died of cancer. Heart disease claimed no more than 8 percent of all deaths. Type II diabetes was rare – almost nonexistent. While the good old days were far from perfect, the older folks among us remember eating perfectly well.

We can't go back in time – and don't want to. As a nation, we have fixed a lot of things and have made many improvements along the way. But cancer and heart disease are taking an increasingly larger toll, and highly touted pharmaceutical drugs and gene therapy won't save us.

It's time to fix our fats and restore the proper role of traditional healthy foods – plant and animal. Make every effort to support the small, mixed family farms before they're gone. We can't go backward – but we can go forward by getting rid of the funny fats that are causing so much harm.

It's time to limit, restrict, or boycott:

- Margarine
- Polyunsaturated cooking oils in clear plastic bottles
- Olestra fake fat
- Hydrogenated or partially hydrogenated vegetable oil
- Trans fatty acids
- Official government low fat diets
- Milk from confined grain-fed dairy cows living on cement floors
- Skim and 2% milk with synthetic vitamin D and oxidized dry milk powder
- Egg-Beaters
- Potatoes deep fried in partially hydrogenated soybean oil
- 70% of all antibiotic drugs used by agribusiness
- Battery chickens eating bakery waste
- Feed lot animals standing in their own dung all day long
- Ultra pasteurized milk, cream, and half and half
- Pepsi and Coke machines in high school entrances throughout the country

21-Day Plan key principle #15:

Use butter, olive oil, coconut butter or lard for cooking

There is nothing unsafe about butter; quite the opposite, butter contains healthful components that are not found in anything else (other than real cream).

Mary Enig, Know Your Fats

"Fat is back: eating butter and drinking milk – in the right amounts – can be good for the heart."

Barnard Christian, M.D.

Butter added to vegetables and spread on bread, and cream added to soups and sauces, ensures proper assimilation of the minerals and water-soluble vitamins in vegetables, grains, and meat.

Sally Fallon, Nourishing Traditions

In *Nourishing Traditions*, Sally Fallon recommends using extra virgin olive oil for cooking and unrefined flax oil for salad dressings. She suggests coconut oil for baking and animal fats like lard for occasional frying. Finally, she says, use as much good quality butter as you like.

In *Know Your Fats*, Mary Enig recommends 100 percent coconut oil for popcorn. For baking, she recommends butter, coconut oil, lard, palm oil, and tallow.

Enig also offers her own all-purpose oil recipe that can be used for sautéing and light frying: One-third each coconut oil, sesame oil, and olive oil. The coconut oil needs to be warmed to about 80 degrees before mixing. Teaspoon, tablespoon and cup measures all work.

You can order coconut oil and other quality products from the following companies:

Omega Nutrition   **800-661-3529**
www.omeganutrition.com

Radiant Life   **888-593-8333**
www.4radiantlife.com

Carotec   **800-522-4279**
www.carotec.com

"Our choice of fats and oils is of extreme importance," says Fallon. Her recommendation is to avoid all processed foods that contain hydrogenated fats and polyunsaturated oils.

Enig's advice is to "consume optimal amounts of fat-soluble vitamins A, D, E, and K, found in animal fats. Adults and children, she says, should eat at least one whole egg a day. Enig recommends full fat diary products, especially for children.

Both Fallon and Enig recommend eating anything made with coconut butter or products made with desiccated or whole coconut, like macaroons or coconut milk. Coconut is the best source of critically important lauric acid.

Finally, both Fallon and Enig emphasize the need to include healthy fats from a wide variety of natural meats, fish, seeds, and vegetables. Do not rely on just one fat or oil exclusively.

Beta Carotene is not vitamin A - synthetic beta carotene may be harmful:

True fat-soluble vitamin A (retinol) is found in animal foods such as liver, other organ meats, fish, egg yolks, and butter and cream from pasture raised cows. Water-soluble carotenes, such as beta carotene, are precursors to vitamin A. Only under optimum conditions do humans convert carotenes to vitamin A.

Diabetics and those with poor thyroid function (tens of millions) cannot make the conversion. Extreme exercise, excess alcohol, excess polyunsaturated fatty acids, excess iron in fortified flour, zinc deficiency, and even cold weather inhibit the conversion. Most Americans are vitamin A deficient.

Low fat diets inhibit carotene conversion to vitamin A because the conversion can only take place in the presence of bile and bile is excreted only when fat is consumed. Low fat = low vitamin A status = poor utilization of protein and minerals, birth defects, cancer, reproductive failure, osteoporosis, and vision problems.

Sound familiar? How many couples, today, do you think, are having difficulty having a baby? Birth defects are on the rise! Cancer is epidemic. Check your multiple vitamin and see whether it contains true vitamin A (fish liver oil) or beta carotene. If it says "beta carotene," you're not getting any vitamin A and the beta carotene is synthetic – unless it states otherwise.

Synthetic beta carotene is worthless, possibly harmful. True retinal vitamin A is critically important for healthy skin, bones, blood and brains. For 40 years, the government and medical profession have warned us to stay away from the very best sources of vitamin A: butter, liver, and organ meats.

For a more lengthy discussion on vitamin A, see "Vitamin A Vagary" at **www.westonaprice.org**.

Know Your Fats, by Mary G. Enig, Ph.D., is the best book available on fats in human nutrition. Find Dr. Enig online at **www.knowyourfats.com**. Dr. Enig's web site contains frequently asked questions, updates, and important links that discuss nutritional issues and food choices we face each day.

Chapter 16

-------- 🐛 --------

Essential omega-3

I believe the essential fatty acids are the primary nutrient missing from the American diet.

Robert C. Atkins, M.D.

Omega-3 and omega-6 are the two essential fat families. Essential fats are polyunsaturated (multiple double bonds) and must come from our diet. They must be consumed fresh and unrefined or they quickly go rancid. Our bodies can manufacturer all other fatty acids, and actually produce twenty different fatty acids from the two parent omega fats.

Alpha linolenic acid (ALA) is the basic omega-3, found in flax-seed (highest source), pumpkin seed, walnuts, green leafy vegetables, wild game, and the meat from ruminant and pasture raised grass-fed animals. Linoleic acid (LA) is the basic omega-6, found in cereal grains, vegetables, sunflower, safflower, corn, and soybean oils, and meat from grain-fed animals.

Omega-3 (technically referred to as *n-3*) means the first double bond is in the 3rd position from the so-called methyl end. Omega-6 (technically referred to as n-6), means the first double bond is in the 6th position from the methyl end (as opposed to the carboxyl end of the carbon chain).[1]

An apt metaphor for what is happening to our fats and our health is the fate of chickens in the 20th century. Free-range chickens, foraging grass, seeds, bugs, and worms, develop optimal amounts of omega fats – in a healthy 1:1 ratio. Battery chickens, force-fed grain, soybean mash, and antibiotics, contain 20 times more omega-6 than omega-3.[2]

Therein lies our problem. Modern agricultural practices, grain-based animal feeds, animal confinement, feed lots, and the widespread use of highly processed commercial omega-6 vegetable fats has caused an unprecedented increase in our ingestion of omega 6 relative to omega-3.

Our ratio of omega-6 to omega-3 has increased from approximately 3:1 to about 20:1. The decrease in omega-3 and the huge increase in omega-6 may explain the explosive growth of cancer and heart disease in the 20th century. In traditional whole food diets, the ratio of omega-6 to omega-3 was about 2:1 or perhaps 1:1.

Felix estimates that our Paleolithic and Native American ancestors consumed small but equal amounts of omega-6 and omega-3, along with plenty of saturated fat. Today, however, according to many researchers, we are consuming 10 to 20 times more omega-6 than omega-3. This is a ratio that spells trouble – and not just for heart health.[3]

Last chapter, we learned that fats are much more than concentrated sources of energy. Specialized fatty acids like those found in tropical fats and butter kill or disable pathogenic invaders. CLA found in pasture raised animals helps the body burn fat and is anti-carcinogenic.[4] Fats police the integrity of intricate cell membrane structures, and with the help of the liver, supervise all the body's chemical transactions.

If cholesterol is the rooster, precursor to all adrenal and sex hormones, omega-6 and omega-3 are the mother hens. Omega-6 and omega-3 are distributed throughout the body's cell membranes and convert into short-lived, jack-in-the-box hormones called eicosanoids. While adrenal and sex hormones circulate long distance in the bloodstream, eicosanoids appear suddenly, perform a function, and then vanish again all within the cell membrane.

The basic omega-6 and omega-3 fats convert in the body into metabolites, which, in turn, are precursors to the eicosanoids. Basic n-6 linoleic acid and n-3 alpha linolenic acid are first converted into new "elongated" forms like n-6 GLA and n-3 EPA, which, in turn, convert into other fatty acids or into the short-lived eicosanoids (also called prostaglandins).

N-3 alpha linolenic acid (ALA) from flaxseed converts into eicosapentaenoic acid (EPA). EPA is the immediate precursor to a series of eicosanoids. ALA also converts into docosahexaenoic acid (DHA). Because these conversions can fail, EPA and DHA are considered conditionally essential. EPA and DHA are found directly in deep-sea cold-water fish and in small amounts in eggs from free-range chickens.

N-6 linoleic acid from seed oils like corn converts in the body into gamma linolenic acid (GLA), which, in turn, converts into dihomo-gamma-linolenic acid (DGLA) and arachidonic acid (AA). Because the conversion to GLA may fail, GLA is considered conditionally essential and is found directly in borage seed and evening primrose oil.

The *desaturase* enzymes your body uses to convert basic fatty acids into their metabolites are often in short supply. You make less as you age, and a diet low in minerals and high in sugar and hydrogenated vegetable fats suppresses their production.

Omega-6 and omega-3 metabolites exert control over arterial tension, blood viscosity (clotting), blood pressure, growth of smooth muscle cells, and the inflammatory response. Optimum control – balance and regulation – occurs when the ratio of dietary omega-6 to omega-3 is about 3:1 or less.

An excess of omega-6, in particular, constricts blood vessels, raises blood pressure, creates life-threatening arrhythmias, and provokes inflammation in the blood vessels. Dietary omega-3 is needed to diminish the negative health effects of excess omega-6.

Paleolithic and Native Americans obtained their essential fats by eating all the fat found in ruminant animals - saturated, monounsaturated, and polyunsaturated. They ate the meat, brain, and internal organs – plus they obtained omega fats in whole, unprocessed nuts, seeds, fish, and occasionally eggs.

For the sake of shelf life and modern production methods, we have processed the omega-3 essential fats out of our food supply and simultaneously increased our consumption of highly processed omega-6. We have too much omega-6 and too much damaged omega-6. The TFAs from excess damaged omega-6 interfere with the conversion of n-3 alpha linolenic acid and n-6 linoleic acid to their elongated forms.

The many benefits of a favorable balance of omega-6 and omega-3 fatty acids includes reduced triglycerides, lower LDL cholesterol, more HDL cholesterol, less arterial plaque, reduced chance of a blood clot, lower blood pressure, and far less risk of sudden death from arrhythmias.

Sufficient omega-3 enables the body to burn storage fat more efficiently. ALA in flaxseed helps the cells of the body, especially muscle cells, respond more effectively to insulin. This helps burn calories, lower blood sugar, lower triglycerides, and, ultimately, reduces the chance of deadly blood clots and heart attacks.

According to Robert Crayhon, "The combination of flaxseed oil with saturated fats yields the most powerful anti-obesity effect in animal studies."[5] Eat fat to burn fat makes metabolic sense. But you must limit excess omega-6 that otherwise blunts the action of omega-3

In *Progress In Lipid Research,* Japan, 1997, Harumi Okuyama discusses the sharp upswing in "Western-type" ailments in postwar Japan, including allergies, bronchitis, cancer, and heart disease. Okuyama links the growth of these degenerative diseases to the introduction in Japan of foods containing omega-6 fatty acids, resulting in a ratio of n-6 to n-3 greater than 4:1.[6]

We need omega-3 and omega-6 in small balanced amounts. We need approximately 2 percent of calories (2 grams) as omega-3 and 3 percent of calories (3 grams) as omega-6. Essential fats can be obtained by eating a wide range of whole, unprocessed foods – plant and animal.[7]

Read labels. Reject all partially hydrogenated fats, commercial cooking oils, and excess grain-fed meat. Use butter not margarine. Emphasize omega-3. Look for grass-fed meat and eggs from foraging chickens. Make flaxseed and deep-sea fish part of your diet.

N-3 Alpha Linolenic Acid deficiency symptoms

- Impaired vision and learning ability
- Motor incoordination
- Tingling/numbness in feet, hands, arms, legs
- Behavioral changes/mental deterioration
- Elevated triglycerides
- High blood pressure
- Sticky platelets
- Low metabolism
- Immune dysfunction

N-6 Linoleic Acid deficiency symptoms

- Skin eruptions
- Hair loss
- Liver/kidney degeneration
- Behavioral disturbances
- Excessive water loss/thirst
- Slow wound healing
- Sterility in males; miscarriage in females
- Growth retardation

from *DHA: The Magnificent Marine Oil*
by Beth M. Ley-Jacobs, Ph.D.

21-Day Plan key principle #16:

Eat two tablespoons of milled flaxseed everyday.

"Wherever flaxseed becomes a regular food item among the people, there will be better health"

Mahatma Gandhi

Milled flaxseed is the best whole food source of the parent omega-3 and omega-6 essential fatty acids. Flaxseed is the highest plant source of omega-3 (alpha linolenic acid), but also contains omega-6 (linoleic acid) and non-essential omega-9 (oleic acid).

The ratio of omega-6 to omega-3 is 1:3. Because most of us are getting excess omega-6, eating flaxseed daily helps restore the natural healthy Paleolithic balance. Flaxseed also provides complex fiber – both soluble and insoluble, complete protein (22 percent), and a wide range of minerals, including calcium, magnesium, potassium, iron, and zinc.

Insoluble fiber (in flax, wheat bran, brown rice) reduces the risk of colon cancer by increasing stool bulk and transit time. Soluble fiber (in flax, apples, oat bran) nourishes friendly bacteria, slows the rate of sugar release, and binds toxins. Both types of fiber help prevent constipation, kidney and gall stones, and degenerative disease.

Flax is the richest plant source of lignans, antioxidant compounds that provide anticancer, antibacterial, antifungal, and antiviral protection. Plant lignans are precursors to mammalian lignans formed in the intestinal tract by hard working beneficial bacteria.

Two level tablespoons of milled flaxseed provides one tablespoon of flax oil. Milled flaxseed can be mixed in tomato juice, water, eggs, oatmeal, hot cereal, smoothies, salads, yogurt, vegetables, and used in baking bread or to thicken soup (add after cooking).

You must mill (grind) whole flaxseed or it will pass undigested right through your body. It's important to mill or grind just the amount you're going to use right away. Do not attempt to store home-milled flaxseed. Home milling pulverizes the seed, introducing oxygen and rapid subsequent oxidation.

Northern Canadian Flaxseed

Because of the higher omega-3 content, Northern Canadian flaxseed is best. *NorthernEdge* milled flaxseed is certified organic, grown north of Prince Albert, Saskatchewan, and is ready to eat. NorthernEdge is sliced – not ground – and is vacuum-packed one bag at a time into a resealable foil bag.

Flaxseed grown in Northern Canada has the highest omega-3 content of any flaxseed in the world. Brown Canadian flax is 45 percent fat, and 60 percent of the fat is omega-3. The further south flax is grown, the higher the omega-6 and the lower the omega-3.

You can store vacuum-packed NorthernEdge in the cupboard or freezer. Once opened, it should be kept refrigerated and used within 45 days. For more information about *NorthernEdge,* check out **www.nokobeach.com or call Nokomis Nutrition, 800-641-6802 in Minneapolis, Minnesota.**

Milling whole flaxseed at home in a coffee grinder is economical - a great nutrition value. Ready-to-eat, *NorthernEdge* is a convenient source of the highest quality milled flaxseed in North America. Both are better everyday options than supplementing with flax oil gel caps, which only contain flax oil. It takes **eleven** gel caps (1,000 mg each) to provide one tablespoon of oil. Gel caps are good when travelling or for use in the office or on the go.

Omega-3 and omega-6 are critically important but are only needed in small, balanced amounts. One tablespoon of flax oil (two level tablespoons of milled flaxseed) per 100 lbs. of body weight is our basic daily requirement. Excess omega fats are not health supporting. Two tablespoons of flax oil (four level tablespoons of milled flaxseed) are sufficient for most people.

You may want to increase your flax intake temporarily for weight loss purposes. Double your flax and water intake when you use L-Carnitine or any other diet support product. Omega-3 promotes weight loss; omega-6 promotes weight gain. Flax oil functions best in a diet that includes healthy natural saturated fats.

Flax is also available as oil, usually in dark plastic bottles. Oil extraction must be done carefully or the oil will oxidize. Flax oil can be used in salad dressings and is added to brown rice, cottage cheese, salads, vegetables, and yogurt. Certified organic **Barleans** is a good choice. Barleans uses Northern Canadian flaxseed that is pressed in small batches under low heat conditions (less than 96 degrees). Approximately 10 percent of the lignans are retained in the extracted oil. Find Barleans online at **www.barleans.com**.

When you purchase the oil in a bottle, make sure it has been refrigerated, and check both the press date and expiration date. Do not use expired product or any oil that produces a slight burning sensation in the throat. It's rancid. You can store bottled flax oil or *NorthernEdge* milled flaxseed in the freezer beyond their expiration dates. Whole flaxseed and flax oil gel caps do not require refrigeration and can be stored indefinitely in a dry cool place.

Gamma Linolenic Acid (GLA)

Extra GLA, a metabolite of n-6 linoleic acid, is an omega fat that may be needed in supplemental gel cap form. Like EPA and DHA (see chapter 18), GLA is a conditionally essential fatty acid. If you're body doesn't make it, you must get if from your diet.

There are few adequate dietary sources of GLA. Diabetics, pre-diabetics, and other people suffering with degenerative conditions may need a direct supplement for optimum health. GLA is found most abundantly in borage seed (starflower) oil and is found in smaller amounts in black current and evening primrose oil.

GLA in supplement form may relieve rheumatoid arthritis, PMS (and other hormonally-related conditions), dry skin, and boost immune function. GLA may be especially effective in reducing joint inflammation and the progression of diabetic neuropathy. Clinicians recommend 240-300 mg daily.

Flaxseed:

- Promotes optimum levels of blood cholesterol.
- Lowers elevated blood pressure.
- Reduces the threat of blood clots.
- Improves laxation.
- Helps control blood sugar.
- Aids in clearing up skin conditions.
- Protects against cancer.
- Aids in the growth and development of the fetus.

NorthernEdge milled flaxseed

A 15 oz. package contains 28 rounded (15 grams each) or 48 level tablespoons of certified organic Northern Canadian flaxseed.

Each rounded **tablespoon** provides over:

- 6 grams of flax oil.
- 3.5 grams of omega-3.
- 4 grams of fiber and mucilage.
- 3 grams of complete protein.
- 300 milligrams of minerals.

Chapter 17

-------- 🦢 --------

The power of protein

Everyone in health food stores looks pale. Everybody at the Carnegie Deli looks healthy.

Jackie Mason, comedian

The anti-protein, anti-saturated fat dogma that grew out of the government's ill-fated National Cholesterol Education Program is coming back to haunt us. The only dietary alternative, grains, do not contain the wide range of sophisticated nutrients that protein and fat provide to build and run our bodies.

The Nurses' Health Study, a long-term survey of over 85,000 female nurses, provides strong evidence that eating more protein protects you from heart disease. The Nurses' Study found that a diet consisting of more protein and less carbohydrate lowered the risk of ischemic heart disease.[1]

More animal protein and less carbohydrate (bread, potatoes, sweets) in the nurses' diets led to a significant reduction in LDL cholesterol and an increase in protective HDL. The researchers found that the nurses who ate more protein also tended to consume more total fat, saturated fat, cholesterol, and folic acid, while eating significantly less carbohydrate, especially sugar.

The nurses with the lowest consumption of folic acid and B-6 had the highest rates of heart attack and heart disease.[2] The highest food sources of these B-complex vitamins are liver and organ meats – forbidden, high cholesterol foods – that just happen to lower elevated homocysteine levels.

The Nurses Study found that women who had high blood pressure and consumed very low levels of animal fat and protein increased their risk of a hemorrhagic stroke 370 percent compared to nurses consuming a high fat, high animal protein diet.[3]

In another recent study involving 10,000 men and women from 32 countries, "When dietary protein intake was higher, blood pressure (systolic and diastolic) was lower." (Circulation 1996; 94: 1629-1634.) These results are consistent with the findings of Gerald Reaven, M.D., Stanford University, who says, "Fifty percent of patients with high blood pressure are insulin resistant."[4]

Insulin resistance is a consequence of excess dietary carbohydrates, says Dr. Reaven. Protein, as we know, has no influence on blood sugar levels or insulin resistance. Conversely, excess carbohydrates raise blood sugar, insulin levels, and blood pressure. Replacing protein with carbohydrates will increase your risk of high blood pressure and heart attack.

"Syndrome X, also known as insulin resistance syndrome, may be the surest route to a heart attack," says Dr. Reaven. If you have Syndrome X, "dieting to lower your total cholesterol…may make a heart attack even more likely." Reaven estimates that 60-75 million people have Syndrome X, a carbohydrate-related cluster of blood fat abnormalities associated with coronary heart disease.[5]

Dr. Reaven's research provides solid proof that a low protein high carbohydrate diet is wrong for 60 to 75 million people. While fruits and low glycemic vegetables provide important antioxidants, the idea that grains – whether whole or refined – can replace animal protein and fat is a serious mistake.

In the last few chapters, we learned that dietary fats are metabolic – have important things to do - like controlling and policing what gets in and out of intricate cell membrane structures. Proteins, on the other hand, make up the body's infrastructure, building blocks for organs, nerves, muscle and flesh.

Proteins are combinations of 22 different amino acids, eight of which are considered "essential." They must come from the diet. Missing just one essential amino acid can lead to problems, even if overall protein intake is high.[6] Other amino acids, like L-Arginine and L-Carnitine, are conditionally essential, in that their production in the body is uncertain.

The enzyme your body uses to produce nitric oxide requires L-Arginine. Nitric oxide, also called "endothelium-derived relaxation factor," allows blood vessels to relax and thereby can reduce high blood pressure. By relaxing arteries, supplemental L-Arginine can promote better blood flow, reduce angina, and preserve and maintain lean muscle tissue.[7]

We discussed the importance of L-Carnitine in the 21-Day Plan, key principle #4. While it's true our bodies can make L-Carnitine, there is a danger that, as we age, our bodies won't make enough. The heart is completely dependent on the fat-burning power of L-Carnitine. Both L-Arginine and L-Carnitine, conditionally essential, are found abundantly only in animal protein.

> Animal protein, containing all eight essential amino acids, is most complete. Eggs and meat are also particularly good sources of the sulfur-bearing amino acids – methionine, cysteine, and cystine, which support detoxification. The body can manufacture 50,000 different proteins when the eight essential amino acids are present.[8]

"Spreading out your protein throughout the day is just as important as getting enough," writes Robert Crayhon, in *The Carnitine Miracle*. Crayhon recommends at least 3-4 ounces of protein, two or three times day - depending on your weight, work, and activities. Experiment to find what's right for you.[9]

Crayhon recommends protein for breakfast, lunch and dinner. "There is no reason to be afraid of protein," he says, "it is good for you." Crayhon's extensive clinical experience proved to him that the best way of balancing the diet is consuming optimal amounts of protein – more than the 15 percent of calories recommended by the American Dietetic Association.

Crayhon says wild game is best. Whenever possible, he says, eat buffalo, elk, venison, duck, goose or any animal that is living in the wild. The rest of the time, make an effort to buy lamb, free-range eggs, chicken and beef directly from the farmer who raises animals the old-fashioned way (See 21-Day plan, this chapter.)

Crayhon, Atkins, and Fallon all dispel the myth that higher protein diets lower calcium levels and cause osteoporosis. The latest research proves that protein from meat does not affect calcium balance and does not cause bone loss. (*American Journal of Clinical Nutrition*, 1995, vol. 62.)

Earlier studies suggesting that high protein diets increased urinary calcium excretion were poorly designed (too short term) and used protein powder instead of the fresh protein people actually eat. More recent studies have shown that as the amount of dietary sugar increases, bone density decreases. High sugar diets acidify the blood, leaching calcium from bone.[10]

Crayhon and Sally Fallon do not recommend soy protein. Soy, like grains, contains phytic acid that blocks mineral absorption, especially zinc, critical for immune response and insulin function. Soy protein lowers cholesterol all right – protective HDL cholesterol. The only safe soy foods to eat, according to Crayhon, are miso and tempeh, both fermented long enough to neutralize the phytic acid.[11]

"High protein diets in no way impair detoxification," says Crayhon. Instead, in his more than ten years of clinical experience, Crayhon has noted how low protein high carbohydrate diets impair detoxification by feeding yeast overgrowth (Candida). Low protein and vegetarian diets lack sulfur-bearing amino acids, crucial for detoxification and liver support.[12]

Today, people on tight budgets may have to stretch their food dollar as far as possible, but eggs, homemade soups, gelatin-rich broths, and small amounts of pasture raised red meat can help fill big nutritional gaps. Small producer brown eggs, even at a dollar or more per dozen, are a great value – the "gold standard" of protein at a reasonable price. See 21-Day Plan, key principle #1.

Eggs from foraging chickens have an ideal 1:1 ratio of omega-6 to omega-3, and contain ten times more lecithin than battery eggs. Raised without antibiotics and pesticide-laden grains, small producer eggs taste better and are safe to eat. Don't throw the yolks away. Eating egg white (protein) without the yolk (cholesterol and fat) will deplete B-complex vitamins. Emphasize protein and don't trim the fat.

Gelatin-rich broths are a must for those who cannot afford large amounts of good quality meat.[13] Fallon reminds us that animal fats and gelatin-rich bone broths spare protein. Meat is more nutritious when eaten in a broth, its own juices, or combined with animal fat.

> Sally Fallon's *Nourishing Traditions* cookbook contains instructions and recipes for making meat, chicken and fish broths. Old-fashioned meat stocks are inexpensive and extremely nutritious. Combining the minerals of bone, cartilage, marrow, and vegetables is strongly health promoting.

If you rely on nuts for protein, which are high in phosphorus, be sure to include plenty of calcium-rich foods in your diet, like Brussels sprouts, broccoli, cabbage (Chinese and green), dry figs, mustard greens, sardines (also high in magnesium), steamed spinach, un-hulled sesame seeds, and high quality cheese, preferably made from raw milk.

Participants in the Nurses' Health Study who snacked on nuts at least five times a week (150 grams) were 35 percent less likely to have heart attacks. Nuts are rich in vitamins, minerals, monounsaturated fats, and protein. Arginine, the amino acid that can dilate arteries and reduce blood pressure, is abundant in nuts.[14]

High quality refrigerated peanut butter or almond butter on celery is a nutritious, low glycemic snack. Almonds and peanuts are particularly good added to stir-fry. Pumpkin seeds and walnuts provide omega-3 fat (refrigerate). Dr. Atkins, calling nuts "the perfect vegetarian food," says they can be substituted for meat and poultry in increasingly popular low carbohydrate diets.[15]

If eaten in large quantities, nuts and seeds are easier to digest if soaked overnight in salt water and then dried in a warm oven (150 degrees) for 12 hours. (Cashews should be soaked no more than 6 hours.) Like grains, nuts and seeds contain enzyme inhibitors. Without soaking, they are harder to digest and strain the digestive system.[16]

> **Avoid highly processed sources of protein**, like protein bars and protein powders. High temperature processing denatures the proteins in powders and renders them hard to assimilate. Like dry egg powder and dry milk powder, protein powders are highly processed and best avoided - even if purchased at your favorite health food store.

Animal protein can be poor quality, over-processed, overcooked, and best avoided at times. Meatless days are a good idea. But don't throw the baby out with the bath water. High quality animal protein is most complete - even if we must take some extra time to learn where to buy it and how to prepare it.

All of us should avoid charred, blackened, or overcooked meat; and pass on bacon, luncheon meat and sausage made with nitrites, nitrates and other chemical preservatives. These overcooked and over processed sources of protein contain oxidized cholesterol and carcinogenic chemicals.

If you can't find old fashioned, 1910-style sausage and bacon, it may be best to avoid these products altogether. Commercial meat today is a far cry from the pasture raised meat widely available in 1910. Cattle today are raised in confinement (feedlot), fed pesticide-laden grains and soybeans, and do not contain the healthy omega-3 fatty acids and fat-soluble vitamins found in pasture raised animals.

The quality of all food, not just meat, has declined during the 20th century. Fruits and vegetables are grown with harmful chemicals and contain far fewer minerals. Vegetables, picked before they are ripe, no longer supply the promised nutrients. Even most tap water is no longer fit to drink.

But we need to eat and feed our families. If you shop the supermarket, just do the best you can – concentrating on the outer aisle. Keep in mind that higher quality meat and eggs are also available direct from the farm. Pasture raised grass-fed red meat is nutritious and health promoting – a much better food value than grain-fed feedlot beef.

You can still eat they way they did in 1910. Consider having liver and onions once a week. Buy high quality liver, preferably from a pasture-raised animal, have it sliced about 1/4 to 3/8 inch thick, and soak it in lemon juice for several hours. This draws out any impurities and leaves a nicer texture.[17]

Liver is the earth's best source of folic acid, vitamin B-6 and vitamin B-12 – nutrients that escort homocysteine out of the bloodstream. Eating liver or other organ meat once a week will promote healthier blood vessels and significantly reduce your risk of heart disease.

Now, take your marinated liver, pat dry, dredge in a mixture of flour, salt, and pepper, and place in a heavy skillet over a high flame and sauté (two slices at a time) in high quality lard. Transfer to a heated platter and keep warm in the oven. In a separate pan, sauté the onions in butter and olive oil over medium heat for about ½ hour or until golden brown.[18]

Liver is an extremely rich source of vitamins A and D, which fight infection, protect the lungs, build bone, and fight cancer. Liver also contains essential fatty acids, copper, zinc, iron, trace minerals, and a wide range of antioxidant nutrients – substances that support your own liver's detoxification capacities.

Omega-3 rich animals foods, like liver, were a critically important part of the 1910 diet – foods that are sadly missing today. But it's not too late. You will be rewarded if you eat liver, especially if you buy direct from the farm. You'll meet some nice people and get high quality food. By supporting the small American mixed farm, you'll protect yourself from heart disease as you help the farmer, the farm, the landscape, and a republic founded in the bosom of small family farms.

21-Day Plan key principle #17:

Choose high quality grass-fed beef, lamb, and wild game

"Protein needs to be the centerpiece of your diet. Your focus should be on eating small amounts of high quality protein throughout the day, preferably at every meal and snack."

Burton Berkson, M.D., *Syndrome X*

"Eating protein increases energy and keeps energy balanced throughout the day. One of the main causes of fatigue in many people, particularly women, is that they are not eating enough protein in the morning and at lunch."

Robert Crayhon, M.S., *The Carnitine Miracle*

Starting in the 1950s, the meat industry began taking animals off pasture and grass and put them into feedlots and on grain. Grass is high in omega-3. In humans or cattle, omega-3 promotes leanness. Grains are high in omega-6. In humans or cattle, omega-6 promotes obesity.

Since the 1950s, our food supply has become overloaded with omega-6: Bakery products, canola oil, corn chips, corn oil, margarine, packaged foods (70 percent of them), potato chips, safflower oil, sunflower oil, and the meat from grain-fed beef, grain-fed chickens, and now even grain-fed lamb

More omega-6 and less omega-3 is a recipe for obesity (and inflammatory conditions like blood vessel damage and cancer). Cattle put on weight more rapidly on a high grain diet than they will in the pasture – even when they consume exactly the same number of calories. The omega-6 rich grain diet creates more *fatty acid synthetase*, an enzyme that promotes fat production

Meat from grain-fed animals has an unhealthy high ratio of omega-6 to omega-3, containing as much as 20 times more omega-6 than omega-3. Grass-fed beef has a ratio of n-6 to n-3 of about 2.5:1 or 3:1, ideal for human health. When we exceed a ratio of 4 (four times more omega-6), fatty acid imbalance and diseases like cancer and diabetes get their start.

More omega-6 fats in our diet increased our ratio of omega-6 to omega-3 from 3:1 to as high as 20:1. All omega-3 originate in the green leaves of plants and algae. Deep-sea ocean fish have large amounts because they eat the fish that eat the algae. Salmon, herring, mackerel, and sardines are excellent sources of the ocean omega-3s: EPA and DHA (see chapter 18).

Grazing animals, getting omega-3 directly from the grass, contain more omega-3 than grain-fed cattle. In fact, pasture raised grass-fed beef provides all healthy fats, including omega-3, monounsaturated omega-9, and stearic acid, a saturated fat. In addition, meat from grass-fed animals is more abundant in beta carotene, vitamin A, vitamin E, and conjugated linoleic acid (CLA).

CLA is concentrated ten times higher in grass-fed animals. CLA is a unique fatty acid found almost exclusively in ruminant animals and in dairy fats. The animals must eat grass to develop CLA. CLA has anti-carcinogenic properties and helps the body burn fat for energy.

Our Native American and Pioneer ancestors ate meat from ruminant animals. Our bodies are superbly adapted to this type of food. Grass-fed meat was the only meat available for thousands of years. In the last 50 years, all of us – humans, cattle, and chicken - have made an abrupt shift away from grass-fed in favor of grain-fed

Over the years, our bodies have come to expect the kinds and amounts of fat found in grass-fed food. Our hearts love the omega-3 and the balance of fats found in the grazing animal. When we switch from grain-fed back to grass-fed, our bodies immediately respond and function better – optimally - once again.

Earth-Be-Glad Farm

A small but growing number of Minnesotans have become acquainted with Earth-Be-Glad Farm located in the bluff country of southeastern Minnesota. The farm is located at the head of "Rupprecht's Valley," settled by Mike Rupprecht's great-great grandfather in 1854.

Mike, his wife Jennifer, and daughter Johanna operate a traditional family farm dedicated to healthy soil, healthy animals, and healthy people. They are busy maintaining pastures and raising cattle, chickens, and eggs without resorting to pesticides, antibiotics, growth hormones, or genetic engineering.

If you drive by the farm when there's no snow on the ground, you will see pastures divided into paddocks so that the cattle can move daily to a lush "salad bar." This carefully managed grazing system provides the least possible negative impact on the environment.

Planned grazing builds up the soil as grass and roots grow and decay, while animal manure fertilizes pastures. This imitates the prairie ecosystem in which the great herds of buffalo existed. The Rupprecht's farm has virtually no soil erosion and uses very little fossil fuel.

The Rupprecht's have experimented with native prairie species in some paddocks, and they always leave a paddock or two un-grazed for ground-nesting birds such as bobolinks. They increase biodiversity by seeding as many as 15 plant species in the pasture. The farm has a lot of nesting habitat for grassland birds and wild-life.

Mike Rupprecht and Al Watson at the *Earth Be Glad Farm* in January 2002.

A walk in May through the pasture may reveal 25 types of birds in sight and song. The Rupprechts have noted the return of the eastern kingbird, Balti-more oriole, and several pair of bluebirds. A fa-vorite, the brown thrasher, is the clown in the treetops with a unique song.

The Rupprechts do not want to compromise the health of the ecosystem by tilling the pasture for any other purpose – whether rows of crops or organic vegetables. They feel that permanent well-managed pasture is the best use of this highly erodible land, and livestock are essential in improving soil fertility.

Their cattle provide the rich manure and nitrogen-bearing urine for the replenishment of the soil. Mike checks on the pastured cattle twice each day, making sure that the water lines and fences are working properly. Mike, Jennifer, and Johanna enjoy watching the young calves playing tag.

In the snowy months, usually late November through March (that's been changing in recent years), three silos provide chopped hay, corn, and other forages. Mike also feeds the cattle tasty ground grains. All feeds are grown right on the farm, with no pesticides, nor do they use genetically engineered seeds.

When weather permits, the cattle are out on winter pasture.

Cattle are very adaptable to cold weather, but Mike takes extra care to provide wind protection.

No artificial growth-promoting hormones, routine antibiotics, or animal by-products are used. "Unknowns" are avoided to help assure that healthy meat can be part of your healthy diet.

The dreaded E.coli bacteria are lower in grass-fed beef because the ruminant animals are eating what their bodies were designed to eat – forages. Commercial animals are force-fed a high grain diet, causing their systems to produce higher E. coli - which is then increasingly present in the meat.

Bypassing much of the conventional food system, which is increasingly controlled by corporate giants, the Rupprecht's are working toward a new consumer paradigm in which the buyer of food knows and trusts the producer of food. Dealing face to face, the buyer provides a living for the producer, and the producer provides clean, nutritious food for the buyer.

When you buy food from the Rupprechts, you're getting their guarantee of environmentally responsible farming, humane animal treatment, and a vision for the future of the land.

Buying beef by the quarter, half, or whole is the best value. If you choose to buy a quarter, you will need freezer space for about 110 pounds of packaged meat (one grocery cart full). When you buy a quarter or more, you choose your own cuts, package sizes, and specialty items.

Your beef will be properly aged, processed at a local plant, and then packaged and frozen according to your specifications. Order at least one month before you wish to pickup your beef. Average final cost for the meat you put in your freezer will be approximately $3.00 per pound, a significant savings compared to prices of individual cuts at natural foods grocery stores.

You can find Earth-Be-Glad Farm and other pastured products in your area online at **www.eatwild.com**

Chapter 18

-------- 🙌 --------

C-Reactive Protein: Inflammation and heart disease

It has been only two years since medical investigators discovered that inflammation is related to heart disease, but we now understand that these markers for inflammation may be better predictors of heart disease than elevated blood cholesterol itself.

Jeffrey S. Bland, Ph.D., *Genetic Nutritioneering*

If cholesterol is the titanic of heart disease dogma, homocysteine is the tip of the iceberg of new ideas. Worldwide, with Dr. Kilmer McCully's discovery that elevated homocysteine caused atherosclerosis, our understanding of coronary heart disease made a giant leap forward.

Insisting that cholesterol was to blame – regardless of the scientific evidence - delayed other solutions and new treatment options. All that is changing now. The role of bacterial and viral agents and the body's inflammatory response to their presence may be no less important than elevated homocysteine in unraveling the causes of heart attack and stroke.

The latest hypothesis: Chronic low-grade bacterial and viral infections are creating an inflammatory response that damages the artery's smooth, slick endothelial surface, attracting blood clotting factors and forming blockages. There's evidence, too, that inflammation can disturb the soft, unstable fast growing plaques, triggering heart attacks and strokes.[1]

Like elevated homocysteine, chronic inflammation in blood vessels is promoting atherosclerosis, and something called C-reactive protein (CRP), a marker in the blood for inflammation, may provide an early warning of the increased risk. Doctors have used the CRP blood test for years to confirm and diagnosis inflammatory diseases such as rheumatoid arthritis.[2]

In the last few years, medical doctors, like Robert C. Atkins, M.D., have come to realize that, "Even moderate elevations of CRP are associated with a high risk of developing heart disease or having a stroke." CRP levels above 2.5 mg/dl can alert us to increased risk and may be used to predict a first heart attack 6 to 8 years in advance.[3]

C-reactive protein is produced in the liver in response to inflammation in the arteries. Risk increases as CRP increases, and high CRP levels dramatically increase the risk that arterial plaque will rupture and cause a heart attack. A major study published in 1997 showed that men with the highest CRP levels had triple the risk of a future heart attack and double the risk of a stroke compared to men with the lowest CRP levels.[4]

Elevated CRP poses an equal or greater risk to women. According to Dr. Atkins, menopausal women using synthetic hormone replacement therapy are most likely to have dangerously high CRP levels. A 1998 study of female health professionals showed that, as with men, the higher the CRP level, the greater the risk of cardiovascular disease. Women with the highest CRP levels had over 7 times the risk of a heart attack or stroke compared to those with normal CRP levels (below 2.5).[5]

Weight gain and obesity are almost certain to increase blood levels of CRP. This suggests that a high carbohydrate diet, high blood sugar, and high insulin levels play an underlying role in blood vessel inflammation (see chapter 10). Obese individuals often have high CRP levels, suggesting that high insulin levels and excess body fat cause chronic, low-grade inflammations.[6]

Elevated CRP is associated with a host of other heart disease risk factors, especially high blood pressure. The 26th International Stroke Conference in Fort Lauderdale, Florida, looked at a Framingham-related study and found that the risk of stroke doubles when a person has both elevated systolic blood pressure (the top number) and high serum CRP.

Framingham participants were measured in 1980 and followed for 14 years. Out of 591 men, those with serum CRP and systolic blood pressure levels in the top 25 percent of values experienced a 2.7-fold increased risk of stroke compared to men with the lowest values. Out of 868 Framingham women, those with serum CRP and systolic blood pressure levels in the top 25 percent of values experienced a 2.06-fold increased risk of stroke compared to women with the lowest values.

Even when data was adjusted for other risk factors, men and women with the highest CRP levels had almost double the risk compared to participants with the lowest levels. The high CRP range for men was 6.9 to 48.3; the range for women was 7.33 to 50.2. Systolic blood pressure levels for men and women were 155 to 225.[6]

Gender	C-Reactive Protein	Systolic Pressure
Men	6.9 to 48.3	155 to 225
Women	7.3 to 50.2	155 to 225

Dr. Atkins recommends low-dose aspirin (81 mg) daily for people with very high CRP levels. For people with lower, less serious levels, he recommends a broad range of nutrients to reduce inflammation, including daily flax oil, fish oil, and GLA, found in borage and evening primrose oil gel caps. See 21-Day Plan, this chapter).

"Inflammation is fundamental to the genesis of atherosclerosis," writes Atkins in his book, *Age-Defying Diet Revolution*. CRP is a marker for inflammation, but where there is inflammation, he says, there is infection. Possible infectious agents include two different bacteria, chlamydia and mycoplasma, and a member of the herpes virus family called cytomegalovirus (CMV).

Because they infect us without producing fever or raised white blood cell count, these various microorganisms are both very common and very hard to detect, states Dr. Atkins. Researchers call these various pathogens "stealth" bacteria or viruses. The only way you know you've been infected is that you will carry antibodies to one or more of the organisms in your blood.

By age 35, as Atkins points out, 50 percent or more of us are infected with one or more of these organisms. The evidence for chlamydia is especially strong. The chlamydia bacterium is often found inside atherosclerotic plaque and may clog arteries by infecting the arterial wall. Antibiotics are often required to knock out entrenched infections.

According to Dr. Atkins, mycoplasma is the stealthiest of the stealth bacteria. They have diminished or missing cell walls and can enter right into your cells – say arterial tissue – where they can hide from both immune system attackers and from most standard antibiotics. If a patient has CHD and no apparent risk factors, cell wall deficient bacteria must be considered.

Stealth pathogens may be causing the underlying damage in many chronic diseases, including multiple sclerosis, fibromyalgia, Alzheimer's and chronic fatigue syndrome.[8] We know, too, that a good share of the inflammatory havoc in our blood vessels is caused by high glucose, high insulin, and the related development of abnormal blood fats and sticky, clot-prone blood.

We may need doctors and antibiotic therapy to fight off entrenched infections, but there's a lot we can do to head off inflammation and drug treatments early on by eating heart-protecting whole foods and restricting the heart and blood vessel damaging refined foods. Carbohydrates and fats must be chosen carefully or they will predispose us to diabetes and blood vessel damage.

The carbohydrate and vegetable fat concoctions we are eating today are nutrient-deficient, nutrient depleting, and pro-inflammatory. Refined foods raise blood glucose and insulin levels and stress many body systems, including blood circulation and the immune system. A weak immune system then opens the doors to these bacterial and viral invaders. The infectious agents, while not the underlying problem, cause the subsequent damage.

Heart disease patients who have had a greater exposure to bacteria and viruses have more advanced atherosclerosis and a far worse prognosis for eventual recovery. A study of 572 hospital patients cited by Dr. Joseph Mercola found that patients who had four to five past infections were nearly twice as likely to have extensive clogging in the arteries as those with fewer infections.[9]

During the study of patients with advanced atherosclerosis, the cardiovascular death rate was 7 percent for patients with zero to three infections and 20 percent for those with six to eight infections. The extent of atherosclerosis and the risk of mortality were significantly related to the presence of multiple infectious agents.

Bacterial and viral invaders take advantage of bodies weakened by nutritional deficiencies and dietary imbalances. Invasion is followed by inflammation, plaque buildup, and blood clots. To prevent this seriously more complicated coronary degeneration, we must lick the sugar habit and give up the highly processed foods that contain excess carbohydrate, excess omega-6 fats, and the dangerous not-found-in-nature TFAs.

21-Day Plan key principle #18:

Eat deep-sea cold-water fish as often as possible

Risk factor	optimum	risk	serious risk
C-Reactive Protein	<2.5	>2.5	>6.9

"Make a habit of eating fish, especially cold water deep sea fish, as often as possible. They are rich in omega-3 fatty acids, fat-soluble vitamins and many important minerals, including iodine, selenium and magnesium."

Sally Fallon, *Nourishing Traditions*

In *The Felix Letter*, Clara Felix says we must counter inflammation and heart disease by eating as close to the Paleolithic diet as possible:

"Lots of fish, shellfish, veggies, fruits, leafy greens, nuts, seeds, starchy roots and tubers, natural sweeteners, not too much reliance on gluten grains. Organically grown whenever possible. Free range beef; lamb and pork raised largely outdoors on pasture and good feed; eggs and meat from free-range poultry; liver and other organ meats from free-range animals or fowl."[10]

Fish are important because, in addition to complete protein, they provide a direct source of the critically important long-chain omega-3 polyunsaturated eicosapentaenoic acid (EPA) and docosahexaenoic acid (DHA). Inside and outside the body, these fats are most sensitive to free radical oxidation.[11]

"House guests and fish smell after three days," but in the case of fish, one day is long enough. Do not buy fish that has sat at the market much more than 24 hours. Eat fresh fish the day you buy it. Fish and fish oils have a very short shelf life. Because they contain a high percentage of polyunsaturated fat, leftover fish and chicken don't last too long in the refrigerator. Eat them up right away.

While EPA and DHA can be made in the body from n-3 alpha linolenic acid, found abundantly in flaxseed, the conversion is never certain, especially in diabetics and people with a high TFA intake. EPA and DHA are common deficiencies, and a regular direct source of both is needed to promote optimum health.

EPA and DHA, like vitamins A and D, are usually found together. Fish tissues are the best source, but DHA is also found in organ meats and in smaller amounts in free-range eggs and good quality lard (from healthy outdoor pigs). The very best sources are the tissues of deep-sea cold-water fish: salmon, sardines, herring, and mackerel.

EPA and DHA can quiet "endothelial activation," a process of inflammatory stimulation in the blood vessels that can spur chain reactions leading to blood vessel damage. According to Felix, "In many trials, less endothelial activation and better vasodilation was seen in patients receiving 4 to 5 grams a day of EPA plus DHA."[12]

Damage to the endothelial layer – endothelial dysfunction – is linked to smoking, high blood pressure, blood sugar disorders, elevated homocysteine, oxidized cholesterol, high lipoprotein(a) levels, and all other risk factors for heart disease.

Avoid fish-farm fish. Like their feedlot friends, they lack the vital omega-3 fats that are only found in animals free to forage – whether at land or sea. Fish is health food (unless you're allergic to it). In a Netherlands study, "Researchers found that just one serving of fish per week substantially reduced the risk of heart disease."[13]

One day per week is a realistic goal. More is better. Ocean fish and sea vegetables are also the best sources of minerals, more reliable than the diminishing quantities found in commercial fruits and vegetables. Consider the Japanese, whose mineral-rich and high fish diet protects them from a variety of inflammation-related diseases, including arthritis, diabetes, and heart disease.

Fish are especially good sources of iodine, magnesium, and zinc. Mackerel, anchovies, and herring are particularly rich in minerals.[14] If vegetarians add just one meat to improve their diet, it should be deep-sea fish.

According to the research of Dr. Weston Price, traditional groups eating seafood were the healthiest people he could find in the 1930s. They consumed ten times more fat-soluble vitamins A and D than Americans did at that time. Red meat eaters scored second in Weston Price's health investment – vegetarian groups came in third.[15]

Mercury and PCB contamination of fish is a serious concern. Sally Fallon recommends avoiding sole and flounder from contaminated shoreline waters or catfish, scavengers, and any other fish from contaminated freshwater sources. Sardines, sole, and flounder from the relatively clean North Atlantic, and deep-sea salmon, tuna, and swordfish are the least contaminated.[16]

Fish is expensive, but even people on tight budgets can include EPA and DHA. Some is a lot better than none. You can stretch a can of Norway sardines between two or three people or eat two sardines a day until they're gone. Less expensive sardines do not carry the Norwegian government's guarantee of no PCB's or mercury.

According to Beth M. Ley-Jacobs, Ph.D., "North Americans have some of the lowest brain DHA levels of any population on earth…" DHA deficiencies are common among people who don't eat enough fish. Relatively inexpensive herring, mackerel and sardines can close this nutritional gap.[17]

EPA and DHA on a regular basis offer many protective benefits for the heart and arteries, including promoting beneficial HDL while reducing triglycerides, LDL cholesterol, blood stickiness, and blood pressure. People with fish-eating ancestors should be especially concerned about not getting their EPA and DHA.[18]

EPA and DHA:

- Reduce inflammation in blood vessels
- Lower triglycerides
- Reduce LDL cholesterol
- Elevate protective HDL
- Reduce clotting factors
- Reduce blood pressure
- Prevent arrhythmia

Hundreds of studies have shown that fish and fish oil reduce inflamation and chronic deseases. The well-known 1989 Diet and Reinfarction Trial (DART) surveyed men who had survived a heart attack. The men who changed their diets and ate fish at least twice per week enjoyed a 29 percent decline in CHD mortality.[19]

In the ongoing Physicians Health Study, researchers have followed the diets and health of about 20,000 male doctors since 1983. Between 1983 and 1994, 133 of the physicians died from sudden cardiac death. The physicians who ate fish at least once a week had a 52 percent lower risk of suffering fatal heart arrhythmias.[20]

Because fish provide direct sources of EPA and DHA, fish are especially important for those at risk of heart disease. Combining two daily tablespoons of milled flaxseed with two weekly servings of deep-sea cold-water fish provides optimum omega protection against diabetes and heart disease.

Atkins says eat fish and take fish oil capsules. Fish oil capsules, according to Dr. Atkins, work better as an anticoagulant than the prescription drug Coumadin, which keeps your blood from clotting by destroying vitamin K. Dr. Atkins recommends fish oil and vitamin E instead of long-term use of Coumadin.

If you have *active heart disease*, and your doctor has you on Coumadin, do not discontinue Coumadin without talking to your doctor. Ask your doctor, though, about switching to fish oil capsules, daily flaxseed, and two weekly servings of deep-sea cold-water fish.

Dr. Atkins' anti-inflammatory supplement program

Nutrient	Dose Range
MSM (methyl sulfonyl methane)	1,500-3,000 mg
Quercitin	800-1,600 mg
Turmeric	200-400 mg
Ginger	200-400 mg
Boswellia Extract	150-300 mg
Bromelain	400-800 mg
Bilberry	100-200 mg
Niacinamide	100-200 mg
Pantethine	100-200 mg
Vitamin C	1,000-2,000 mg
EPA/DHA (fish oil)	800-1,600 mg
GLA (borage oil)	800-1,600 mg
ALA (flax oil)	800-1,600 mg

PART IV

Putting it all together

Chapter 19

-------- 🐟 --------

Hormones and the heart

For the first time in history, women may share the promise of tomorrow as biological equals of men…Thanks to hormone therapy, they may look forward to extended well being and extended youth."

Robert A. Wilson, M.D., *Feminine Forever*

Feminine Forever?

In 1964, doctors enthusiastically began prescribing synthetic estrogen to menopausal women. Paid advertising and planted media stories promised women they would be *feminine forever.* "Oh What A Lovely Pill, heralded *Cosmopolitan* in July, 1965, *"No more menopause."*

Drug company salesmen were passing out free copies of *Feminine Forever*, a book by gynecologist Robert A. Wilson, M.D., to doctors' offices throughout the country. John R. Lee, M.D., Mill Valley, California, who initially prescribed estrogen, remembers getting his copy.[1]

Later, when his patients were experiencing serious side effects that he was powerless to explain, let alone treat, Dr. Lee decided to investigate. There was something "wrong with the synthetic hormone picture," he thought, and he was determined to solve the puzzle.

Lee discovered that estrogen's approval as a prescription drug was based largely on a small study of women in Puerto Rico who took birth control pills. Twenty percent of the participants complained of side effects and three died. No autopsies were performed. Other subsequent evidence of synthetic hormones causing blood clots and strokes was simply ignored, says, Dr. Lee.[2]

By the mid-1970s, dark clouds dimmed the hoopla. Large numbers of women using synthetic estrogen had developed uterine (endometrial) cancer at a rate four to eight times greater than untreated women. Researchers confirmed the link between synthetic estrogen and uterine cancer. The estrogen bandwagon temporarily stalled.[3]

When doctors began adding synthetic *progestin* to oppose the estrogen, the uterine cancer "side effect" was effectively reduced. Estrogen therapy became *hormone replacement therapy* (HRT), and the practice of prescribing HRT to women over fifty became virtually automatic for many physicians.

Synthetic hormones perform some of the functions of natural hormones, but not all of them. While *progestin* (synthetic progesterone) balances unopposed estrogen and works as a birth control pill, it will not promote bone remodeling. Synthetic progestin, occupying progesterone receptor sites, is not easily metabolized from the body.

Synthetic, patented hormones have altered shapes not found in nature. "We don't have enzymes designed to handle any of the synthetic steroids," says Dr. Lee. Unlike natural progesterone, which is multifunctional and capable of transforming into many other related hormones, progestins are biological dead ends.

Calling menopause a disease and treating it with synthetic estrogen and progestin is now entrenched medical practice. Thumb through just about any women's magazine today and you'll see the ads for HRT, promising relief from the symptoms of menopause – plus protection against bone loss and heart disease. Synthetic hormones are among the top selling drugs in the world.[4]

Estrogen Effects

Causes breast stimulation

Increases body fat

Salt and fluid retention

Depression/headaches

Interferes w/ thyroid hormone

Increases blood clotting

Decreases sex drive

Impairs blood sugar control

Zinc loss/copper retention

Reduces cell oxygen

Increases endometrial cancer

Increases breast cancer risk

Progesterone Effects

protects against fibrocystic breasts

helps use fats for energy

natural diuretic

natural antidepressant

facilitates thyroid hormone action

normalizes blood clotting

restores sex drive

normalizes blood sugar levels

normalizes zinc/copper levels

restores proper oxygen levels

prevents endometrial cancer

helps prevent breast cancer

From *What Your Doctor May Not Tell You About Menopause*, by John R. Lee, M.D.

But – we should ask - does estrogen deficiency cause heart disease, bone loss, and osteoporosis? No, to all three, says Dr. Lee, "There are very, very few western women truly deficient in estrogen; most become deficient in progesterone." And, according to Dr. Lee, progesterone levels start declining first, years before menopause.[5]

Dr. Lee states, "A large percentage of advertising and research dollars are spent trying to convince women that estrogen will cure everything from heart disease to Alzheimer's, but there is scant evidence for any of these claims and realms of evidence that synthetic estrogens are highly toxic and carcinogenic."

"The real tragedy," says Dr. Lee, "is that the natural forms of these hormones, used widely and in moderation, could be of very real benefit to millions of women. I believe that the present synthetic hormones are making millions of women sick and putting them at risk for cancer, strokes, and heart disease."[6]

Menopausal Estrogen and Estrogen-Progestin Replacement Therapy and Breast Cancer Risk," published in the January 26, 2000 issue of *JAMA,* showed that women on HRT (synthetic estrogen and progestin) have a higher breast cancer risk than women using estrogen alone – and a much higher risk than women using no hormones.

The study found that women on conventional HRT for five years have a 40 percent higher risk of breast cancer than women not using HRT. As Dr. Lee points out, "Unopposed estrogen is dangerous and estrogen combined with synthetic progestins is even more dangerous in terms of breast cancer risk."[7]

> *"Research dating back to the 1980s and now exploding in more recent medical literature shows that estrogen dominance (relative progesterone deficiency) accounts for 80 percent of all breast cancers."*
>
> John R. Lee, M.D.

Nor does HRT cure or correct osteoporosis. Bone loss actually begins years before menopause when estrogen levels are still high. Estrogen at menopause may slow bone loss for a few years, but it does not promote bone remodeling. According to Dr. Lee, progesterone – not estrogen - is needed to slow bone loss and promote optimum bone density.[8]

"The more important factor in osteoporosis is the lack of progesterone, which causes a decrease in new bone formation. Adding progesterone will actively increase bone mass and density and can reverse osteoporosis," writes Dr. Lee in What *Your Doctor May Not Tell You About Menopause.* Lee hastens to add that curing osteoporosis also depends on "proper diet, weight-bearing exercise, and some vitamin and mineral supplements."[9]

According to Robert C. Atkins, M.D., HRT does not reduce the risk of heart disease, and may even promote it. "If you're on the borderline for an insulin-related disorder," says Dr. Atkins, "HRT could tip you over into a full-blown version of it." HRT has an adverse effect on glucose/insulin metabolism, sharply elevates triglyceride levels, and promotes diabetes, blood clots, and heart attacks.[10]

Progesterone is a steroid hormone made by the ovaries and in smaller amounts by the adrenal glands. Progesterone is manufactured in the body from pregnenolone, which, in turn, is made from cholesterol. Progesterone is a precursor hormone to estrogen (there are three) and testosterone.

In women, years before menopause, progesterone levels begin to decline sooner and more precipitously than estrogen levels, which continue to be produced in fat cells. Levels of other hormones – such as DHEA, pregnenolone, and testosterone – peak in our 20s and then decline gradually, especially after age 40.

Women and men can restore a healthy hormone balance by supplementing with natural progesterone, synthesized in the laboratory from wild yam extract. Supplemental natural progesterone matches body made progesterone, eases menopausal symptoms, and offers natural protection against osteoporosis and heart dis-

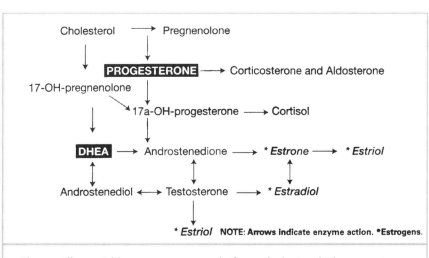

Above: All steroid hormones are made from cholesterol. There are two major steroid pathways - via DHEA or Progesterone.

ease - without any side effects.

Progesterone is not a female sex hormone. It boosts the immune systems of women and men, supports bone remodeling, forms the myelin sheath, and is a precursor to other steroid hormones, including testosterone. Men, too, can experience better overall health and restored sexual libido using natural progesterone.

Natural progesterone is to estrogen what magnesium is to calcium: A vital, balancing co-factor. Without sufficient progesterone, estrogen becomes a bull in the china shop. And, without sufficient magnesium, calcium migrates into soft tissues, causing artery damage. Bone building and heart health depend on supplemental progesterone and magnesium – not estrogen and calcium.

DHEA

The most abundant hormone in the body, DHEA is an important marker for age-related health problems. DHEA levels decline faster than any other hormone. The lower your DHEA, the more likely you will develop cancer, coronary heart disease, diabetes, osteoporosis, and lowered immunity.

After age 40, our bodies gradually produce fewer and fewer hormones. We can lose muscle mass and tone, bones may become brittle, blood vessels stiffen, libido flags, short term memory wanes, and we become less able to fend off bacterial and viral invaders.

Your adrenal glands manufacture DHEA from cholesterol. By the time you're forty or so, you're making only half the DHEA you did at age 20. At age 65, you're down to about 10 to 20 percent of peak. Besides normal aging, many things deplete DHEA levels - especially excess alcohol, beta blockers, calcium channel blockers, coffee, corticosteroid drugs (prednisone), insulin, synthetic hormones, and stress.[11]

Stress is the enemy, and DHEA is the silent victim. Low DHEA may cause migraine headaches, raise LDL cholesterol and insulin levels, and suppress the immune system. Any stressful event can stop the body's production of DHEA, including a death in the family, divorce, financial worries, job changes, physical trauma, public speaking, relocations, strenuous exercise, and surgery.

DHEA (dehydroepiandrosterone), often called the "mother hormone," converts to or stimulates the production of 40 other adrenal hormones, including androstenediol, testosterone, and the estrogens. In men, there is evidence that DHEA is a precursor to testosterone, but the DHEA pathway in women is less certain.

Dr. Lee cautions that women should emphasize progesterone and be cautious with DHEA. According to Lee, "Most of the [DHEA] studies have been done on men, and many in the health care fields are making the mistake of thinking that what applies to a man applies to a woman. When it comes to how sex hormones behave, this is almost never true and DHEA is no exception."[12]

With decades of clinical experience using natural progesterone cream, Dr. Lee speaks with well-earned authority on women's health issues. Supplemental progesterone's safety and efficacy are backed by Dr. Lee's extensive clinical data.

According to Dr. Lee, DHEA converts into many other adrenal hormones, but does not convert into progesterone in men or in women. At the same time, says Lee, there is strong evidence that progesterone increases DHEA in both women and men.

DHEA has its advocates and wide-scale testing programs and clinical trials are under way. DHEA may be the hormone of choice for men. For both men and women, testing and close monitoring are strongly advised. Some people may not achieve optimum hormone balance without the use of two or more hormones.

DHEA and other androgen hormones (testosterone, DHEA, and androstenedione) play important roles in tissue regeneration, especially in the proper growth of brain cells, skin, bones, and muscles. DHEA may inhibit the conversion of carbohydrates to fats (triglycerides), reduce blood clotting, and help lower blood pressure. Restoring healthy levels of DHEA protects you from and even reverses a wide range of degenerative diseases.[13]

Optimum levels of DHEA can:

- regulate hormones
- lower blood pressure
- decrease platelet stickiness
- increase testosterone in men
- lower LDL cholesterol
- enhance immune function
- reduce enlarged prostate
- promote fat burning
- increase muscle mass
- stabilize blood sugar
- discourage overeating
- boost endurance
- restore collagen
- and fight cancer, fatigue and depression.

Adapted from *DHEA*, by Rita Elkins, M.H.

Low Thyroid can increase the risk of heart disease:

Symptoms of low thyroid function (hypothyroidism) include: sensitivity to cold, weight gain, inability to lose weight, fatigue and lethargy, depression, dry skin, headaches, inability to concentrate – and elevated total cholesterol – especially *high HDL and low triglycerides.*

T-4 and T-3 are two active thyroid gland principles. T-3 is most active but is secreted in tiny amounts. The body converts less active T-4 to T-3. For many reasons, T-4 may fail to convert to T-3 or converts instead to *reverse* T-3, which incorrectly registers as T-3 in blood tests. When this occurs, you may experience various symptoms of sluggish thyroid, but test OK for thyroid hormone.

According to Dr. Atkins, the slowdown in the conversion of T-4 to T-3 is a common response to stress. Prolonged dieting can cause the slowdown, as well as selenium, zinc, and vitamin A deficiencies. Remember, zinc is abundant only in red meat. People on high carbohydrate diets are often deficient in both retinol vitamin A (animal source) and zinc.

Doctors may prescribe *Synthroid*, a synthetic version of T-4 (and only T-4). Atkins says this prescription "is the perfect way to develop T-3 failure." Atkins recommends natural thyroid hormone (as in Armour or Thyrolar), which includes T-4, T-3, and other thyroid compounds.

If natural hormone therapy is successful for just a few months - and relapse occurs - you may have Wilson's Syndrome, a low thyroid condition that requires more precise hormone therapy. A treatment protocol and further information can be found at **www.wilsonsyndrome.com.**

At Home Thyroid Test:

The lower your average body temperature, the more likely you have a sluggish thyroid. Use a glass-bulb thermometer and take your temperature under the tongue four times a day for three days – just before you eat and right before you go to bed. After the third day, calculate the average of the 12 readings and compare to the following chart. Be sure to schedule a visit with your doctor if your average temperature is below 98.

Temperature average	Chance of a thyroid problem
98.5 or higher	unlikely
98.1 to 98.4	possible
97.8 to 98	50-50
97.7 or lower	highly likely

Ask your doctor to read *Dr. Robert Atkins Health Revelations*, Volume V, Number 4, April, 1997. Find Dr. Atkins online at **www.atkinscenter.com.**

21-Day Plan key principle #19:

Monitor and, as necessary, restore health-promoting hormone levels.

Synthetic hormones are dangerous. Used wisely, natural hormones help prevent cancer, heart disease, osteoporosis, and extend longevity. We can nutritionally support healthy hormone levels and supplement with natural hormones to restore youthful beneficial levels. This can be done at home, preferably in conjunction with saliva testing, or under the guidance of a knowledgeable, experienced physician.

Too little of a hormone does nothing and too much can be dangerous. Hormones work within a narrow range. When in balance, hormones - like minerals, fats and proteins – work together in team fashion to run our bodies harmoniously. When out of balance – whether minerals, fats, proteins or hormones – trouble begins.

You can disrupt hormone balance by eating a high sugar, high carbohydrate diet, spending too much time at fast food restaurants, not eating fish or flaxseed, buying too much commercial meat, using synthetic hormones, living in constant haste, suffering excess stress, and by supplementing with a single hormone. You can monitor your own hormone levels at home with a *Saliva Test Kit*.

Home Testing:

Saliva testing measures the active, bioavailable "free hormones" circulating in your body. Most routine blood tests, in contrast, measure storage hormones (bound to blood proteins) that are not available to the body. The saliva method uses a proprietary process that cleans all toxins and impurities first.

The Evalu8 saliva tests profile from one to ten hormones. The kit contains saliva collection supplies, step-by-step information booklet, requisition form, and prepaid mailing tube. Saliva testing should be done at the start of hormone therapy.

The saliva test results are presented numerically and are mailed directly to you or your medical practitioner. Normal hormone levels are listed in the report. Medical insurance and HMO's will only reimburse tests ordered by a doctor. To order an Evalu8 saliva test, call **888-999-7440**, or go online at **www.life-flow.com**.

Evalu8 Saliva Test Options:

Estradiol	Testosterone
Estriol	DHEA
Estrone	Cortisol
Progesterone	Melatonin
Dihydrotestosterone	Androstenedione

Saliva testing services are also available from ZRT Laboratory. A minimum of two hormone tests is required per order. You can find ZRT online at **www.salivatest.com** or obtain further information by calling: **503-466-2445**.

The hormones

Dr. Lee recommends hormone cream for absorption through the skin (transdermal). Hormones are taken up by the fatty layer beneath, and then transferred to the bloodstream – bypassing the liver and digestive system.

If taken orally, as little as 5 percent of a hormone will survive the stomach, liver, and digestive system. Creams are easy to use. Simply rub into the skin anywhere you blush – face, neck, upper chest, thighs, etc. Rotate the application for best results.

Good quality progesterone creams – like *Elan Vitale's Bio Balance* – are also excellent face creams. Natural Progesterone, DHEA, Pregnenolone and information and books about hormone supplements are available by calling Nokomis Nutrition at **800-641-6802** or online at **www.nokobeach.com**.

Progesterone

Rub about a teaspoon into the skin. About 15 mg daily is a maintenance dose. More (up to 50 mg) or less may be appropriate. Use for 21-days, take a seven-day break and then start again. You want to use a product that contains approximately 1,500 mg of progesterone per 2 oz. container. Progesterone is excellent for women of all ages and for men age 40 and older.

Progesterone is used for hormone balance, PMS, menopause, male andropause, and to promote bone remodeling and heart health in both women and men. Pregnenolone is the precursor molecule, but supplemental pregnenolone – due to possible enzyme conversion failure - may not increase progesterone levels in all cases.

For more information about natural progesterone, read *What Your Doctor May Not Tell You About Premenopause* or *What Your Doctor May Not Tell You About Menopause*, both by John R. Lee, M.D. You can find Dr. Lee online at **www.johnleemd.com** or call **800-528-0559** to subscribe to his newsletter.

DHEA/testosterone

DHEA is also available as a cream. Apply same as progesterone. A high dose of DHEA is more than 25 mg per day. Women make 20 percent less DHEA then men and supplement with a smaller amount. Doses up to 50 mg daily may be appropriate but should be verified with saliva testing.

High levels of DHEA are associated with optimum body functioning. DHEA is especially important for preventing a wide range of degenerative conditions, including diabetes and heart disease. DHEA may promote fat burning by accelerating metabolism and enhance the immune system's ability to defend against viral and bacterial infections.

Testosterone protects the cardiovascular system by reducing the tendency of blood to clot. According to Dr. Lee, a low testosterone to estradiol ratio is strongly associated with the inability of the body to dissove clots.

As men age, progesterone levels fall, testosterone converts to dihydrotestosterone (DHT), and estradiol rises. This results in weight gain, greater risk of heart attack, enlargement of the prostate, and increased risk of prostate cancer. It is very beneficial and important for men to test their testosterone, DHT, progesterone, and estradiol levels together.

Of all the hormones we have discussed, only testosterone is a prescription drug, but natural testosterone is available from the doctor. According to Dr. Atkins, androstenedione and DHEA, in combination, significantly increase testosterone and no prescription is needed. DHEA and/or progesterone may increase testosterone in women as well.

Testosterone levels begin falling off in men (and women) in their late 40s – just as progesterone and estrogen levels are declining in women. These declining hormone levels are associated with various symptoms of aging, such as weight gain, loss of muscle tone, declining libido, blood sugar elevations, depression and fatigue.

For more information about DHEA and anti-aging, read *Dr. Atkins Age-Defying Diet Revolution*, by Robert C. Atkins, M.D. You can find Dr. Atkins online at www.atkinscenter.com.

Pregnenolone

Pregnenolone is the precursor or base material the body uses to make progesterone, DHEA, testosterone, and estrogen. Pregnenolone is at the very beginning of the hormonal chain – to the right of the king of hormones – none other than the big cheese – CHOLESTEROL. People on low cholesterol diets take warning: You need cholesterol to make hormones and you need hormones to run your bodies.

Dr. Atkins uses equal amounts of DHEA and pregnenolone in combination for pain and inflammation instead of prednisone - the dreadful side effect-laden first choice of most mainstream doctors.

As we age, pregnenolone declines, DHEA declines, and the enzyme that converts pregnenolone to DHEA declines as well. Everybody packs up and leaves the party at the same time – leaving you with inevitable symptoms of aging – flat butt and all! Atkins says taking both pregnenolone and DHEA together will increase levels of both hormones and decrease cortisol – DHEA's ancient antagonist.

DHEA and cortisol counteract in a complex manner. Excess cortisol, the hormone that takes over when your blood sugar remains too high, suppresses and even stops DHEA production. Too much blood sugar or stress will result in a cascade of problems as cortisol becomes dominant over DHEA.

Excess cortisol accelerates the aging process. That may explain why some mellow, content people eating white bread and luncheon meat daily live just as long or longer as someone obsessing about doing everything right. The protective power of DHEA is lost in the face of sustained, unremitting stress of any kind.[14]

High circulating cortisol also inhibits the production of the eicosanoids, those short, lived jack-in-the-box hormones that function within cell membranes (chapter 16). Stress, excess omega-6 fats, and TFAs in partially hydrogenated vegetable fats all interfere with eicosanoid functioning.

This illustrates the double whammy served up by high stress and poor nutrition - the disease trail that links our emotions, hormones, and the food choices we make. By putting a 21-Day Plan together, we can prevent and reverse diabetes and heart disease.

It's time to meet Maria E.

Chapter 20

-------- 🐛 --------

Proof of the pudding: Maria E.

"If I'd known I would live this long, I would have taken better care of myself."

- anonymous -

Maria weighed 332 pounds in March 2001. She had fasting blood sugar levels in the neighborhood of 150 to 220 – and even over 500 a couple of times! Her doctor ordered a **HbA1c** test (average blood sugar over time) and learned that Maria had been running over 125 fasting glucose for 3-4 months.

She was diagnosed with Type II diabetes. Her pancreas was putting out insulin but her cells were resisting it. Further testing revealed first-degree blockage in a main coronary artery. She felt bloated and was holding water – edema around her ankles. The doctor would not prescribe diuretics so she began self-medicating with caffeine-laden over the counter diuretics.

She bought *Coke* in one-liter bottles and shifted back and forth all day between Coke and orange juice. She started each day with a *Coke* and a cigarette. She was in the habit of eating a lot of candy. Her car seats and floors were full of empty snack wrappers. *Slim Jim's*, *Twizzlers* (red candy licorice), and fast food were daily fare.

Maria was suffering tremendous stress. She was in a failing marriage and had other serious family problems. She didn't sleep well – often not at all. She was plagued with painful muscle spasms – charley horses she had come to believe were normal for someone her age.

Overweight, diabetic, and living in constant haste, Maria was just 33 years old. Looking and feeling closer to 50, Maria had many aches and pains. She had been through several surgeries in the past 12 months, including a hysterectomy. She had several painful diabetes-related abscesses removed, including two that were malignant.

Her doctor prescribed *Glucophage* for Type II diabetes, which she took sporadically, and Prozac for depression. She became allergic to the Prozac and addicted to painkillers. She tried illegal speed for weight loss – and through it all, managed to keep her job at a small town restaurant, where her work ethic, friendly nature, and aura of plight endeared her to customers and employees alike.

The nurse taught her how to use a home blood sugar monitor and a nutritionist gave her a specific food plan.

Maria E., March 2002

The first two pages of the food plan contained a long list of "carbohydrate choices," including bread, cereal, hot dog bun, skim milk, potato chips, glazed doughnut, and artificially sweetened low-fat yogurt. Instructions said to spread carbohydrate intake throughout the day – and "eat consistent amounts of carbohydrates at meals and snacks from day to day."

With the admonition to "follow your food plan," it was OK for Maria to include 3-4 carbohydrate choices (45-60 grams) at each meal and one to two carbohydrates choices (15-30 grams) for each snack. Maria's food plan (dated January 24, 2001) encourages her to consume fifteen to seventeen (15-17) carbohydrate choices per day.

Maria could eat several slices of bread, bagels, and English muffins a day. Baked potato, chocolate candy bar, granola bar, honey, pasta, white rice, and sugar were all permitted. The basic plan: Eat anything – just count the servings and spread your poison out throughout the day.

"Free foods" include diet soft drinks (unlimited) and sugar substitutes (unlimited). Maria's plan offered one free tablespoon serving of catsup or taco sauce – high fructose corn syrup notwithstanding – and one free tablespoon of *fat free* - high sugar salad dressing.

The illustrated USDA Food Pyramid – complete with 6-11 servings of grains, beans, and starchy vegetables daily – was her official road map to good nutrition – the federal government's best advice for getting and maintaining "manageable" diabetes.

We discussed the findings of Gerald Reavan, M.D., who, after 20 years of research at Stanford University Medical School, states: "Carbohydrates become glucose, and glucose must be herded into certain cells. That requires insulin. More carbohydrates equal more glucose equal more insulin: that's the formula for disaster …"[1]

… for the 60-75 million insulin resistant and diabetic people like Maria!

Unsaturated fats, which contain TFAs, are the food plan's recommended dietary fats, said to be "better choices" than saturated fats, which do not contain TFAs.

Maria's choices here included soft margarine, reduced fat margarine, reduced fat mayonnaise, and two teaspoons (one serving) of peanut butter. No distinction is made between *Jif* and *Skippy* peanut butters, which contain sugar and TFAs, and refrigerated *Real* peanut butter, which contains only peanuts and salt.

Hasn't Maria's nutritionist or medical doctor heard about trans fatty acids? Maria's food plan doesn't mention – even in fine print - *"partially hydrogenated vegetable oil"* or *"trans fatty acids."* In fact, by recommending margarine, reduced fat salad dressing, graham crackers, glazed doughnuts, pretzels, and just about any other processed food, the registered dietitian, in effect, was recommending that Maria load up on trans fatty acids – and, indeed, she was.

Earlier in this book (chapter 14), we presented the well-documented evidence of Mary G. Enig, Ph.D., who concluded that TFAs "decrease the response of red blood cells to insulin," and "increase blood insulin levels in humans in response to glucose load, increasing risk for diabetes."[2] Is this something Maria ought to know about?

We also learned from the Harvard Nurses' Health Study that the risk of a heart attack is *nearly double the average* if you get just 2 percent of total calories from TFAs. On the basis of solid evidence, Dr. Enig says the average American diet averages 11 percent of fat as trans fat – which would work out to be at least 4 percent of Maria's total daily calories.[3]

Maria's food plan says, "*You can ignore the total grams of sugar listed on the label,*" but warns against any and all fat: "Choose lower fat foods, such as snacks, cereals, dairy products, side dishes, deserts, and low-fat packaged meats with 3 grams or less of fat per serving."

Eating less fat and low fat can only mean ingesting more sugar. Maria's plan said, try "*light, low-fat, and fat free products in place of regular products.*" *Twizzlers* became Maria's low fat (less than 3 grams) snack of choice, providing a whopping 27 grams of carbohydrate if she could keep it down to just three (3) sticks.

High sugar *Pop Tarts*, with less than 3 grams of fat per serving, qualify under Maria's food plan, but nutritious, fatty avocados do not. Promoting sugar (ignore it) and warning only about fat (no more than 3 grams), Maria's food plan fails to even mention that essential fatty acids must come from the diet.

Wholesome natural fats are nutritious - excellent daily sources of a wide range of critically important nutrients. But encouraged to eat carbohydrates all day long, Maria is violating the food plan when she consumes her two daily tablespoons of milled flaxseed, which contain 10-12 grams of fat.

In October 2001, nine months after being diagnosed with Type II diabetes, Maria was near the end of the line. Suffering with anxiety, depression, high blood sugar, and cancerous abscesses, she and her well-meaning doctor were getting nowhere. Her misguided food plan, bad dietary habits, high fasting glucose, and high anxiety were teaming up – and taking over.

Without testing (women are tested less than men) we can only guess that Maria's triglycerides were high – well over 200 – and her HDL cholesterol was dangerously low - in the 30s. Undoubtedly, the stress hormone cortisol was high and protective DHEA was low. Maria's hormones were surely out of balance, and she was feeling sick.

A New Day

Scared, alone, and halfway to Texas on a rainy night in October, Maria decided it was time to quit running. She stopped to make a call, turned her car around, and headed home. She had one last cigarette and threw the pack away. Tired and weary, Maria was going to change her ways.

Right away, it was no more Coke, no more sugary orange juice, Twizzlers, Slim Jim's, Fudge Brownies, or visits to Burger King, McDonalds or Taco Bell. Her Country Crock, Uncle Ben's Quick Rice, Corn Pops and Spaghetti O's are things of the past.

Her sugar consumption dropped from a pound a day to virtually zero. In November and December, Maria restricted carbohydrates and lost 25 pounds. Going completely against the grain (pun intended), Maria eliminated all cake, cookies, chips and cereals.

In January, she began incorporating small amounts of brown rice, potatoes, and sprouted grain bread back into her diet. Her weight loss, promoted with L-Carnitine (two 500 mg capsules two or three times a day), is progressing the best way - slow and sure.

For breakfast, she is eating free-range brown eggs purchased at *Down Home Foods* in Wadena, Minnesota. She's a regular now, going in weekly for raw nuts, seeds, green tea, good quality cheese, those nutritious brown eggs, occasional brown rice, and frozen *Ezekiel 4.9 Sprouted Grain Bread* (made without flour).

She prepares a salad of leafy greens, cucumbers, tomatoes, garlic and onions almost everyday. Instead of croutons, she sprinkles two or three tablespoons of milled Canadian flaxseed on her salad and *Eden's Gomazio*, an ancient Japanese combination of sea salt and roasted sesame seeds.

Maria has switched to the full fat refrigerated salad dressings. She has learned to be leery of processed, packaged foods, almost anything, that is, not in the outer aisle of the supermarket. Maria has gotten into the habit of reading food labels, looking out for sugar, corn syrup, high fructose corn syrup, and partially hydrogenated vegetable oil.

When a Sebeka area sheep rancher sold lamb this winter, I split one with Maria and her sister. We also split some grass-fed beef from the Earth-Be-Glad Farm (see chapter 17). Instead of Corn Pops or *Toaster Strudels* for breakfast, Maria is now enjoying a 3 to 4 egg omelet with a lamb chop or two. (A hearty Minnesota winter breakfast.)

Her diet includes plenty of butter, fresh brown eggs, omega-3 rich grass-fed beef and lamb, chicken, tuna and other fish. She still restricts most grains, emphasizing brown rice and occasional toast made from certified organic *French Meadow* sourdough or low glycemic *Ezekiel 4.9*: flourless bread.

Her vegetables are low glycemic: Asparagus, brocolli, cauliflower, Brussel sprouts, cabbage, and leafy greens. Snacks include apples, grapefruit, oranges, peanuts, nuts (especially almonds) and cheese.

She is using *ConcenTrace* Mineral Drops daily. She squirts 10 or more drops to a glass of water or green tea and has about six glasses a day. Once magnesium deficient – with chronic, painful charley horses, Maria is slowly becoming magnesium sufficient and the charley horses are going away.

Green and herb tea and filtered water have replaced Coke and orange juice. She's adding slices of real lemon to her water and tea. The lemon provides flavor and is good for the liver, facilitating cellular hydration. Other daily supplements include mineral ascorbate

216

vitamin C with bioflavonoids, 500 mg tablets, up to four per day.

Maria takes vitamin E (mixed tocopherols), 400-800 IU's daily and Alpha Lipoic Acid, a free radical fighter that enhances the antioxidant activity of vitamins C and E. To promote circulation and reduce triglycerides that increase after meals, Maria takes *Quinn's Blend All-In-One*, the late Dick Quinn's near legendary combination of cayenne, garlic, and hawthorn.

The big surprise - discovered by chance - Olive Leaf Extract (18 percent strength) – 4 per day – dropped her blood sugar dramatically. Feeling a cold or flu coming on, Maria began taking 4 olive leaf extract capsules daily. Almost immediately, her fasting blood sugar, which had been in the 105-115 neighborhood, fell below 100.

Throughout March 2002, her fasting blood sugar was consistently below 100 – even in the upper 80s several days in a row - optimum blood sugar control on a high protein high natural fat diet. April 2, 2002, with spring in the air, Maria gets the best news of all.

She visits her doctor for an HbA1c test, which measures average blood sugar going back 120 days. The result - 5.4% - placed her in the "nondiabetic" category (3-6%) for the first time in 12 months. She weighed 218 pounds, a 100 pound drop in a year, much of it during the last 6 months.

Very surprised about Maria's excellent recent blood sugar history, her doctor speculated that it was the Glucophage - which she hadn't taken for 6 months - and the weight loss - accomplished only by eating hefty amounts of wholesome natural fat.

Yes - Maria has reversed Type II diabetes. Her cure: Tossing out the medical establishment's food plan and eating like her grandmother did on a farm years ago. Maria is still taking nutritional supplements, especially *ConcenTrace Mineral Drops,* vitamins C and E, and smaller doses of L-Carnitine and Olive Leaf Extract.

If you ask Maria what has made the biggest difference, she'll say: "It was changing my diet - getting away from the sugar, fast

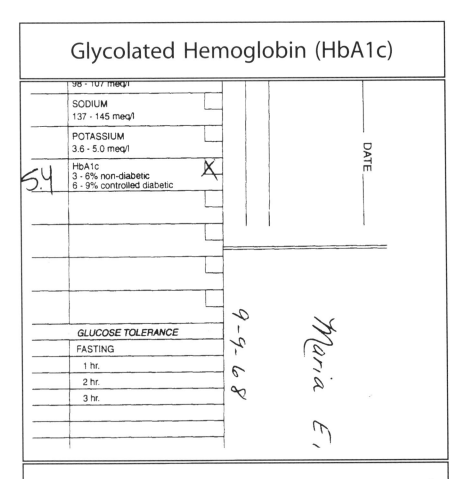

Glycolated Hemoglobin (HbA1c)

98 - 107 meq/l	
SODIUM 137 - 145 meq/l	
POTASSIUM 3.6 - 5.0 meq/l	
HbA1c 3 - 6% non-diabetic 6 - 9% controlled diabetic	X

5.4

DATE

GLUCOSE TOLERANCE
FASTING
1 hr.
2 hr.
3 hr.

9-9-68

Maria E.

HbA1c is a blood test that measures the average amount of glycated homoglobin (red blood cells damaged by sugar) in the bloodstream over a 4-month period. A high percentage indicates poor blood sugar control. Maria's result was **5.4**, which indicates that she is now "nondiabetic."

food, and all the junky carbs and snack foods I was eating."

Along with dramatically improved blood sugar readings, Maria feels calm – "more together." She sleeps much better and is looking forward to a Minnesota summer and the opportunity to get more daily outdoor exercise. The dietary changes have been relatively easy; preparing wholesome meals is a joy for Maria – something that is coming along naturally.

Maria is not out of the woods. Diabetic abscesses still flare and cancerous lesions remain a threat. While diabetes is technically gone, the damage in its wake – sugar and free radical induced glycosylation – is still taking a toll. Post diabetic detoxification is slow. Scores of small, red sores are slowly clearing from her back and arms.

Maria is managing stress by reordering her life with new priorities, fashioning new and hopeful plans for herself and her daughter. Weekly counseling for "*Post Traumatic Stress Syndrome*" is helping her reduce the stress of the past.

Maria, who has stopped running, is moving forward again. While too many people resist breaking old carbohydrate ways, Maria quickly embraced her own 21-Day plan and reversed Type II diabetes. She created her own food plan, rich in complete protein, low glycemic vegetables, omega-3, CLA, and nutritious saturated and monounsaturated fats.

Good nutrition - fabulous fat - is helping Maria live a full, healthy life once again.

21-Day Key principle #20:

Replace excess coffee and soft drinks with green tea, herb tea, and plenty of pure water.

High quality red wine and small amounts of alcohol are beneficial for some people.

Some people need to reduce or phase out coffee. Caffeine signals the liver to release stored sugar. Caffeine is a stimulant that in excess and over the long run may stress the adrenal glands, raise homocysteine, and increase blood sugar levels. Tea contains less caffeine and is less potentially harmful than coffee.

Green tea, the natural beverage of Japan, may even reduce your risk of both cancer and heart disease. All tea comes from the same plant (Camellia sinensus) but green tea is least processed and retains more health-promoting *polyphenols*, powerful antioxidants. *Sencha* is a high quality green tea. You steep sencha leaf just a few minutes and use hot – but not boiling – water.

If you are using liquid herb extracts - say cayenne for blood flow, hawthorn for the heart or gotu kola for peripheral circulation, you can add the drops to your steeping green or herb tea. Spiking tea with concentrated liquid herbal extracts adds interesting flavor and more certain medicinal benefits.

Green tea polyphenols include flavanels (catechins), flavonels, and proanthocyanidins. These antioxidants team up to ward off free radical oxidation and may be especially important in suppressing cancer formation. Green tea contains 35 to 52 percent catechins and flavonels, and each cup provides up to 400 mg of polyphenols.[4] Green tea also contains essential oils and a small amount of caffeine

Research in Japan has proven that green tea, consumed for centuries, is protecting the Japanese against various cancers. Other research suggests that polyphenols in green tea may help keep arteries free of plaque, as reported in Lancet, vol 349: 360-361, 1997). Green tea extract (powder) is also available in capsules or tablets.

Water is the best daily beverage for sure, especially mineral-rich hard water. Softened and fluoridated water should be avoided. It's almost mandatory these days for all of us to filter tap water to remove as many contaminants as possible but without reducing the mineral content.

Distilled and reverse-osmosis water are pure, but you must restore the essential minerals with *ConcenTrace* liquid minerals. *ConcenTrace* is a concentrated magnesium-emphasized liquid trace mineral product that safely provides all minerals in a ready-to-absorb "ionic" form (see chapter 7).

Remember to flavor your water and increase cell hydration with a pinch of lemon or lime. Also, you can add those herbal extracts to your water too. Starting out each day with a tall glass of mineral water is a critically important habit to form. Don't force yourself to drink 6-8 glasses a day; just be sure to have pure water (with added minerals) available to drink throughout the day.

A balanced plant and animal whole foods diet reduces thirst. Excess water may needlessly stress the kidneys. And avoid water, especially ice water, 30 minutes before and after meals. Excess water at mealtime can dilute stomach acid and strain the digestive system.[4] It's probably best to avoid any liquids while eating – with the possible exception of a glass or two of high quality red wine.

Alcohol in small amounts can be beneficial as part of a healthy heart program. In *50 Ways To A Healthy Heart*, Christian Barnard, M.D. cites evidence (more than 60 studies) that drinking two glasses of good quality red wine daily reduces the risk of heart disease up to 40 percent. Red wine also reduces the risk of cancer.

According to Barnard, drinking one or two glasses of beer daily (unpasteurized *Guinness* is best) may also reduce the risk of heart disease. The studies he cites show no benefit drinking hard liquor or drinking more than two glasses of red wine daily. Alcohol has a very narrow range of benefit; even a little too much can damage the liver.

This might be a good time to make another plug for Julia Ross's book, *Diet Cure*. Ross deals with the topic of addiction –alcohol and sugar. She provides detailed advice for people plagued with cravings for sweets, starches, and alcohol. She recommends L-glutamine, for example, for low blood sugar-related (hypoglycemia) carbohydrate cravings.

Hence, the recommendation to drink alcohol does not apply to people with sugar cravings, upset body chemistry, or nutritional deficiencies. Small amounts of alcohol – especially red wine – are beneficial in the context of an overall healthy lifestyle that includes stress reduction, whole foods, and pleasurable exercise (the Crete lifestyle comes to mind).

In *Nourishing Traditions*, Sally Fallon provides recipes for preparing traditional lacto-fermented beverages, made from fruits, the sap of trees, herbs, and grain. For centuries, these drinks have been used to strengthen the sick, enhance digestion, and promote overall well being. Traditional root beer and ginger brew, for example, were considered superior to plain water in their ability to relieve thirst and rejuvenate the body.

The bottom line with beverages and heart disease is to absolutely limit fruit juices and both sugary and so-called "diet" soft drinks. All are extremely bad for you – whether they contain 9 teaspoons of sugar or some synthetic chemical sweetener. Fruit juices and soft drinks upset body chemistry and create life threatening sugar cravings and blood sugar disorders.

Just ask Maria.

NEED HELP WITH WEIGHT LOSS?

New Diet Revolution (Atkins) and *The Diet Cure* (Ross) are excellent overall reference books for promoting good eating habits and extending wellness and longevity. In essence, they are anti-diet books – food for thought for everyone.

Dr. Atkins' New Diet Revolution is the best selling book of all time, after the Judeo-Christian bible. It is a mistake to judge Dr. Atkins by what you may have heard in the media. He is not a "fat doctor" and the Atkins diet is not a "fad diet." Those characterizations are simply expressions of media ignorance. Dr. Atkins is trained in cardiology (Yale) and has decades of clinical experience with thousands of patients. Atkins offers a 1910 style-eating plan.

The Atkins plan is not a high protein diet; it is a balanced fat and protein diet with low glycemic index carbohydrates appropriate to your metabolism. Atkins endorses eating healthy green leafy vegetables, cabbage salads, and a wide range of low glycemic vegetables. He advises against eating sugar, refined carbohydrates, excess starchy carbohydrates, grains, and fast and junk foods.

The Diet Cure by Julia Ross, MA, is an excellent complement to the Atkins book and is based on ten years of proven clinical results. Julia Ross is a pioneer in the field of nutritional psychology. Her *Diet Cure* is based on correcting impaired brain chemistry challenged by too much dieting, inadequate protein, unstable blood sugar, low thyroid function, hormonal irregularities, food addictions and a deficiency of natural fat.

Chapter 21

-------- 🪢 --------

Summary of coronary heart disease risk factors

"The supposed mission of the National Cholesterol Education Program is to get Americans to reduce their cholesterol levels in order to reduce the incidence of heart disease, even though a direct link between high cholesterol and dying from a heart attack has never been made."

John R. Lee, M.D.

Recently, my older brother Jim, age 59, talked to his doctor about the results of his lipid evaluation. His doctor did not mention Jim's high normal fasting glucose (104), elevated triglycerides (207), and relatively low HDL cholesterol (44). Noting only Jim's high total cholesterol (308), the doctor recommended Zocor, a cholesterol-lowering drug.

Since most people who die of heart attacks have low or average levels of cholesterol, reducing Jim's relatively high cholesterol will do little or possibly nothing to reduce Jim's risk of heart disease. The doctor could have served Jim better by focusing on his high normal fasting blood sugar, elevated triglycerides, and low HDL.

"Cholesterol is overemphasized to the point where the other risk factors are too often ignored," says Robert C. Atkins, M.D. This hurts two groups of people: Those with high cholesterol who are overtreated with drugs, and those with low and average cholesterol who, mistakenly, are not treated at all.

In the Cardiovascular Health Study discussed in chapter 11, we learned that high fasting glucose was "significantly and independently associated with mortality." High blood cholesterol was not. In fact, people with higher LDL cholesterol (more than 153 mg/dl) had just two thirds of the mortality risk of those with so-called desirable levels - less than 96 mg/dl.

In the long term Framingham Study, we learned that declining cholesterol over time was the best predictor of overall mortality. "For each 1 mg/dl drop of cholesterol, there was an 11 percent increase in coronary and total mortality."

With elevated triglycerides (207) and relatively low HDL cholesterol (44), my brother Jim is already at risk of heart disease. Forcing his LDL cholesterol down with Zocor would not address the greatest risk Jim faces: A 4.7 ratio of triglycerides to HDL, and fasting glucose that has climbed into the high normal range (104).

Only excess carbohydrates- especially simple sugars – raise glucose. High glucose levels are associated with elevated triglycerides and low HDL cholesterol. Jim doesn't need Zocor; instead he needed to replace the English muffins and other enriched flour products that he had been eating at breakfast with fresh farm eggs.

A truck driver who rises every morning when some people are just getting to bed, Jim was drinking too much coffee (all day long), eating too much bread, and was having trouble resisting the junky snacks that line the shelves of truck stops and convenience stores.

On the plus side, his good overall nutrition and nutritional supplement program are reflected in his low C-reactive protein (0.8) and reasonably safe homocysteine level (8.3).

Jim's best chance of reducing his risk of a heart attack is by restricting carbohydrates, especially simple sugars and starches, and by replacing the excess coffee with herb and green tea. Finally, daily exercise - walking around the school running track several times - would make a big difference. Given the family history on our father's side of the family, these are reasonable things to do.

21-Day Plan key principle #21

Ask your doctor for a complete lipid evaluation.

"It's a national scandal. I'd estimate that only 5 percent of doctors in the United States are using these specialized blood tests."

Thomas Yannios, M.D.

"Lab test results by themselves are useless, however; you must have them analyzed by a doctor who recognizes that there are many paths to heart disease."

Robert C. Atkins, M.D.

Summary CHD Risk Factors

Risk Factor	Optimum	Risk	Serious Risk
C-Reactive Protein	-	>2.5	>6.5
Fasting Glucose	87	>100	>110
Fibrinogen	<235	>235	>350
Homocystine	<8	>8	>12
Lipoprotein(a)	<20	>25	30
LDL Cholesterol	-	>240	-
Total Cholesterol	-	>350	-
HDL (men)	>60	<60	<40
HDL (women)	>70	<70	<50
Triglycerides (TG)	<100	>100	>150

The above tests can be ordered during "blood work." Costs vary. If your insurance company will not pay for all tests, discuss the relative importance of each one with you doctor. You may have to consider paying for at least one additional test or two.

Approximate Test Costs In Minnesota:

Cholesterol/TG panel	$76
C-Reactive Protein	$37
Fasting glucose	$22
Glucose Tolerance Test 3-hr	$86
Homocysteine	$128
HDL Cholesterol	$43
Lipoprotein(a)	$90
Triglycerides	$11

You may want to schedule your blood work or lipid evaluation in the A.M. In order to get valid baseline values, you must fast (water only) at least 12 hours before blood is drawn.

If you have a family history of premature coronary heart disease or diabetes, evaluating your risk is especially important. Let the doctor know that you need as much information as possible in order to (1) learn what is going on in your arteries, and (2) take preventive measures to protect yourself.

A "lipid panel" typically includes tests for total cholesterol, LDL cholesterol, HDL cholesterol and triglycerides. Total cholesterol is a composite number that includes LDL (low density lipoprotein), IDL (intermediate density lipoprotein), VLDL (very low density lipoprotein) and HDL (high density lipoprotein).

Total cholesterol (TC) and triglycerides (TG) are measured directly from your blood sample. Here's how it's currently done. After TC and TG are measured, LDL, VLDL, and IDL float to the top and are removed from the sample. HDL remains in solution and is measured directly.

Next, non-HDL is calculated. The formula goes like this: IDL and VLDL = TG divided by five. With these three numbers known (TG divided by 5, TC, and HDL), LDL can be calculated. (This method is accurate when triglycerides are less than 400.)

HDL cholesterol is most important. HDL protects us from heart attacks. You want as much HDL as possible. HDL is reverse transport – garbage trucks hauling cholesterol back to the liver for recycling. HDL reuptakes cholesterol from plaque.

HDL of 60 or more protects men – 70 or more protects women. Men with readings below 40 and women below 50 are at much greater risk of heart disease.

In *The Heart Disease Breakthrough,* Thomas Yannios, M.D., wrote, "The physicians Health Study also produced interesting results. Though heart attack victims were found to have the same cholesterol levels as the control population, people developing heart attacks were distinguishable by their low HDL levels. Yet most therapy for heart disease prevention is directed at lowering LDL – rather than raising HDL."

Triglycerides, ideally, are under 100 mg/dl. The more carbohydrates you eat, the greater your triglycerides. Readings above 100 signal increased risk of CHD. Risk is linear – the higher the number, the greater the risk, especially for women. For both men and women, readings above 150 signal serious increased risk of coronary heart disease. (See 21-Day Plan, key principle #10.)

The **TG/HDL ratio** is the very best predictor of heart attack risk. You can calculate the TG/HDL ratio by dividing triglycerides by HDL. For example, if your triglycerides are 80 and your HDL is 80, your TG/HDL ratio is 1:1, which is ideal. If your triglycerides are 180 and your HDL is 60, the ratio is 3:1 (180 divided by 60 = 3). If your TG is 207 and your HDL is 44, the result is 4.7 (nearly 5:1). A ratio this high represents serious increased risk of heart disease.

In most people, a high carbohydrate low fat diet will increase triglycerides and reduce protective HDL. When triglycerides go up, HDL goes down. This is one of the most consistent antagonisms you will find in blood work. If you have high triglycerides and low HDL, you can assume that LDL cholesterol is more likely to oxidize (become rancid or damaged).

Currently, there is no test for oxidized cholesterol, but the presence of high triglycerides signals the increased risk of oxidized LDL

– whether LDL is high or not. Elevated TC and elevated LDL are not major independent risk factor for heart disease. Don't let your doctor focus on lowering total cholesterol, and then ignore your overall lipid picture.

You can die of heart disease with high or low LDL. In *Heart Disease Breakthrough*, Thomas Yannios, MD, wrote, "In other studies of people who developed heart disease, 46 percent had LDL levels below 160 – the level at which the National Cholesterol Education Program recommends no further intervention beyond a prudent diet."[1]

Many doctors are saying that healthy people should simply ignore total cholesterol if it's below 300 mg/dl. "In the case of older people, there is absolutely no relevant study concerning cholesterol as a factor for heart and circulatory problems," wrote Christian Bernard, M.D., in his book, *50 Ways To A Healthy Heart.*

C-reactive Protein (CRP) is produced by the liver in response to inflammation in the arteries. If monitored early enough, elevated CRP can be an early warning of heart attack risk – 6 or more years in advance. A faulty diet can damage or "inflame" arterial tissue, weaken the immune system, and make the body vulnerable to bacterial or viral infections.

Robert C. Atkins, M.D., recommends low-dose aspirin (81 mg) to lower dangerously high CRP levels. Eating deep sea fish and using fish oil supplements can reduce inflammation in the heart and arteries. See 21-Day Plan, key principle #19.

Aspirin may be recommended to help prevent blood clots in late stage active heart disease or to lower elevated CRP, but the scientific evidence in support of daily aspirin is inconclusive.

Recent meta-analyses of the anti-platelet activity of aspirin suggest that the value of aspirin's effectiveness and safety have been overvalued. According to Dr. John G.F. Cleland, "All the large long term trials of aspirin after myocardial infarction show no effect on mortality." Dr. Cleland states that aspirin may simply change the way vascular events present themselves; i.e., a reduction in nonfatal events and an increase in sudden death.[2]

Diets emphasizing high quality protein and natural fat and nutritional supplementation are the best long term anti-blood clot strategies. On a regular basis, use avocados, flaxseed/oil, cold-water deep-sea fish/oil, magnesium and trace minerals, cayenne, ginger, garlic, onion, and vitamins C and E.

These nutrients promote free flowing blood and provide a wide range of other nutrients. Aspirin, as we know, has no nutritional value, and increases the risk of hemorrhaging-type strokes. To succeed, however, we must replace refined carbohydrates with a variety of low glycemic vegetables and eliminate trans fatty acids from the diet.

Fasting glucose is a measurement of how well your body is managing glucose (blood sugar). Ideal fasting glucose is 87.1. High normal (between 100 and 109) represents significant increased risk of CHD. Impaired blood sugar control leads to diabetes. More than 80 percent of Type II diabetics die of heart disease. See 21-Day Plan, key principle #10.

Fibrinogen is the protein molecule that traps the red blood cells and locks them into a blood clot. The more fibrinogen - the thicker the blood. Thicker blood flows less easily, especially through partially blocked arteries. Fibrinogen, especially in combination with other risk factors, is a predictive risk factor for coronary heart disease.

Testing for fibrinogen is easy and inexpensive; however, your doctor may hesitate to order the test because fibrinogen levels fluctuate a lot – rising and falling rapidly in response to many stimuli. Stress, trauma, infections and recent heart attacks, for example, all cause fibrinogen to increase.

But, consistent elevated fibrinogen - highest third in the range - conveys a 250 percent increased risk of CHD compared to levels in the lowest third. People with active heart disease and high levels of fibrinogen are in danger of disease instability and a dramatically increased chance of repeated clotting and blockages.[3]

Platelets are tiny cells that are attracted to injured tissue of any kind, where they accumulate to stop the flow of blood and then chemically stimulate the clotting cascade. Multiple clotting factors are then sequentially activated to convert circulating fibrinogen into the latticework of fibers called fibrin.

Homocysteine, a by-product of amino acid metabolism, is normally cleared rapidly from the bloodstream. Elevated homocysteine is a result of vitamin deficiency, especially folic acid and vitamins B-6 and B-12. Elevated homocysteine damages arteries and dramatically increases the risk of heart attack and stroke. Levels greater than 8 micomoles per deciliter signal increased risk of heart disease. See 21-Day Plan, key principle #3.

Lipoprotein(a) has been called the "heart attack" cholesterol. Lipoprotein(a) is actually a sticky protein that attaches to LDL and accumulates rapidly at the site of arterial lesions or ruptured plaque. Readings of 30 or more indicate serious risk of heart disease, especially in the presence of elevated fibrinogen (>350).

Lipoprotein(a) promotes blood-clotting and inhibits plasminogen, your body's natural clot-dissolving enzyme. Eating large amounts of margarine and partially hydrogenated fats are known to increase lipoprotein(a). Butter and saturated fats reduce lipoprotein(a). See 21-Day Plan, key principle #14.

For a detailed analysis of all 7 sub-fractions of LDL and 3 types of HDL, read *The Heart Disease Breakthrough* by Thomas Yannios, M.D. Learning about and testing for these sub-fractions is critically important for patients with "good numbers" but who have persistent, aggressive coronary heart disease. Dr. Yannios goes beyond "good" and "bad" cholesterol and describes genetically determined LDL and HDL particle characteristics.

LDL is a particle that consists of cholesterol and varying amounts of triglycerides. Steering the LDL is a protein called, "Apoprotein B." Because each LDL particle has an Apoprotein B marker, the number of LDL particles can be counted in a laboratory test. The cholesterol level in routine tests (milligrams of cholesterol in a given volume of blood) does not reveal the number or size of the particles.

At the same cholesterol level in the blood – say 220 mg/dl – a person can have a different distribution of LDL particle count and density (size). LDL "B" particles, for example, are smaller, more dense, and contain more triglycerides, which, induce chemical changes that make the LDL more much more likely to oxidize and damage artery walls.

If your triglycerides are low (below 75), your LDL is most likely subclass A. If your triglycerides are high (over 180), your LDL is most likely small, dense subclass B. High triglycerides are a warning sign that you may have this more oxidized-prone form of LDL cholesterol, regardless of the level of cholesterol circulating in the blood.

Once oxidized, LDL is more likely to attract foam cells, clotting factors and develop into atherosclerotic plaque. While elevated triglycerides suggest the presence of these more malignant "B" particles, only further laboratory testing can document their presence and exact number.

As Dr. Yannios points out, "many of the people with the most aggressive heart disease have total cholesterols under 200." They could more accurately assess their risk by carefully scrutinizing glucose and triglycerides levels or, even better, by testing specifically to identify LDL, subclass B.[3]

Less triglycerides available to the liver means less triglycerides in the LDL particle. Reducing your intake of carbohydrates reduces the amount of glucose available to the liver. Restricting carbohydrates – especially simple sugar and high glycemic grains – is the best way of reducing your risk of heart disease.

Bibliography

Atkins, Robert C., M.D. *Age Defying Diet Revolution*. New York: St Martin's Press, 2000.

Atkins, Robert C., M.D. *Health Revelations Newsletter*. Maryland: Agora Inc.

Appleton, Nancy Ph.D. *Lick The Sugar Habit*. New York: Avery Publishing Group, 1996.

Barnard, Christiaan, M.D. *50 Ways to a Healthy Heart*. London: Thorsons, 2001.

Bergner, Paul *The Healing Power of Minerals*. California: Prima Publishing, 1997.

Bland, Jeffrey S., Ph.D. *Genetic Nutritioneering*. Los Angeles: Keats Publishing, 1999.

Bucco, Gloria *"The Heart of the Matter,"* Delicious Living, February 2001, pp. 42-45.

Challem, Jack; Berkson, Burton M.D.; and Smith, Melissa Diane. *Syndrome X*. New York: John Wiley & Sons, 2000.

Crayhon, Robert M.S. *The Carnitine Miracle*. New York: M. Evans and Company, Inc., 1998.

DeFelice, Stephen L. M.D. *The Carnitine Defense*. USA: Rodale Press Inc., 1999.

Douglass, William Campbell M.D. Dr. William Campbell Douglass' *Real Health Newsletter*. Maryland: Agora Inc.

Duke, James A. Ph.D. *The Green Pharmacy*. Pennsylvania: Rodale Press, 1997.

Enig, Mary Ph.D. *Know Your Fats: The Complete Primer for Understanding the Nutrition of Fats, Oils, and Cholesterol*. Maryland: Bethesda Press, 2000.

Fallon, Sally *Nourishing Traditions*. Washington D.C.: New Trends Publishing, 1999.

Fallon, Sally; Enig, Mary *"What Causes Heart Disease?"* Wise Traditions, Spring 2001, pp.14-26.

Fallon, Sally; Enig, Mary *"Guts and Grease"* Wise Traditions, Spring 2001, pp. 40-47.

Felix, Clara *The Felix Letter: A Commentary on Nutrition*. California: Publisher, Clara Felix.

Lee, John R. M.D. *Common Sense Guide to a Healthy Heart.* Arizona: Hormones Ect. Inc., 1999.

Lee, John R. M.D. *What Your Doctor May Not Tell You About Menopause.* New York: Warner Books Inc., 1996.

Lee, John R. M.D. *http://www.johnleemd.com* "HRT and Breast Cancer Déjà vu."

Ley-Jacobs, Beth M. Ph.D. *DHA: The Magnificent Marine Oil.* California: BL Publications, 1999.

Medosa, Rick *http://www.mendosa.com* "Glycemic Index Lists."

Mercola, Joseph M.D. *http://www.mercola.com* "How to Best Test for Undiagnosed Diabetes."

McCully, Kilmer M.D. *The Heart Revolution.* New York: HarperCollins Publishers, Inc., 1999.

Moore, Thomas J. *"The Cholesterol Myth,"* The Atlantic Monthly, September 1989, pp. 37-69.

Pierce, James B., Ph.D. *Heart Healthy Magnesium.* New York: Avery Publishing Group, 1994.

Reaven, Gerald M.D.; Strom, Terry Kristen M.B.A.; and Fox, Barry Ph.D. *Syndrome X - The Silent Killer: The New Heart Disease Risk.* New York: Simon and Schuster, 2000.

Robinson, Jo *http://www.eatwild.com* "Super Healthy Milk."

Ross, Julia M.A. *The Diet Cure.* New York: Penguin Putnam Inc., 1999.

Sardi, Bill *"The Cholesterol Conundrum,"* Nutrition Science News, September 1998, pp. 492-498.

Schneider, Mier; Maureen Larkin *The Handbook of Self-Healing.* New York: Penguin Books Inc., 1994.

Shealy, C. Norman M.D., Ph.D. *Sacred Healing: The Curing Power of Energy and Spirituality.* Boston: Element Books Inc., 1999.

Stacey, Michelle *"The Rise and fall of Kilmer McCully,"* New York Times Magazine, August 9, 1997, pp. 27-29.

Uffe, Ravnskov, M.D. PhD. *The Cholesterol Myths.* Washington DC: New Trends Publishing Inc., 2000.

Wayne, Howard H. M.D., F.A.C.C. *How to Protect your Heart From Your Doctor.* California: Capra Press, 1994.

Notes

Introduction

1. Peskin, Brian Scott. *Beyond The Zone.* Houston: Noble Publishing, 2000, p. 18.
2. Atkins, Robert C., M.D. *Dr. Atkins Age-Defying Diet Revolution.* New York: St Martin's Press, 2000, p. 6.
3. Ibid, p. 7.
   Fallon, Sally; Enig, Mary G., Ph.D. *"What Causes Heart Disease?"* Wise Traditions, Spring 2001, p. 15.
4. Ibid.
5. Barnard, Christian, M.D. *50 Ways To A Healthy Heart.* London: Thorsons, 2001, p. cbxiii.
6. Atkins, *Dr. Atkins Age-Defying Diet Revolution,* p. 9.
7. Yannios, Thomas, M.D. *The Heart Disease Breakthrough.* New York: John Wiley & Sons, 1999, p. 65.
8. Atkins, *Dr. Atkins Age-Defying Diet Revolution,* p. 9.
9. Yannios, p. 34.
10. Lee, John R. M.D. *Common Sense Guide to a Healthy Heart.* Phoenix: Hormones Etc. Inc., 1999, pp. 7-8
11. Wayne, Howard H. M.D. *How to Protect your Heart From Your Doctor.* Santa Barbara: Capra Press, 1994, p. 14.
12. Yannios, pp. 12-13.
13. Ibid, p. 10.
14. McCully, Kilmer, M.D. *The Heart Revolution.* New York: HarperCollins Publishers, Inc., 1999, p. 13.
15. Howard, p. 68.
16. Enig, Mary G. Ph.D. *Know Your Fats: The Complete Primer for Understanding the Nutrition of Fats, Oils, and Cholesterol.* Silver Springs: Bethesda Press, 2000, p.92
17. Peskin, pp. 21-27.
18. Barnard, p. xiv.

Chapter 1

1. Fallon, Sally; Enig, Mary G., Ph.D., *"What Causes Heart Disease?"* p. 19
2. Ibid, p. 49.
3. Atkins, *Dr. Atkins Age-Defying Diet Revolution,* p. 25.
4. DeFelice, *The Carnitine Defense,* p. 11
   Yannios, *The Heart Disease Breakthrough,* pp. 26-28.

Fallon, Sally; Enig, Mary G., Ph.D., *"What Causes Heart Disease?"* p. 17

5. Enig, *Know Your Fats* pp. 56 & 187.
6. Ibid, p. 56.
7. Ibid, p. 50.
8. Wayne, *How to Protect your Heart From Your Doctor, p. ???*.
9. Fallon, Sally. *Nourishing Traditions.* Washington D.C.: New Trends Publishing, 1999, p. 445.
10. Ibid, p. 436.
11. Uffe, Ravnskov, M.D., PhD. *The Cholesterol Myths.* Washington DC: New Trends Publishing Inc., 2000, p. 45.
12. Ibid, p. 41.
13. Bland, Jeffrey S., Ph.D. *Genetic Nutritioneering.* Los Angeles: Keats Publishing, 1999, p. 146.
14. Ibid.
15. Shealy, C. Norman M.D., Ph.D. *Sacred Healing: The Curing Power of Energy and Spirituality.* Boston: Element Books Inc., 1999, p. xxii
16. Bland, p. 148.
17. Moore, Thomas J. *"The Cholesterol Myth."* The Atlantic Monthly, September 1989, p. 38.
18. Ibid.
19. Atkins, Robert C., M.D. *Health Revelations Newsletter.* Maryland: Agora Inc., June 2002.
20. Yannios, pp. 139-146.

Chapter 2

1. Moore, *"The Cholesterol Myth,"* p. 39.
2. Ibid, p. 40.
3. Ibid.
4. Ibid.
5. Moore, p. 42
6. Ravnskov, *The Cholesterol Myths,* p. 56.
7. Yannios, *The Heart Disease Breakthrough,* p. 28.
8. Ibid.
9. Ravnskov, p. 57
10. Sardi, Bill, *"The Cholesterol Conundrum."* Nutrition Science News, September 1998, pp. 492-493.
11. Ravnskov, p. 59
12. Moore, p. 65.
13. Ibid, p. 42
14. Fallon, *Nourishing Traditions,* p. 5.

Chapter 3

1. McCully, Kilmer, M.D., *The Heart Revolution,* p. 9.
2. Ibid, p. 10.
3. Bucco, Gloria *"The Heart of the Matter,"* <u>Delicious Living,</u> February 2001, p. 44.
4. Stacey, Michelle *"The Rise and fall of Kilmer McCully."* <u>New York Times Magazine,</u> August 9, 1997, p. 28.
5. McCully, p. *mcxviii.*
6. Stacey, p. 28.
7. Ibid, p. 29.
8. Ibid, p.28
9. Ibid.
10. DeFelice, *The Carnitine Defense,* p. 129.
11. Stacey, p. 29.
12. Ibid, p. 28.
13. Ibid.
14. Ibid.
15. Atkins, *Dr. Atkins Age-Defying Revolution*, p. 32.
16. McCully, p. 23.
17. DeFelice, p. 130.
18. Ibid, p. 131.
19. Ibid.
20. McCully, p. 11.
21. Yannios, *The Heart Disease Breakthrough,* p. 40.
22. Atkins, *Dr. Atkins Age-Defying Revolution*, p. 32.
23. Ibid.
24. Yannios, p. 40.
25. Ibid, p. 41

Chapter 4

1. Moore, *"The Cholesterol Myth,"* pp. 44-46.
2. Ravnskov, *The Cholesterol Myths,* p. 56.
3. Ibid, p.162.
4. Moore, p. 47.
5. Ravnskov, p. 161
6. Ibid, p. 162.
7. Moore, p. 47
8. McCully, *The Heart Revolution*, p. 18.
9. Ravnskov, p. 16.
10. DeFelice, *The Carnitine Defense,* p. 90.

Chapter 5

1. Ravnskov, *The Cholesterol Myths,* p. 165.
2. Ibid, p. 167.
3. Wayne, *How to Protect your Heart From Your Doctor,* p. 76.
4. Ibid, p. 75.
5. Ibid.
6. Ibid.
7. Ravnskov, *The Cholesterol Myths,* p. 168.
8. Wayne, p. 73.
9. Ibid.
10. Ravnskov, p. 168.
11. Moore, "*The Cholesterol Myth,*" p. 51.
12. Wayne, p. 75.
13. Yannios, *The Heart Disease Breakthrough,* p. 27.
14. Ravnskov, p. 171.
15. Barnard, Christian, M.D., *50 Ways To A Healthy Heart, p. 30.*
16. DeFelice, *The Carnitine Defense,* p. 111.
17. Ibid, p 118.
18. Ibid.
19. Ibid, p. 119.
20. Ibid. p. 120.
21. Ibid, p. 116.
22. Ibid, p. 123.

Chapter 6

1. Moore, "*The Cholesterol Myth,*" p. 56.
2. Ibid.
3. Wayne, *How to Protect your Heart From Your Doctor,* p. 80.
4. Yannios, *The Heart Disease Breakthrough,* pp. 70-71.
5. Ibid, p. 129.
6. Wayne, p. 72.
7. Ravnskov, *The Cholesterol Myths,* p. 168.
8. Moore, p. 51.
9. Ibid, p. 52.
10. Fallon, *Nourishing Traditions,* p. 34.
11. Robinson, Jo http://www.eatwild.com "Super Healthy Milk," p. 1
12. Ibid, p. 2.
13. Ibid, p. 3.
14. Lee, John R. M.D. *Common Sense Guide to a Healthy Heart* Phoenix: Hormones Etc. Inc., 1999, p. 13.
15. Ibid, p. 14.

Chapter 7

1. Appleton, Nancy Ph.D. *Lick The Sugar Habit.* New York: Avery Publishing Group, 1996, p. 11.
   Peskin, *Beyond The Zone*, pp. 4-6.
2. Appleton, p.7.
3. Ibid, p. 18
4. Challem, Jack; Berkson, Burton M.D.; and Smith, Melissa Diane, p.40.
   Syndrome X. New York: John Wiley & Sons, 2000, p. 40.
5. Appleton, p. 11.
6. Ibid, p. 88.
   Challem, Jack; Berkson, Burton M.D.; and Smith, Melissa Diane. *Syndrome X.* New York: John Wiley & Sons, 2000, p. 44.
7. Ibid, p. 46.
8. Appleton, p. 10.
9. Ibid, p. 57.
10. Enig, Know Your Fats, p. 43
11. Appleton, p. 88.
12. Ibid, pp. 25-27. *American Journal of Clinical Nutrition* 1989; 50 (5): 955-61).
13. Appleton, p. 27
14. Newcorn, Claudia D. "For Your Heart's Health," *Minneapolis/St. Paul Business to Business Journal*, p.7
15. Ibid.

Chapter 8

1. Atkins, *Dr. Atkins Age-Defying Revolution*, p. 15.
2. Ibid, p. 16.
3. Ibid.
4. Ibid.
5. Ibid.
6. McCully, *The Heart Revolution*, p. 50.
7. Ibid, p. 51.
8. Ibid, p. 68
9. Challem, Jack; Berkson, Burton M.D.; and Smith, Melissa Diane, Syndrome X, p. 84.
10. Mercola, Joseph M.D. http://www.mercola.com Issue #254, "How to Best Test for Undiagnosed Diabetes."
11. Ibid.
12. Reaven, Gerald M.D.; Strom, Terry Kristen M.B.A.; and Fox, Barry Ph.D. *Syndrome X-The Silent Killer: The new Heart Disease Risk* New York: Simon and Schuster, 2000, p. 153
13. Atkins, *Dr. Atkins Age-Defying Revolution*, p. 53.
14. Ibid, p. 44.
15. Challem, and others, p. 18.

Chapter 9

1. Challem, Jack; Berkson, Burton M.D.; and Smith, Melissa Diane, Syndrome X, pp. 86-87.
2. Ibid, pp. 82-83.

Chapter 10

1. Reaven, Gerald M.D.; Strom, Terry Kristen M.B.A.; and Fox, Barry Ph.D. *Syndrome X-The Silent Killer, p. 18.*
2. Challem, Jack; Berkson, Burton M.D.; and Smith, Melissa Diane, *Syndrome X*, p. 48.
3. Ibid, p. 20.
4. Atkins, *Dr. Atkins Age-Defying Revolution*, p. 24.
5. Ibid, p. 25.
6. Ibid, p. 26.
7. Yannios, *The Heart Disease Breakthrough*, pp. 92-94.
8. Ibid.
9. Atkins, *Dr. Atkins Age-Defying Revolution*, pp. 24-25.
10. Ibid.
11. Ibid.
12. Reaven, and others, p. 152
13. Ibid, pp.44-45.
14. Challem, et.al., p. 31.
15. Atkins, *Dr. Atkins Age-Defying Revolution*, p. 136.

Chapter 11

1. Felix, Clara *The Felix Letter: A Commentary on Nutrition.* California: Publisher, Clara Felix, Issue #102, 1999.
2. Ibid.
3. Ibid.
4. Atkins, *Dr. Atkins Age-Defying Revolution*, p. 52.
5. Ibid, p. 49.
6. Ibid, p. 54.
7. Atkins, Robert C., M.D. *Health Revelations Newsletter*. Maryland: Agora Inc., April 2001.
8. Ibid.
9. Atkins, *Dr. Atkins Age-Defying Revolution*, p. 54.
10. Atkins, *Health Revelations Newsletter*, April 2001.
11. Atkins, *Dr. Atkins Age-Defying Revolution*, p. 56.
12. Challem, Jack; Berkson, Burton M.D.; and Smith, Melissa Diane, *Syndrome X*, p. 43.
13. Atkins, *Dr. Atkins Age-Defying Revolution*, p. 60.
14. Ibid, p. 66.
15. Douglass, William Campbell M.D. *Real Health Newsletter*. Maryland: Agora

Inc., December 2001.

16. Schneider, Mier; Maureen Larkin *The Handbook of Self-Healing.* New York: Penguin Books Inc, 1994, p. 266.

17. Douglass, *Real Health Newsletter*, December 2001.

18. Ibid.

19. Ibid.

20. Atkins, *Health Revelations Newsletter,* November 2000.

21. Scheider, p. 266.

Chapter 12

1. Felix, Clara *The Felix Letter,* Issue #102.

2. Fallon, Sally. *Nourishing Traditions,* pp. 21-25.

3. Ibid, p 476.

4. Ibid, pp. 452-453.

5. Ibid, pp. 452-454.

6. Ibid, p. 453.

7. Ibid.

Chapter 13

1. Fallon, Sally; Enig, Mary *"Guts and Grease,"* <u>Wise Traditions.</u> Spring 2001, p. 40.

2. Ibid, p. 43.

3. Ibid, p. 42.

4. Ibid, p. 45.

5. Ibid, p. 41.

6. Enig, *Know Your Fats*, p. 96.

7. Ibid.

8. Fallon, *Nourishing Traditions*, p. 5.

9. Enig, *Know Your Fats,* pp. 93-96.

10. Fallon, *Nourishing Traditions*, p. 17.

11. Enig, *Know Your Fats,* p. 166.

12. Ibid, p. 167.

13. Atkins, *Age Defying Diet Revolution*, p. 7.

14. Enig, *Know Your Fats,* pp. 133 & 193.

Chapter 14

1. Fallon, *Nourishing Traditions,* p. 14.

2. Enig, *Know Your Fats*, p. 21.

3. Ibid, p. 44

4. Atkins, *Age Defying Diet Revolution*, p. 187.

5. Ibid.

6. Enig, *Know Your Fats*, pp. 85-87.

7. Ibid, p. 44.
8. Ibid, p. 43.
9. Ibid, p. 85
10. Ibid, p. 42.
11. Yannios, *Heart Disease Breakthrough,* p. 39.
12. Ibid, p. 55.
13. Ibid, p. 57.
14. Atkins, *Age Defying Diet Revolution*, p. 28.
15. Ibid, p. 29.
16. Enig, *Know Your Fats*, p. 101.
17. Ibid, p. 45.
18. Ibid, pp. 39.
19. Ibid, pp. 42-44.

Chapter 15

1. Fallon, *Nourishing Traditions,* pp. 8-9.
2. Ibid, p. 18.
3. Ibid.
4. Enig, *Know Your Fats*, p. 37.
5. Fallon, *Nourishing Traditions*, p. 19.
6. Ibid.
7. Enig, *Know Your Fats*, p. 115.

Chapter 16

1. Enig, *Know Your Fats*, p. 25.
2. Fallon, *Nourishing Traditions*, p. 436.
3. Felix, Clara *The Felix Letter,* Issue #94-95, 1997.
   Challem, Jack; Berkson, Burton M.D.; and Smith, Melissa Diane, *Syndrome X*, pp. 92-93.
4. Enig, *Know Your Fats*, p. 46.
5. Crayhon, The Carnitine Miracle, p. 100.
6. Felix, The Felix Letter, Issue #116/117, 2001.
7. Enig, *Know Your Fats*, p. 66.

Chapter 17

1. *American Journal of Clinical Nutrition* 1999; 70(2): 221-227).
2. McCully, *The Heart Revolution,* p. 24.
3. Atkins, *Health Revelations Newsletter,* March 2001.
4. Reaven, and others, *Syndrome X-The Silent Killer*, p. 51.
5. Ibid, p. 18.
6. Fallon, Nourishing Traditions, p. 26.
7. Felix, Clara *The Felix Letter,* Issue #115, 2001.
8. Fallon, Nourishing Traditions, p. 26.

9. Crayhon, The Carnitine Miracle, p. 87.
10. Atkins, <u>Health Revelations Newsletter</u>, September 1999.
11. Crayhon, p. 93.
12. Ibid.
13. Fallon, Nourishing Traditions, p. 29.
14. Atkins, <u>Health Revelations Newsletter</u>, April 2000.
15. Ibid.
16. Fallon, Nourishing Traditions, p. 512.
17. Ibid, p. 307.
18. Ibid.

Chapter 18

1. Mercola, Joseph M.D. http://www.mercola.com "Antibiotics May Improve Heart Disease," Issue #307.
2. Atkins, *Age Defying Diet Revolution*, p. 34.
3. Ibid, p. 35.
4. Ibid.
5. Ibid.
6. ibid.
7. Atkins, <u>Health Revelations Newsletter</u>, April 2001.
8. Atkins, *Age Defying Diet Revolution*, p. 37.
9. Mercola, Joseph M.D. *http://www.mercola.com* "Bacteria and Viral Exposure Linked To Heart Disease," Issue #293.
10. Felix, Clara <u>The Felix Letter</u>, Issue #102, 1999.
11. Ley-Jacobs, Beth M. Ph.D. *DHA: The Magnificent Marine Oil.* Temecula: BL Publications, 1999, p. 14.
12. Felix, <u>The Felix Letter</u>, Issue #115, 2001.
13. Fallon, *Nourishing Traditions*, p. 258.
14. Ibid.
15. Ibid.
16. Ibid.
17. Ley-Jacobs, p. 17.
18. ibid, p. 73.
19. Atkins, Age-Defying Diet Revolution, p. 177.
20. Ibid.

Chapter 19

1. Lee, John R. M.D. (with Virginia Hopkins). *What Your Doctor May Not Tell You About Menopause.* New York: Warner Books Inc., 1996, pp. 22-23.
2. Ibid, pp. 24-25.
3. Ibid, pp. 25-26.
4. Ibid, p. 4.
5. Ibid, pp. 43-45.
6. Ibid, p. 5

7. Lee, John R. M.D. http://www.johnleemd.com. "HRT and Breast Cancer Déjà vu"
8. Lee, *What Your Doctor May Not Tell You About Men*opause, p. 152.
9. Ibid, p. 169.
10. Atkins, *Age Defying Diet Revolution*, p. 152.
11. Elkins, Rita M.H. *DHEA.* Pleasant Grove: Woodland Publishing, 1996, p. 9.
12. Lee, *What Your Doctor May Not Tell You About Men*opause, p. 140.
13. Elkins, p. 9.
14. Atkins, *Age Defying Diet Revolution*, p. 141.

Chapter 20

1. Reaven, and others, *Syndrome X-The Silent Killer*, pp. 19-20.
2. Enig, *Know Your Fats,* pp. 85-86.
3. Atkins, *Atkins Age-Defying Diet Revolution,* p. 187.
4. Fallon, *Nourishing Traditions*, p. 583.

Chapter 21

1. Yannios, *Heart Disease Breakthrough*, p. 28.
2. Mercola, Joseph M.D. http://www.mercola.com "Aspirin Not Recommended for Heart Disease Anymore," Issue #293.
3. Yannios, p. 110.
4. Ibid, pp.29-34

Quick Order Form
21 Days To A Healthy Heart

Fax orders: 612-721-9946. Send this form, or copy.

Telephone orders: Call 800-641-6802 toll free.
Have your credit card ready.

Order from website: www.nokobeach.com

Postal Orders: Nokomis Nutrition, 2720 East 50th Street
Minneapolis, MN 55417

Name:_____

Address:_____

City:_____State:____Zip:_____

Telephone:_____

Sales tax: Please add 7% for orders shipped to Minnesota addresses.

Shipping
U.S. $3.00 for the each book.

Payment: ☐ Check ☐ Credit Card
☐ Visa ☐ MasterCard ☐ Amex ☐ Discover

Card number:_____

Name on card:_____Exp. date_____

Diet Heart Publishing

PO Box 330
Sebeka, MN 56477-0330

218-837-6175 ph
218-837-6191 fax

noko@wcta.net